Question&Answer

MEDICAL LAW

Question&Answer

MEDICAL LAW

Michelle Robson
Kristina Swift
Helen Kingston
Carolyn Fyall

Harlow, England • London • New York • Boston • San Francisco • Toronto • Sydney • Auckland • Singapore • Hong Kong
Tokyo • Seoul • Taipei • New Delhi • Cape Town • São Paulo • Mexico City • Madrid • Amsterdam • Munich • Paris • Milan

Pearson Education Limited
Edinburgh Gate
Harlow CM20 2JE
United Kingdom
Tel: +44 (0)1279 623623
Web: www.pearson.com/uk

First published 2016 (print and electronic)

ISBN: 978-1-292-00209-7 (print)
978-1-292-00292-7 (PDF)
978-1-292-00290-3 (eText)
978-1-292-06598-4 (ePub)

British Library Cataloguing-in-Publication Data
A catalogue record for the print edition is available from the British Library

ARP Impression 98

Front cover bestseller data from Nielsen BookScan (2009–2013, Law Revision Series).

Print edition typeset in Helvetica Neue by 71
Printed in Great Britain by Ashford Colour Press Ltd., Gosport

NOTE THAT ANY PAGE CROSS REFERENCES REFER TO THE PRINT EDITION

Contents

Supporting resources

Visit the **Law Express Question&Answer** series companion website at **www.pearsoned.co.uk/lawexpressqa** to find valuable learning material including:

- **Additional essay and problem questions** arranged by topic for each chapter give you more opportunity to practise and hone your exam skills.
- **Diagram plans** for all additional questions assist you in structuring and writing your answers.
- **You be the marker** questions allow you to see through the eyes of the examiner by marking essay and problem questions on topics covered in the book.
- Download and print all **Before you begin** diagrams and **Diagram plans** from the book.

Also: The companion website provides the following features:

- Search tool to help locate specific items of content.
- Online help and support to assist with website usage and troubleshooting.

For more information please contact your local Pearson sales representative or visit **www.pearsoned.co.uk/lawexpressqa**

Acknowledgements

Michelle Robson wishes to thank Hannah Marston at Pearson for always being extremely flexible with deadlines and for her advice throughout this process. I would like to thank Tim for patiently reading draft material and for all his love and support. And a final thanks to Joe, Angus, Dan, Grace, Mum and Jacqui for never failing to make me smile.

Kristina Swift would like to express her gratitude to Hannah Marston at Pearson for her guidance. I would also like to thank my parents, Sandra and Dave, for their help and support. And a final big thank you to my amazing daughters, Hannah and Millie, for their love and patience.

Carolyn Fyall would like to thank Dave, Logan and her parents, June and Dave Snr, for all their love and support and for always making her laugh when she needs it the most.

Publisher's acknowledgements

Our thanks go to all reviewers who contributed to the development of this text, including students who participated in research and focus groups which helped to shape the series format.

What you need to do for every question in Medical Law

HOW TO USE THIS BOOK

Books in the *Question and Answer* series focus on the *why* of a good answer alongside the what, thereby helping you to build your question answering skills and technique.

This guide should not be used as a substitute for learning the material thoroughly, your lecture notes or your textbook. It *will* help you to make the most out of what you have already learned when answering an exam or coursework question. Remember that the answers given here are not the only correct way of answering the question but serve to show you some good examples of how you could approach the question set.

Make sure that you regularly refer to your course syllabus, check which issues are covered (as well as to what extent they are covered) and whether they are usually examined with other topics. Remember that what is required in a good answer could change significantly with only a slight change in the wording of a question. Therefore, do not try to memorise the answers given here, instead use the answers and the other features to understand what goes into a good answer and why.

Medical law is a patchwork of many things: law, ethics, morality and science. It continues to evolve, reacting to (ponderously so a lot of the time) scientific advancements and public concern, as well as managing on occasions not medical but social issues. Students of medical law struggle in an exam situation with this fragmented picture. While an understanding of legal principles is often evident, the application of these is frequently patchy with little regard for the ethical principles which have moulded the subject into its present form. With this in mind we have the following advice.

When answering a problem question in a medical law exam consider:

1 Are you required to advise a party or simply to discuss the issues in the scenario?
2 Are you asked to identify only the legal issues, or both legal and ethical issues?
3 What information do you have and what information is missing or ambiguous?

In your answer, adopt the following approach:

1 Ordinarily, work through the problem chronologically, following the order of the facts in the question. There will be some situations, however, where an alternative approach may work more effectively, e.g. to group related issues together.
2 Focus on the issues in the problem; do not discuss other matters peripheral to the subject area, e.g. if asked to discuss causation then don't discuss duty or damages.
3 Always define the area of law to be discussed at the outset, e.g. 'Surrogacy is . . . '. This serves as an introduction and reminds you (and the examiner) of the focus of the question.
4 Discuss the legal and then the ethical issues, referring to professional guidelines, e.g. GMC/BMA Guidance, if appropriate.
5 Identify what information is missing.
6 Conclude with your advice or opinion. If a firm conclusion cannot be reached say so and why.

In an essay question remember that you are not being asked to state all that you know on a point – you are being asked to focus on a particular question and discuss specifically the identified issue arising from that question. You must adopt a clearly defined structure; if the question is charting a development in the law then a chronological approach always works best. You must refer to the issue in the question, constantly weaving this into your essay, but then you must go further and critically analyse the law, discussing areas of controversy or that have been the subject of reform. To do this, you must be knowledgeable of current legal developments, mindful of ethical guidance and always have an eye on the news.

Guided tour

What to do for every question – Identify the key things you should look for and do in any question and answer on the subject, ensuring you give every one of your answers a great chance from the start.

What you need to do for every question in Medical Law

HOW TO USE THIS BOOK

Books in the *Question and Answer* series focus on the *why* of a good answer alongside the what, thereby helping you to build your question answering skills and technique.

This guide should not be used as a substitute for learning the material thoroughly, your lecture notes or your textbook. It *will* help you to make the most out of what you have already learned when answering an exam or coursework question. Remember that the answers given here are not the only correct way of answering the question but serve to show you some good examples of how you could approach the question set.

Make sure that you regularly refer to your course syllabus, check which issues are covered (as well as to what extent they are covered) and whether they are usually examined with other topics. Remember that what is required in a good answer could change significantly with only a slight change in the wording of a question. Therefore, do not try to memorise the answers given here, instead use the answers and the other features to understand what goes into a good answer and why.

Medical law is a patchwork of many things: law, ethics, morality and science. It continues to evolve, reacting to (ponderously so a lot of the time) scientific advancements and public concern, as well as managing on occasions not medical but social issues. Students of medical law struggle in an exam situation with this fragmented picture. While an understanding of legal principles is often evident, the application of these is frequently patchy with little regard for the ethical principles which have moulded the subject into its present form. With this in mind we have the following advice.

2 Judicial review

How this topic may come up in exams

Claims challenging the allocation of healthcare resources have increased in popularity. This may be attributed to the public's changing awareness of what it means to be in good health and increased knowledge of available treatments, as well as the underlying perception that there is a right to health care. Problem and essay questions focus on challenges to rationing decisions and the decision-making process. This chapter considers both the claims for judicial review and for breach of a Convention Right under the Human Rights Act 1998, two actions available to claimants challenging funding allocation decisions.

How this topic may come up in exams – Understand how to tackle any question on this topic by using the handy tips and advice relevant to both essay and problem questions. In-text symbols clearly identify each question type as they occur.

Essay question

Problem question

Before you begin – Use these diagrams as a step-by-step guide to help you confidently identify the main points covered in any question asked. Download these from the companion website to add to your revision notes.

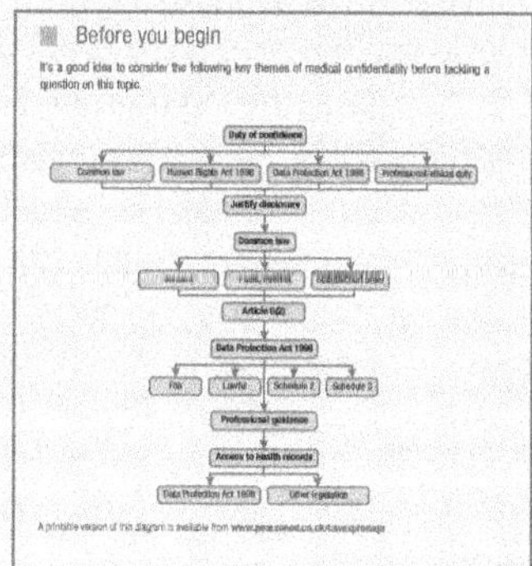

Answer plans and Diagram plans – A clear and concise plan is the key to a good answer and these answer and diagram plans support the structuring of your answers, whatever your preferred learning style.

Answer plan

- Explain that there are two pieces of legislation currently dealing with this area.
- Explain the limits of common/statute law to impose treatment.
- Consider why compulsory detention and treatment might be necessary.
- Concentrate on the Mental Health Act in its current form.
- Consider briefly the ethical issues – autonomy versus paternalism; public and individual safety in light of impaired judgement; patient's right to treatment.

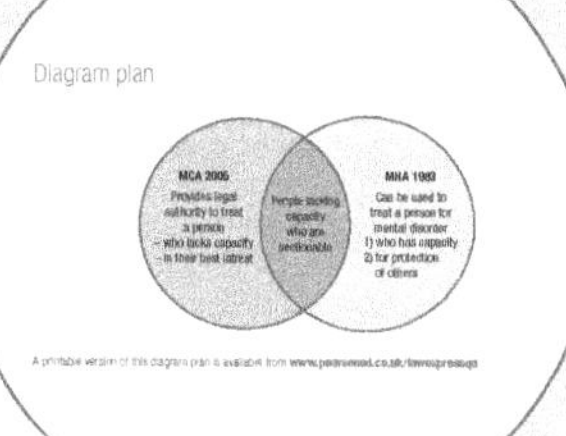

Answer with accompanying guidance – Make the most out of every question by using the guidance to recognise what makes a good answer and why. Answers are the length you could realistically hope to produce in an exam to show you how to gain marks quickly when under pressure.

[1] The examiner would expect you to introduce what is meant by surrogacy.

Answer

[1] The examiner would expect you to introduce what is meant by surrogacy.

[2] This is a relevant issue as Angela and Bob seek advice regarding their legal position ... cinct coverage here will ... ce. This would require ... attention if there is a ... (e.g. if it appears likely ... rogate mother will ... to hand the child over).

The issues arising from this proposed surrogacy arrangement will be discussed. Surrogacy involves one woman carrying a child where she intends to hand the child over after birth.[1] Carla will carry a child, and then hand the child to the intended parents, Angela and Bob. Surrogacy arrangements are not enforceable (Surrogacy Arrangements Act 1985, section 1B).[2] At this stage there is no reason to suspect that either Carla would refuse to hand the child over or that Angela and Bob would refuse to pay the money.

The issues regarding parentage will be complicated.[3] We must consider the parenthood provisions contained in the Human Fertilisation and Embryology Act 2008 (HFE Act 2008) which apply to determine parentage where a woman is treated using donated gametes. Here an embryo will be created using Angela's egg and donor sperm. The Human Fertilisation and Embryology Authority (HFEA) Code of Practice (8th edn) is also relevant.

Case names clearly highlighted – Easy-to-spot bold text makes those all important case names stand out from the rest of the answer, ensuring they are much easier to remember in revision and an exam.

note the immediate reference to the question

Generally, in both tort and contract claims, the courts have awarded damages for loss of a chance – see, for example, ***Chaplin v Hicks*** [1911] 2 KB 786 and ***Allied Maples Group Ltd v Simmons & Simmons*** [1995] 1 WLR 1602 which awarded damages for the loss of a 'real or substantial chance'. Yet, long before the decision in ***Gregg v Scott*** the courts had ruled that the loss of chance claim was not sustainable in a clinical negligence claim.[2]

[2] One of the more significant issues with a loss of chance claim is that clinical negligence cases are dealt with on a different basis from tort and contract cases

In ***Hotson v East Berks AHA*** [1987] 2 All ER 909, a boy alleged that a four-day delay in diagnosis deprived him of a 25 per cent chance of

Make your answer stand out – Really impress your examiners by going the extra mile and including these additional points and further reading to illustrate your deeper knowledge of the subject, fully maximising your marks.

✓ Make your answer stand out

- Adopt a structure such as the one suggested here. You are asked to consider the situation and discuss – this is pointing you in the direction of identifying the legal options and making a comparison.
- Discuss whether section 2 or section 3 of the Mental Health Act would be most appropriate in the circumstances of this case. Don't forget this is a problem question and you need to apply the law to the facts you have been provided with.
- When discussing informal admission, point out that this is the case for every admission to hospital for a physical health problem; the Mental Health Act is an exception to the usual rules in medical law.
- Consider the implications of Annie being deprived of her liberty in hospital – and refer to Article 5 ECHR.

Don't be tempted to – Points out common mistakes ensuring you avoid losing easy marks by understanding where students most often trip up in exams.

! Don't be tempted to . . .

- Just explain the ethical concerns – remember this is a medical *law* question!
- Forget about a structure – this model answer has no subheadings, but answers the question in the first paragraph and ties the general discussion in the subsequent paragraphs neatly together in a strong conclusion.
- Ignore the European Convention – it is usually relevant to any discussion of mental health law.
- Focus on one case (i.e. *DL-H v Devon*) which you think answers the question. Poorer students will do this, setting out at length the facts of a particular case. Your examiner is asking you here for a more general discussion, and if (like in the suggested answer here) you do mention the case, explain the *ratio*, not the facts.

Bibliography – Use this list of further reading to really delve into the subject and explore areas in more depth, enabling you to excel in exams.

Bibliography

Alghrani A. and Harris J. (2006) Reproductive liberty: should the foundation of families be regulated? *Child and Family Law Quarterly*, 18(2): 191.

Asch A. (2003) Disability Equality and Prenatal Testing: Contradictory or Compatible? *Florida State University Law Review*, 30: 315–42.

Guided tour of the companion website

Book resources are available to download. Print your own **Before you begin** and **Diagram plans** to pin to your wall or add to your own revision notes.

Additional Essay and Problem questions with **Diagram plans** arranged by topic for each chapter give you more opportunity to practise and hone your exam skills. Print and email your answers.

You be the marker gives you a chance to evaluate sample exam answers for different question types and understand how and why an examiner awards marks. Use the accompanying guidance to get the most out of every question and recognise what makes a good answer.

All of this and more can be found when you visit **www.pearsoned.co.uk/lawexpressqa**

Table of cases and statutes

Cases

Statutes

Table of statutory instruments

Table of international conventions

1 Themes in medical law

How this topic may come up in exams

Throughout your studies of medical law you will have appreciated that particular themes and issues emerge across the topics you have covered. You may be asked a question (most likely an essay question) which focuses on a particular theme or issue.

A question may require discussion of the extent to which different ethical principles (e.g. beneficence and non-malfeasance) are reflected in medical law. You might have to compare different principles, for example, to consider the tension between patient autonomy and medical paternalism.

The impact of the Human Rights Act 1998 is also a key issue. A question could focus on the relevance of a particular article of the European Convention on Human Rights to medical law.

Such questions often require a broad knowledge across different topics. Time restraints mean you will need to be selective in your choice of material, but also be prepared to justify your approach to the examiner.

Before you begin

It's a good idea to consider the following key themes in medical law before tackling a question on this topic.

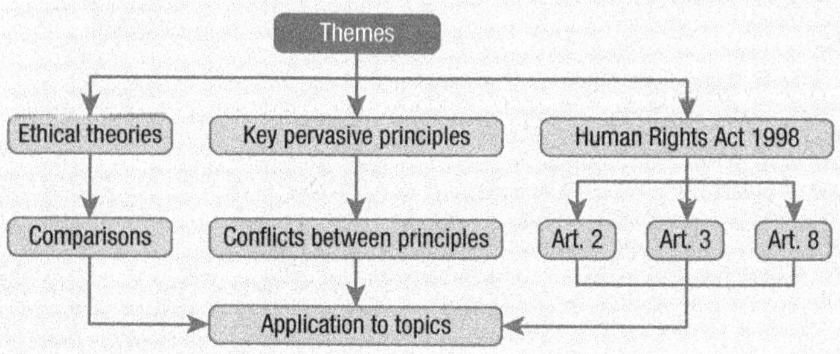

A printable version of this diagram is available from **www.pearsoned.co.uk/lawexpressqa**

Question 1

Critically evaluate the impact of Article 8 of the European Convention on Human Rights on medical law.

Answer plan

- Introduce Article 8.
- Consider the impact of the Human Rights Act 1998.
- Discuss whether Article 8 has been used successfully in cases challenging refusal to fund treatment.
- Analyse the impact Article 8 has had in relation to medical confidentiality.
- Consider the role Article 8 has played in challenges to the law on assisted suicide.

Diagram plan

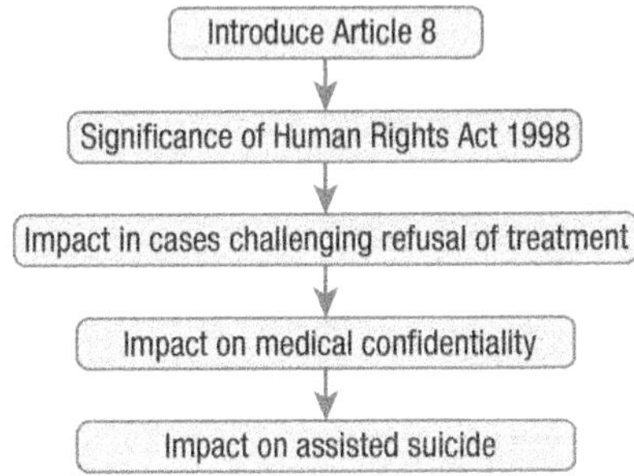

A printable version of this diagram plan is available from **www.pearsoned.co.uk/lawexpressqa**

Answer

The Human Rights Act 1998 has incorporated Articles of the European Convention on Human Rights into domestic law, including Article 8. Article 8 of the Convention may have effect in various ways. For instance, the courts may make a declaration of incompatibility where legislation is incompatible with Article 8 (s. 4) and it is unlawful for a public authority (such as NHS bodies) to act incompatibly with the Convention (s. 6).[1] Article 8(1) provides that 'everyone has the right to respect for his private and family life'. This is not an absolute right.

[1] It is worthwhile to confirm how Article 8 may be used following introduction of the Human Rights Act 1998.

It can be interfered with if the interference is in accordance with the law, necessary in a democratic society and for a legitimate aim (Art. 8(2)).[2] Article 8 will be relevant to many areas. I will consider its impact in challenges to treatment refusal decisions, medical confidentiality and assisted suicide.[3]

[2] You should introduce Article 8. It is important to stress this does not establish an absolute right and the examiner will be pleased if you refer to the significance of Article 8(2).

[3] Introduce the areas you will focus on. The examiner will understand you will not have time to cover all areas, so you should highlight what will be tackled in your answer.

1. Resource allocation[4]

Has Article 8 helped patients challenge decisions refusing treatment?

It is difficult to demonstrate a positive obligation owed to a particular individual. In ***Sentges v Netherlands*** (App. No. 27677/02) the applicant unsuccessfully challenged the refusal to provide a robotic arm. It was held that 'the fair balance that has to be struck between the competing interests of the individual and the community as a whole' must be considered.[5] It was stressed that states had a wide margin of appreciation, particularly regarding the allocation of limited funds.

Article 8 was used to frame a different type of challenge[6] in ***R (Condliff) v North Staffordshire Primary Care Trust*** [2011] EWCA Civ 910. The applicant had been refused bariatric surgery as he failed to satisfy Body Mass Index (BMI) criteria. The Primary Care Trust's (PCT) policy to determine eligibility for treatment considered only clinical criteria, not social factors. He argued the policy breached Article 8 which imposed a positive obligation on the PCT to consider his private and family life and by excluding social factors the PCT had fettered its discretion. The Court of Appeal disagreed and held that the policy did not show a lack of respect for his private and family life. In any event, there were 'legitimate equality reasons' to use the policy and this fell within the 'margin of appreciation'.

[4] As you are dealing with different areas of law, the use of headings may help to divide your commentary.

[5] Section 2 of the 1998 Act states that courts must take into account Strasbourg jurisprudence where relevant, so it is appropriate to refer to this decision.

[6] The examiner will be impressed if you try to identify the different types of argument that have been advanced using Article 8.

2. Medical confidentiality

Has Article 8(1) helped to protect patient information? It has been used to protect 'private' information. Article 8 is relevant when 'there is a reasonable expectation that the information in question will be kept confidential' (***Campbell v MGN Ltd*** [2004] 2 All ER 995). Medical information is, however, protected in any event under the common law of confidentiality and the Data Protection Act 1998.[7]

[7] This is a key point to make. You are asked to comment on whether Article 8 has had any impact, so it is apt to point out that there are alternative avenues of protection in any event.

The common law duty of confidence and Article 8(1) do not provide absolute rights, so comparisons should be made between the justifications for disclosure at common law and under Article 8(2). For instance, at common law disclosure is justified where serious crime has been committed or a third party is at risk of serious harm (***W* v *Egdell*** [1990] Ch 359). Article 8(2) permits disclosure where there is a 'legitimate aim' and it is 'necessary in a democratic society'. In ***Z* v *Finland*** (1997) 45 BMLR 107 the medical records of an HIV-positive patient (Z) were used during the investigation and prosecution of Z's husband for attempted manslaughter and sexual offences. Z argued that her rights under Article 8 were violated. It was held there was a legitimate aim (the prevention of crime) and this was proportionate to the legitimate aim pursued. Parallels exist between the common law justifications and the Article 8(2) position.[8]

[8] The comparison is developed further to assess the 'impact' or 'added value' of Article 8 by exploring the justifications for disclosure.

There may be 'extra' procedural safeguards under Article 8(2). ***Re General Dental Council's Application*** [2011] EWHC 3011 (Admin) decided the General Dental Council could use dental records without patients' permission to investigate a dentist's conduct. The court addressed whether the GDC was obliged to tell patients what it proposed to do with the records under Article 8(2). At common law it would be good practice to inform the person in advance if information was going to be disclosed. ***Re GDC's Application*** went one step further and held prior notification may be 'required' under Article 8(2) as 'procedural obligations' may arise so individuals are involved before Article 8 rights are interfered with.[9]

[9] This develops coverage of the 'impact' of Article 8 even further, and shows the examiner you have considered a range of issues by also evaluating the procedural safeguards that Article 8(2) may establish.

3. Assisted suicide

It is an offence to intentionally encourage or assist the suicide of another (Suicide Act 1961, s. 2). The consent of the Director of Public Prosecutions is required before prosecution (s. 2(4)).

Diane Pretty sought assurance from the DPP that her husband would not be prosecuted if he helped her commit suicide. As this was refused, she commenced legal action arguing that the 1961 Act and the DPP's action were incompatible with her Convention rights. I will focus on the arguments raised regarding Article 8.[10] The House of Lords (***R* v *Director of Public Prosecutions*** [2001] UKHL 61) held that Article 8(1) was not engaged as it protected the way individuals lived their lives, not the way they died. Anyway

[10] *Pretty* is a complex case which deals with various Articles of the Convention. It is important to ensure you focus on the Article 8 issues in light of the question set.

Article 8(2) would provide justification as protecting vulnerable persons constitutes a legitimate aim (as others would be affected if assisting suicide was permitted). However, the European Court of Human Rights found Article 8(1) was engaged (***Pretty* v *UK*** (App. No. 2346/02)), confirming private and family life was a broad term covering a person's 'physical and psychological integrity'.[11] Applying Article 8(2), however, the approach taken could be justified. The measures had a legitimate aim (to protect the rights of others), were 'necessary in a democratic society' and within the state's margin of appreciation.

[11] The examiner will be impressed if you compare the decisions of the House of Lords and the European Court of Human Rights.

In ***R (Nicklinson)* v *Ministry of Justice*** [2014] UKSC 38 the Supreme Court addressed whether the current law on assisted suicide is incompatible with Article 8[12] and held this issue fell within the UK's margin of appreciation. Five of the nine judges considered the court *could* make a declaration of incompatibility regarding the Suicide Act 1961, however only two of the five judges would have done so.[13] Lady Hale would have made such a declaration as she found the current law was discriminatory and disproportionate. Foster (2014) considers this is 'judicially brave' but could be viewed as either 'a breach of the separation of powers' or 'an example of innovative judicial activism' (see Foster S. (2014) Case Comment (*R (on the application of Nicklinson)* v *Ministry of Justice*) [2014] UKSC 38. *Coventry Law Journal*, 19(1): 73–76). The four minority judges thought the issue of compatibility with Article 8 should be left to Parliament. Foster suggests the minority's view that it is 'constitutionally inappropriate' to apply section 4 of the 1998 Act in individual cases goes against the Act's purpose.

[12] As *Nicklinson* is a difficult case which raised a wide range of issues you will need to be selective. This discussion highlights a key Article 8 point in the case.

[13] It is worthwhile spending some time highlighting the majority and minority approach regarding whether a declaration of incompatibility *could* be made. This is a relevant issue regarding the 'impact' of Article 8.

Conclusion[14]

Despite extensive consideration of the impact of Article 8, assisted suicide remains unlawful. Regarding medical confidentiality Article 8 may have some impact although this may be limited to procedural safeguards. Even if there was interference with a patient's Article 8(1) right following treatment refusal, this could be justified using Article 8(2) bearing in mind the margin of appreciation and demands on finite funds.

Overall, Article 8 has had little impact.[15]

[14] This brings together the conclusions drawn following coverage of the three different areas.

[15] A different conclusion may have been drawn if alternative medical law topics had been considered.

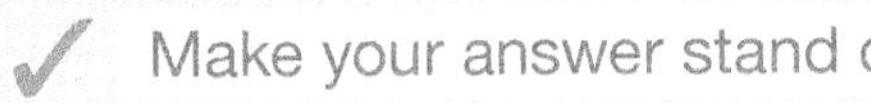

Make your answer stand out

- Refer to authority from the European Court of Human Rights where appropriate given section 2 of the 1998 Act provides that the courts should consider it. Also show you understand that states enjoy a significant margin of appreciation.
- You could consider alternative Article 8 arguments that have been raised regarding assisted suicide. In *R (Purdy)* v *DPP* [2009] UKHL 45 it was held that the DPP's Code for Crown Prosecutors did not satisfy Article 8(2) as it was not sufficiently clear enough – a successful outcome using Article 8(2) albeit on a more limited issue. Contrast the later unsuccessful Article 8 challenge to the revised DPP guidance in *Nicklinson*.
- Draw comparisons with the existing common law. If significant protection exists from another source in any event perhaps this will affect your view of Article 8's impact. What added value does it provide? May its value be limited to strengthening procedural safeguards?
- Address the significance of the different approaches of the majority and minority in *Nicklinson* regarding whether a declaration of incompatibility *could* be made. If some members of the judiciary would prefer to leave the matter for Parliament, perhaps this could reduce the potential impact of Article 8 in the courts?

Don't be tempted to . . .

- Forget to introduce Article 8 and its significance following introduction of the 1998 Act. The temptation is to begin discussing the areas of medical law without first explaining the content of Article 8.
- Try to cover too many areas of medical law. If you cover too much ground your discussion is likely to lack detail. Be selective. Explain you have chosen to focus on particular areas – the examiner will understand.
- Stray from the Article 8 focus when discussing case law. For instance, the *Pretty* litigation also dealt with Articles 2, 3, 9 and 14. Try not to stray from the question.

Question 2

To what extent does the law sufficiently protect patients' rights in relation to medical treatment?

Answer plan

- ➜ Introduction – define patients' rights and the parameters of what you will discuss.
- ➜ Adults – discuss their right to refuse treatment but not the right to demand.
- ➜ Children – discuss their right to consent but not the right to refuse.
- ➜ End of life – consider the right to life but not the right to die.
- ➜ Conclusion.

Diagram plan

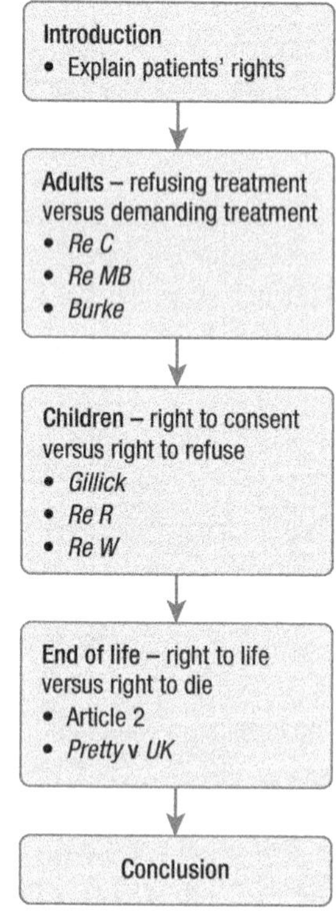

Introduction
• Explain patients' rights
Adults – refusing treatment versus demanding treatment
• Re C
• Re MB
• Burke
Children – right to consent versus right to refuse
• Gillick
• Re R
• Re W
End of life – right to life versus right to die
• Article 2
• Pretty v UK
Conclusion

A printable version of this diagram plan is available from **www.pearsoned.co.uk/lawexpressqa**

Answer

[1] Begin by simply defining what are 'patients' rights'.

Patients' rights may be thought of as a moral entitlement to a justifiable claim.[1] Patients' rights are seen from the individual's perspective and cannot be outweighed by the interests of others.

Patients may claim negative rights; that is a claim against unwanted interference, or patients may allege positive rights, often thought of as a demand for assistance. The law has recognised the concept of patients' rights by enacting the Human Rights Act 1998 incorporating Articles of the European Convention on Human Rights into domestic law. Society also has embraced the idea of patients' rights in the form of the NHS Constitution. This essay examines patients' rights in three areas: the right of a capable adult to refuse and demand treatment; a child's right to consent and refuse treatment; and the right to life and to end one's life.[2]

[2] A clearly defined structure is essential. The answer has five distinct sections; an introduction, discussion of the three areas and then a conclusion. Although this is not a prescriptive model it is a format you should consider when tackling 'theme' essays.

1. Adults: right to refuse treatment versus right to demand[3]

[3] Where the answer is in distinct parts it is a good idea to use sub-headings.

The law recognises that a capable adult has the right to refuse treatment. In ***Re C (Adult: Refusal of Treatment)*** [1994] 1 All ER 819, a schizophrenic patient refused to consent to an amputation. The court held that as C was mentally competent his refusal should be upheld. Echoing this decision, Butler-Sloss LJ said in ***Re MB (An Adult: Medical Treatment)*** [1997] 8 Med LR 217: 'A mentally competent patient has an absolute right to refuse to consent to medical treatment for any reason, rational or irrational or for no reason at all, even where that decision may lead to his or her own death . . .'[4]

[4] This quote succinctly states the nature of the right and also demonstrates that you know the law.

The right of a capable adult to refuse treatment is unrestricted; the consequences of the refusal are disregarded, see ***St George's Healthcare NHS Trust* v *S*** [1998] 3 All ER 673 where the court upheld a mother's right to refuse even though her refusal had the potential to kill her unborn child.[5] Only if a patient lacks capacity under the Mental Capacity Act 2005 may a refusal be ignored if it is deemed to be in the patient's best interests.

[5] The paragraph continues by discussing any limits to the right to refuse. It is advisable that you give other case law examples to demonstrate to the examiner that you are aware that for all intents and purposes an adult's right to refuse treatment is indeed absolute.

While the law acknowledges the negative right to refuse treatment, the same protection is not afforded to the right to demand treatment.[6] In ***R (Burke)* v *General Medical Council (Official Solicitor intervening)*** [2005] 2 WLR 431, Leslie Burke sought judicial review of the General Medical Council's guidance to doctors that artificial feeding and hydration could be withdrawn from him against his wishes. Mr Burke was ultimately unsuccessful. In the Court of Appeal Lord Phillips stated, 'If . . . he . . . informs the doctor that he wants a form of treatment which the doctor has not offered him . . . if the doctor concludes that this treatment is not clinically indicated he is

[6] Having discussed the negative right to refuse, the answer then continues by examining the second half of the statement referred to in the sub-heading, namely the positive right to demand treatment, again quoting from case law to support the argument. Always ensure that the sub-heading mirrors the discussion to follow and that a balanced view is given.

not required . . . to provide it . . .' No-one has an indisputable right to healthcare treatment and/or facilities as judicial review cases challenging healthcare resource allocation have demonstrated (see ***R* v *Cambridge District Health Authority, ex parte B*** [1995] 2 All ER 129).

2. Children: right to consent versus right to refuse medical treatment

In ***Gillick* v *West Norfolk and Wisbech AHA*** [1985] 3 All ER 402 the House of Lords held a child under the age of 16 who was '***Gillick*** competent' had the right to consent to treatment. Children between the ages of 16 and 18 years also had the right to consent to treatment under the Family Law Reform Act 1969, s. 8. The converse of the ***Gillick*** rule and section 8, namely that if you are competent to consent you are competent to refuse, does not hold good. In ***Re R (A Minor)*** [1992] Fam 11 Lord Donaldson contended if a child declines or refuses to give consent, consent can be given by someone with parental responsibilities. Similarly in ***Re W (A Minor) (Medical Treatment: Court's Jurisdiction)*** [1992] 4 All ER 627 he argued that adolescents do not have the maturity to appreciate the risks and consequences associated with refusal of medical treatment and that the court has the power to 'override the refusal of a minor, whether over the age of sixteen or under that age'.[7] This approach was followed in ***Re E (A Minor: Wardship) (Medical Treatment)*** [1993] 1 FLR 386; ***Re M (Child: Refusal of Medical Treatment)*** [1999] 2 FLR 1097.

[7] As for point 3, this quote aptly sums up the limits of the 'right' and the law.

This reasoning has been the subject of much academic criticism. Furthermore, with the introduction of the ECHR into English Law Lord Donaldson's conclusion hints of discrimination under Article 14 and possibly breaches Article 8. As Freeman (1992) opines, 'To believe in autonomy is to believe that anyone's autonomy is as morally significant as anybody else's. Nor does autonomy depend on the stage of life a person has reached . . . To respect a child's autonomy is to treat that child as a person and as a rights-holder' (see Freeman, M. (1992) Taking children's rights more seriously. *International Journal of Law, Policy and Family Law*, 6(1): 52–71).[8]

[8] There is a wealth of academic writing in this area; try and include at least one source in your answer.

3. Right to life versus right to die

Article 2 of the ECHR provides 'Everyone's right to life shall be protected by law'.[9] This has been interpreted as imposing a positive obligation on the state to take positive steps to protect life (***Osman* v *UK***

[9] As a preliminary begin by setting out Article 2 and the right to life.

(2000) 29 EHRR 245. Article 2 does not confer a right to demand every form of medical treatment required to preserve life (***Burke* v *UK*** (Application No. 19807/06), but it at least creates universal, minimum standards that must be adhered to by each member state to protect life. All persons are protected by this right but the foetus is not (***Vo* v *France*** [2004] 2 FCR 577).[10] Article 2 does not, however, bestow the right to determine how one should die or a right to commit suicide. In ***Pretty* v *UK*** (2002) 35 EHRR 1, Diane Pretty, who was dying of motor neurone disease and was unable to commit suicide without assistance, argued that the right to life included or implied a right to die. The European Court ruled that Article 2 did not confer on an 'individual the entitlement to choose death rather than life'.[11] A capable adult has the right to refuse medical treatment resulting in their death (***Re B (Adult: Refusal of Medical Treatment)*** [2002] 2 FCR 1), but not as yet the right to demand assistance to die.

[10] This demonstrates to the examiner that you are aware that the courts have imposed some limits on the applicability of Article 2.

[11] As before a direct quote from case law clarifies the nature of the right being discussed.

There is no common theme running through the courts treatment of patients' rights.[12] What may be discerned is the courts will err on the side of preservation of life. There is no right to die and the courts will ensure children reach adulthood at the expense of affording them the right of unfettered decision making. Few rights appear absolute. The right to refuse is available to a capable adult only, and even the right to life may be qualified in a healthcare context. Patients' rights are recognised by the courts but not afforded unmitigated protection.

[12] Always conclude with reference to the question, even if your conclusion is to say there is no definitive answer!

✓ Make your answer stand out

- Try using sub-headings; it makes the essay more reader-friendly and also reminds you what you have to discuss!
- Look at more than one area in your answer otherwise your essay is not about medical law but simply a discussion of your chosen area.
- A thorough knowledge of the case law again is essential. Throughout this answer directly quoting from cases has neatly summed up the 'right' or argument.
- There is a wealth of academic commentary in the area of consent, children and assisted suicide. Try and include at least one source in your answer. Examples of further reading are: Gilmore, S. and Herring, J. (2012) Children's refusal of treatment: the debate continues. *Family Law*, 42: 973–78; Coggon, J. (2006) Could the right to die with dignity represent a new right to die in English Law? *Medical Law Review*, 14; Coggon, J. and Miola, J. (2011) Autonomy, liberty and medical decision making. *Cambridge Law Journal*, 70: 523–47.

! Don't be tempted to . . .

- Discuss too many areas; you will spread yourself too thinly. Breadth of coverage should not come at the expense of depth of coverage.
- Only look at positive or negative rights – you should aim for a balance.
- Write a purely ethics-based essay; you are asked to consider the law.

www.pearsoned.co.uk/lawexpressqa

Go online to access more revision support including additional essay and problem questions with diagram plans, You be the marker questions, and download all diagrams from the book.

2 Judicial review

How this topic may come up in exams

Claims challenging the allocation of healthcare resources have increased in popularity. This may be attributed to the public's changing awareness of what it means to be in good health and increased knowledge of available treatments, as well as the underlying perception that there is a right to health care. Problem and essay questions focus on challenges to rationing decisions and the decision-making process. This chapter considers both the claims for judicial review and for breach of a Convention Right under the Human Rights Act 1998, two actions available to claimants challenging funding allocation decisions.

Before you begin

It's a good idea to consider the following key themes of judicial review before tackling a question on this topic.

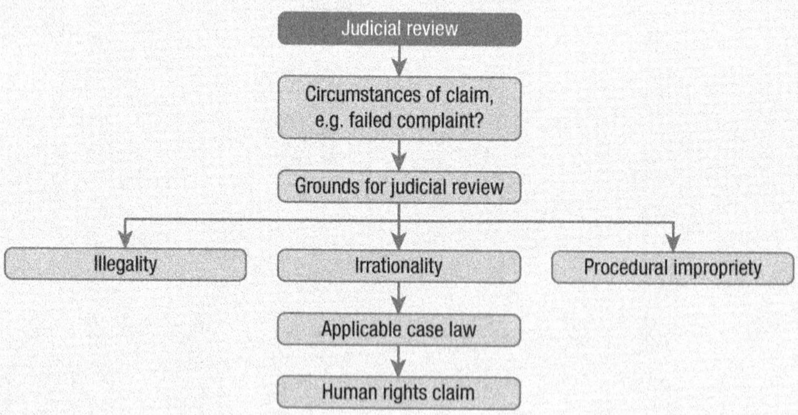

A printable version of this diagram is available from **www.pearsoned.co.uk/lawexpressqa**

Question 1

'. . . the courts are not, contrary to what is sometimes believed, arbiters as to the merits of cases of this kind. Were we to express opinions . . . as to the merits of medical judgement then we should be straying far from the sphere which under our constitution is accorded to us. We have one function only, which is to rule on the lawfulness of the decisions that is a function to which we should strictly confine ourselves.' (per Sir Thomas Bingham in *R* v *Cambridge Health Authority, ex parte B* [1995] 1 WLR 898)

In light of this statement critically discuss the role of judicial review in the healthcare setting.

Answer plan

- Define the judicial review claim and the grounds on which it may be sought.
- Briefly discuss early case law and courts' approach to judicial review claims to include the *Wednesbury* unreasonableness test.
- Analyse the conflicting approaches between the first instance and Court of Appeal judgments in *ex parte B*.
- Critically analyse case law following *ex parte B*.
- Consider the impact, if any, of the Human Rights Act on judicial review claims.

Diagram plan

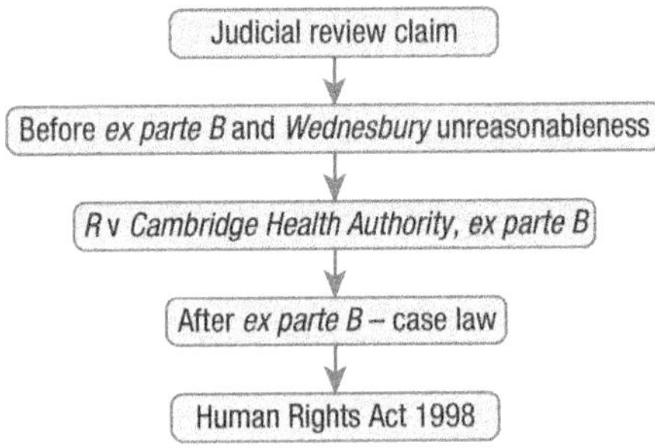

A printable version of this diagram plan is available from **www.pearsoned.co.uk/lawexpressqa**

Answer

In ***R* v *Cambridge Health Authority, ex parte B*** [1995] 1 WLR 898 Lord Bingham said the court's role in judicial review applications was only to examine the lawfulness of the decision-making process. The judicial review action may challenge a decision by alleging it was illegal, irrational or unreasonable or there was procedural irregularity in the decision-making process. Judicial review claims are not a new phenomenon but what is, is the approach of the courts in their handling of often very public debates. Do the courts stray outside the remit of Lord Bingham and consider matters other than the lawfulness of the decision?[1]

[1] Always ensure the introduction refers to the quote in the question and identifies any key words, in this case 'lawfulness'.

Early attempts challenging healthcare decisions were unsuccessful. In ***R* v *Secretary of State for Social Services, ex parte Hincks*** (1980) 1 BMLR 93 four patients alleged that the Minister of Health had failed in his duty (then under the National Health Service Act 1977) in providing facilities for orthopaedic surgery. The Court of Appeal emphasised that financial constraints must be considered in deciding whether the service was reasonable, the courts only intervening if the decision was unreasonable so as to frustrate the policy of the Act. This approach was followed in ***R* v *Central Birmingham HA, ex parte Walker*** (1987) 3 BMLR 32, Sir John Donaldson MR declaring that in matters of resource allocation the court could only intervene if the decision was ***Wednesbury*** unreasonable 'so outrageous in its defiance of logic or accepted moral standards that no sensible person . . . could have arrived at it'.[2] By setting the ***Wednesbury*** test as the benchmark, the courts rejected any involvement where resource allocation was in issue, a reminder that the statutory duty to provide health care is not absolute. Put more simply the courts were rejecting claims requiring a ruling on which child should receive treatment first, a medical decision which they are ill-equipped to make.

[2] As the *Wednesbury* test is central to judicial review claims try and set it out in as much detail as possible.

In ***R* v *Cambridge District Health Authority, ex parte B*** in the glare of intense publicity the court examined their role again.[3] B, a ten-year-old girl suffering from non-Hodgkin's Lymphoma had received a bone marrow transplant but had relapsed and doctors considered no life-prolonging treatment should be given. Her father disagreed and obtained expert advice which indicated that with chemotherapy a second bone marrow transplant was possible. Both treatments had a 10–20 per cent chance of success. Cambridge HA refused to fund the £75,000 for further treatment. At first instance Laws J rejected the unreasonableness test where the right to life was at stake asserting that the health authority must do more than 'merely toll the bell of tight resources'.[4] This approach implicitly examining the merits of the clinical decision, was rejected by the Court of Appeal, Lord Bingham reiterating the court's function was to assess the decision-making process and only in exceptional circumstances could the courts intervene. He commented,

[3] Given that *R* v *Cambridge* is referred to in the question it is appropriate to set out the facts and the judgment.

[4] *R* v *Cambridge* is a landmark case in the area of judicial review and challenges to funding allocation decisions. It is noteworthy for the markedly different approach taken by the High Court and the Court of Appeal and the essay addresses both.

'difficult and agonising judgments have to be made as to how a limited [hospital] budget is best allocated to the maximum advantage of the maximum number of patients. That is not a judgment which the court can make.'

For some, ***ex parte B*** was a landmark decision, 'The case took on a symbolic importance, helping people to grasp the reality that expectation and demand had now outstripped their publicly funded systems without regard to the opportunity cost' (Thornton, S. (1997) The Child B case – reflections of a chief executive. *British Medical Journal*, 314: 1838).[5] Yet subsequent decisions have inadvertently questioned the decision in line with the approach of Laws J. In ***R* v *NW Lancashire HA, ex parte A, D and G*** [2000] 1 WLR 977 a policy against funding gender reassignment surgery was held unlawful as the authority had failed to evaluate the medical evidence relating to trans-sexuality. Auld LJ commented that before formulating its policy the authority must examine the nature and seriousness of each individual's illness and the effectiveness of the varying treatment. In ***R (Rogers)* v *Swindon NHS Primary Care Trust*** [2006] EWCA Civ 392 the Court of Appeal held the defendant's funding policy for, at the time, the unlicensed cancer drug Herceptin was irrational and unlawful. In stating that cost was not a factor in refusing Mrs Rogers's treatment the court found no rational basis for treatment being denied, declaring that the PCT should focus only on the patient's clinical needs in funding decisions. Christopher Newdick asserts courts are now more demanding in the procedures required justifying refusal of life saving or life prolonging treatment. He argues the more severe the patient outcome the more intense the judicial scrutiny.[6] Undeniably these decisions demonstrate that, as Lord Bingham asserts, the court will rule on the lawfulness of the decision but will also intently scrutinise the decision-making process. They also send a signal that a decision not to fund treatment on the basis of resources is acceptable but hiding behind ill-thought-out policy is not.

The courts will intervene if the decision ignores relevant factors; in ***R* v *North Derbyshire HA, ex parte Fisher*** [1997] 8 Med LR 327 the court found it unlawful not to prescribe Mr Fisher with Beta Interferon contrary to an NHS circular.[7] If a body has created an expectation that a service will be provided and an individual has relied on that assurance, the court will not permit a body to renege on that promise (***R* v *North and East Devon HA, ex parte Coughlan*** [2001] QB 213).

[5] In an essay try and quote from a range of sources, although in an exam situation paraphrasing is perfectly acceptable.

[6] Again use academic commentary to further your argument and here Christopher Newdick is an excellent choice.

[7] The answer continues by stating those instances which are unrelated to resources where the court will rule in the applicant's favour.

[8] The impact, if any, of the Human Rights Act should be finally considered.

Has the Human Rights Act made a difference?[8] ***R* v *NW Lancashire*** held that Article 8 could not be relied on to found a right to receive treatment. In ***R (Condliff)* v *North Staffordshire PCT*** [2011] EWHC 872 (Admin) a trust's policy not to consider non-clinical social factors was not in breach of Article 8, the court ruling that unless evidently unworkable a trust may define a policy as it sees fit. Before dismissing the influence of the Human Rights Act note the judgment of Grenfell J in ***R (Ross)* v *West Sussex PCT*** [2008] EWHC 2252 (Admin): 'where life and death decisions are involved, the courts must submit the process to rigorous scrutiny . . . the more substantial the interference with human rights, the more the court will require by way of justification before it is satisfied that the decision is reasonable.'

[9] Always ensure that the conclusion refers to the question and in this case the quote of Lord Bingham.

Lord Bingham's assertion that the courts' role is to rule only on the lawfulness of the decision is fundamentally correct.[9] Yet the judgment of Laws J has been reinvented in ***NW Lancashire*** and ***Rogers***. Christopher Newdick believes the court will find a procedural flaw should they wish to. The Human Rights Act may not have inexorably altered the courts' approach in their inspection of healthcare decisions but it has encouraged more rigorous judicial scrutiny and in doing so the courts have unconsciously questioned both policy and medical judgment.

✓ Make your answer stand out

- Structure is all important – an introduction setting out what will feature in the discussion, the main body of the work and a conclusion again referring to the question.
- Adopt a chronological approach. This question is essentially asking if Lord Bingham's approach is still applicable or if the courts' handling of judicial review claims has changed. By looking at the cases chronologically you can chart any changes more easily.
- The work of Christopher Newdick is particularly informative in this area. See for example: Newdick, C. (2005) *Who Should We Treat? Rights, Rationing and Resources in the NHS*, (2nd edn). Oxford: Oxford University Press; Newdick, C. (2007) Judicial review: low priority treatment and exceptional case review. *Medical Law Review*, 15(2): 236.
- Refer to the question throughout the essay – weave it in and out of the paragraphs, see for example the discussion after *R* (Rogers) v *Swindon NHS Primary Care Trust*.
- Look at other instances other than policy when a judicial review claim has succeeded, e.g. reliance on a promise, see *R* v *North Devon HA ex parte Coughlan* above. In so doing you are demonstrating that you are aware of on what grounds a judicial review application may succeed.

Don't be tempted to . . .

- Write a history of judicial review claims.
- Write a case review of *R* v *Cambridge, ex parte B* – ensure you discuss the case but the question requires much more than an analysis of the case only.

Question 2

Sonia has been diagnosed with cancer of the small intestine. She has already received treatment using conventional drugs and chemotherapy but with limited success. She has recently heard of a new anti-cancer drug being made available for patients with her condition and her consultant recommends that she should receive the drug as additional therapy. Although the drug had been licensed for second- and third-line treatment of patients with similar level of illness it has yet to have been appraised by the National Institute for Health and Care Excellence. Clinical trials indicated that the drug could lengthen Sonia's life expectancy by two years, however the medical evidence is incomplete and there is concern that the drug could cause respiratory problems in some patients. The cost of the new drug is £2,500 per month.

Sonia's application for her trust to fund the cost of this treatment was rejected, the trust citing that the drug is too expensive. As the drug is not in general use the trust state they may, however, still fund the treatment if a patient presents exceptional circumstances enough to justify treatment. The Exceptional Case Committee has ruled that Sonia is not an exceptional case as her circumstances are identical to other patients with her illness. In reaching this decision the committee indicated that the cost of the treatment was not a relevant factor.

Sonia wishes to apply for judicial review of the decision as being in breach of her human rights. She and her treating clinician contend that Sonia will benefit from the drug and are aware of patients with similar conditions being prescribed it. She would also like the committee to consider that she is the sole carer for her eight-year-old daughter who suffers from cerebral palsy.

Advise Sonia.

Answer plan

→ Identify the judicial review claim.

→ Consider relevant case law and apply it to the facts.

→ Discuss any potential claim under the Human Rights Act.

→ Conclude ensuring that you have advised Sonia.

Diagram plan

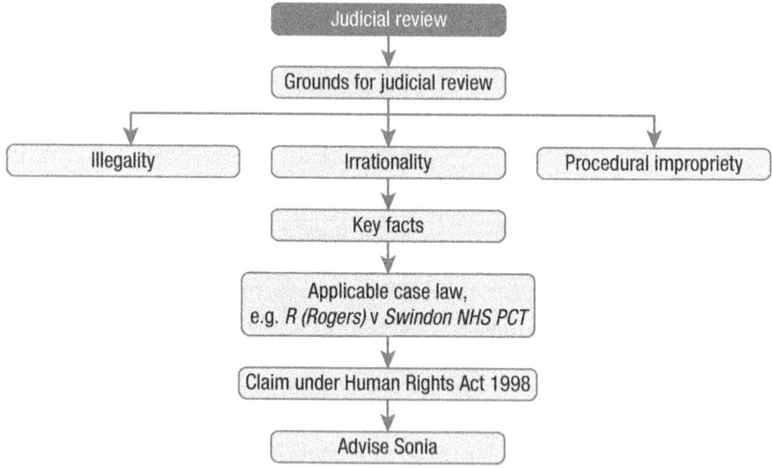

A printable version of this diagram plan is available from **www.pearsoned.co.uk/lawexpressqa**

Answer

Sonia's application for judicial review of the trust's decision not to fund her treatment with the new anti-cancer drug should ordinarily be made within three months from when the grounds of the application first arose (***St George's Healthcare NHS Trust* v *S*** [1998] 3 All ER 673) and should be the last resort (***R* v *Portsmouth Hospitals NHS Trust*** [1999] All ER 836). Sonia has already had an application rejected by the Exceptional Case Committee therefore a judicial review application is her only remaining option to challenge the decision.

The application may be made on one of three grounds:[1]

[1] It is not necessary to set out a detailed explanation of the law on judicial review but the answer should identify the grounds for making an application.

1 The trust's decision to refuse to fund the treatment was illegal.

2 The trust's decision was irrational or unreasonable. Unreasonable in the context of judicial review means satisfying the ***Wednesbury*** unreasonableness test, a decision 'so outrageous in its defiance of logic or accepted moral standards that no sensible person . . . could have arrived at it'.

3 There was procedural impropriety in the making of the decision.

Sonia's application to receive the anti-cancer drug was refused on the grounds of expense.[2] Sonia would have little prospect of success should she be challenging this preliminary decision. The courts have stated repeatedly that health authorities may consider financial constraints in reaching treatment decisions, see ***R* v *Central Birmingham HA, ex parte Walker*** (1987) 3 BMLR 32 and ***R* v *Cambridge District HA, ex parte B*** [1995] 2 All ER 129 where the Court of Appeal stressed that their function was not to consider the merits of the decision but rather the process by which it is reached.

[2] The answer begins with setting out the first argument in denying Sonia's application. The reasons given by the Exceptional Case Committee are discussed in the subsequent paragraphs.

Sonia may challenge the decision of the Exceptional Case Committee whose remit is to establish whether she presents exceptional circumstances enough to justify treatment notwithstanding the general rule. On the information provided, Sonia may allege that the decision to refuse her treatment was irrational similar to the ruling in ***R (Rogers)* v *Swindon NHS Primary Care Trust*** [2006] EWCA Civ 392.[3] In ***Rogers*** the applicant appealed against a decision not to fund the cost of treatment with the breast cancer drug Herceptin despite the Secretary of State and Mrs Rogers's consultant endorsing the treatment. As in Sonia's situation Mrs Rogers was denied treatment on the grounds that she was not an exceptional case and in reaching that decision the cost of the treatment was not a relevant factor. The Court of Appeal found in favour of Mrs Rogers, ruling that the policy of the PCT was irrational as it failed to consider each individual case, endorsing the approach of ***R* v *NW Lancashire HA and ex parte A, D, G*** [2000] FCR 525. Having excluded Mrs Rogers from treatment as she was not an exceptional case, the Committee could not suggest what amounted to 'exceptional' and for this reason the policy was deemed irrational as it amounted essentially to a blanket ban. Once financial considerations are ruled out Sir Anthony Clarke MR said: '. . . the only reasonable approach was to focus on the patient's clinical needs and fund patients within the eligible group who were properly prescribed Herceptin by their physician'.[4]

[3] It is not usually necessary to set out the facts of a case but here the point is made that Sonia's case is very similar to that of *Rogers*.

[4] In a problem question, paraphrasing the judgment will suffice but if you can quote directly from the judgment then do so.

Therefore unless the Committee produce more guidance as to why Sonia is not exceptional and furthermore what is an exceptional patient then she may challenge the decision as being irrational simply as 'exceptionality' as a workable concept is impossible to envisage.[5] If the Committee's decision was reached on the basis of cost, or that the drug is yet to be approved by the National Institute for Health and Care Excellence and

[5] Always state if further information is necessary to give a definitive answer and explain why.

there is evidence that it may cause respiratory failure then the decision may not be deemed irrational. The court in ***Rogers*** confirmed if the trust had decided not to fund the treatment because of financial constraints and on the basis that the drug had yet to be approved by the National Institute for Health and Care Excellence then it would have been unlikely that the policy would have been found irrational.

Sonia hopes the new drug will extend her life expectancy. Her situation is similar to a number of cases (see ***R (Otley)* v *Barking and Dagenham NHS PCT*** [2007] EWHC 1927 (Admin); ***R (Gordon)* v *Bromley NHS PCT*** [2006] EWHC 2462 (Admin)) and the courts have emphasised that where there was a chance that a drug could extend life then a patient should not be denied treatment because of spurious decision making. In ***R (Ross)* v *West Sussex PCT*** [2008] EWHC 2252 (Admin) the court held if the decision was a matter of life and death the courts would rigorously scrutinise the decision-making process. However, should the trust return to court with a more reasoned decision for denying treatment Sonia may find that continued funding of the drug is withdrawn particularly if the reasons for denying treatment are resource based (see the judgment of Ousely J in ***Bromley*** above).[6]

[6] The answer notes that the decision could change should the trust provide additional information.

Sonia also wants the court to consider that she is a single parent of a disabled child. In ***Rogers***, Clarke MR said a trust subject to financial constraints could legitimately elect to fund treatment for a woman caring for a disabled child and not for a woman with different personal circumstances. ***R (Gordon)* v *Bromley PCT*** similarly stated that exceptional circumstances may include where short-term survival mattered citing the example of someone who needed to make care arrangements for young children. Finally, in ***R (Murphy)* v *Salford PCT*** [2008] EWHC 1908 (Admin) the court said the applicant's submission that she was the main carer for her husband would be considered with all other factors. However, in ***Rogers*** Sir Anthony Clarke MR emphatically stated: 'Where the clinical needs are equal, and resources are not an issue, discrimination between patients in the same eligible group cannot be justified on the basis of personal characteristics not based on healthcare.'[7]

[7] The answer continues by discussing the relevance of personal characteristics in the decision-making process. Here it is good practice to refer to a few decisions to illustrate the varying factors the court may consider.

Furthermore, Sonia could not argue that in failing to consider social factors the trust breached her human rights.[8] In ***R (Condliff)* v *North Staffordshire PCT*** [2011] EWCA Civ 910 the Court of Appeal found that the PCT policy of excluding social factors was not in contravention

[8] The answer would not be complete without considering the impact, if any, of the Human Rights Act.

of Article 8 and furthermore even if Article 8 was engaged the PCT policy was in the margin of appreciation as it had attempted to reach a fair compromise between the needs of the individual and the general public.

In conclusion, Sonia's claim for judicial review has a reasonable prospect of succeeding on the basis that the trust's policy of exceptionality appears irrational given that they have specifically excluded cost as being a relevant factor.[9] However, her argument that a failure to consider social factors in breach of her human rights on the basis of the decision in ***Condliff*** is not sustainable.

[9] Always conclude reiterating your advice. The examiner may not agree with your conclusions but this does not matter providing you give a reasoned opinion.

✓ Make your answer stand out

- Have a defined structure, dealing with the arguments for and against each strand of the claim ensuring you anticipate the arguments likely to be raised by the trust.
- Identify if further information is required and say why, e.g. more information as to why Sonia is not considered to be 'exceptional'.
- Use a breadth of case law to support your argument. For example, Rogers was quoted extensively as the facts and issues in dispute are very similar to Sonia's case but also use other case law when discussing exceptionality.
- Remember your task is to advise Sonia, hence give a reasoned conclusion. If you are unable to come to a definitive conclusion, say why and state what further information is required.

! Don't be tempted to . . .

- Give an extensive résumé of the law on judicial review.
- Cite every case that you can recall on judicial review whether it has any bearing on the facts of the problem.
- Get into a discussion of the appropriateness of the court's role, for example should they be more interventionist; this is the function of an essay not a problem – your task is to advise.

www.pearsoned.co.uk/lawexpressqa

Go online to access more revision support including additional essay and problem questions with diagram plans, You be the marker questions, and download all diagrams from the book.

3 Clinical negligence

How this topic may come up in exams

This is a topic of enormous importance as it is the likely area of practice for medical law students. Essay questions will focus on two main issues. The first is the *Bolam* test and the courts' treatment of medical expert evidence. The second theme is causation. Questions may feature the loss of a chance claim, risk disclosure or simply the complications in proving causation. Problem questions will require you to advise a party on the merits of a clinical negligence claim. Here, knowledge of the law is essential, but so is an ability to apply it.

Before you begin

It's a good idea to consider the following key themes of clinical negligence before tackling a question on this topic.

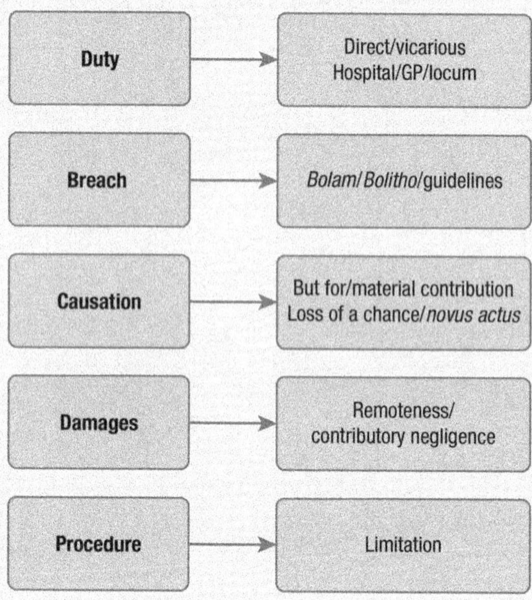

A printable version of this diagram is available from **www.pearsoned.co.uk/lawexpressqa**

Question 1

In *Gregg* v *Scott* Lord Nicholls comments that the decision not to award damages for loss of a chance is 'rough justice indeed'. (*Gregg* v *Scott* [2005] UKHL 2, para. 49)

To what extent do you consider that the approach taken by the judiciary to the legal principles in proving a loss of a chance in clinical negligence claims is an example of 'rough justice'?

Answer plan

- Introduce causation.
- Define the claim for loss of a chance.
- Set out the courts' approach in tort and contract cases.
- Introduce *Hotson* and percentage rule.
- Critically analyse the judgments in *Gregg* v *Scott*.
- Evaluate the role of policy versus legal certainty.
- Conclude – should the courts recognise a loss of chance claim in clinical negligence? Is there an alternative?

Diagram plan

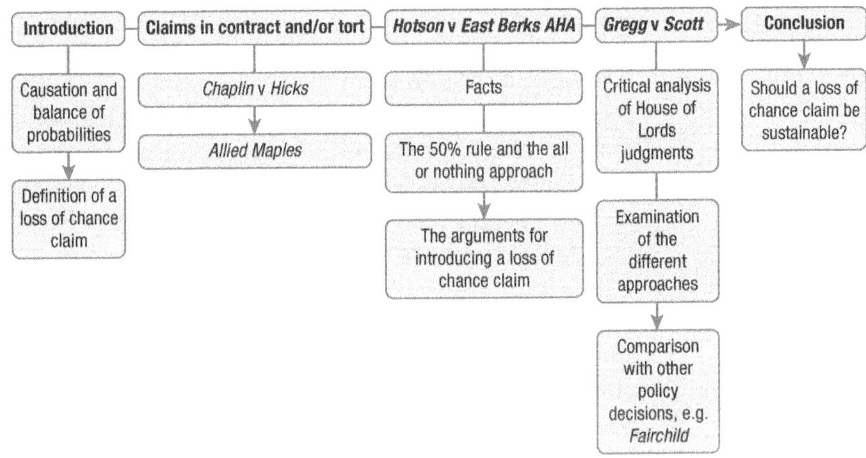

A printable version of this diagram plan is available from **www.pearsoned.co.uk/lawexpressqa**

Answer

For a clinical negligence claim to succeed the claimant must establish a causal link between the breach and the resulting damage on a balance of probabilities. A loss of a chance claim contends that because of a delay in treatment or diagnosis, the claimant lost the chance of making a full or a better recovery. A loss of a chance claim is not a new phenomenon, however it is peculiar in that it generates problems for clinical negligence claims not encountered in other areas of tort. It is these difficulties that are alluded to in Lord Nicholls's judgment and which will be the focus of the discussion in this essay.[1]

[1] It is sensible to introduce the test for causation at the outset together with a brief explanation of the loss of a chance claim. Additionally, note the immediate reference to the question.

Generally, in both tort and contract claims, the courts have awarded damages for loss of a chance – see, for example, ***Chaplin* v *Hicks*** [1911] 2 KB 786 and ***Allied Maples Group Ltd* v *Simmons & Simmons*** [1995] 1 WLR 1602 which awarded damages for the loss of a 'real or substantial chance'. Yet, long before the decision in ***Gregg* v *Scott*** the courts had ruled that the loss of chance claim was not sustainable in a clinical negligence claim.[2]

[2] One of the more significant issues with a loss of chance claim is that clinical negligence cases are dealt with on a different basis from tort and contract cases.

In ***Hotson* v *East Berks AHA*** [1987] 2 All ER 909, a boy alleged that a four-day delay in diagnosis deprived him of a 25 per cent chance of avoiding developing avascular necrosis. The Court of Appeal awarded him 25 per cent of the damages in line with the 25 per cent chance he had lost. The House of Lords, however, pointedly held that causation should be decided on an all or nothing approach. Therefore, unless the claimant could show that he had lost a chance in excess of 50 per cent, his claim would fail, something which the claimant in ***Hotson*** was unable to establish. ***Hotson*** signalled that the courts would not award proportionate awards of damages. Consequently, notwithstanding the extent of the negligence, this approach means that the loss of chance claim can never succeed unless the claimant can show he had a greater than 50 per cent chance of recovery. This differs drastically from a non-clinical negligence case where once the claimant has established that a chance has been lost the courts then go on to evaluate that loss. Is this indeed 'rough justice'?[3]

[3] *Hotson* is the forerunner of the *Gregg* decision and thus is essential to the discussion.

In ***Gregg* v *Scott*** the claimant had developed non-Hodgkins Lymphoma. He saw his GP who negligently diagnosed it as a benign lymphoma and failed to refer him to a specialist. This failure to refer was negligent and it delayed treatment by nine months, reducing the claimant's chance of surviving for five years from 42 per cent to 25 per cent. Applying ***Hotson***, however, loss of a less than even chance was not an actionable injury. The claimant could not show on the balance of probabilities that the negligent failure to refer had a material effect on the outcome of the disease, because the prospects of a cure were in any event less than 50 per cent.

Gregg was a 3–2 majority decision echoing perhaps the amount of discord among legal commentators.[4] Lord Nicholls and others argued there was an over-reliance on statistical evidence, saying 'statistics do not show whether the claimant patient would have conformed to the trend or been an exception from it'. But more significantly there was a realisation by some members of the judiciary that in situations where it is impossible to predict what the outcome would have been if the negligence had not occurred, then it was appropriate to develop the law. At paragraph 42 Lord Nicholls commented that: 'A patient should have an appropriate remedy when he loses the very thing it was the doctor's duty to protect.' He continued: 'It cannot be right to adopt a procedure having the effect that, in law, a patient's prospects of recovery are treated as non-existent whenever they exist but fall short of 50 per cent. If the law were to proceed in this way it would deserve to be likened to the proverbial ass.'[5]

It is the last comment in particular that has prompted academics such as Charles Foster to agree with the sentiments expressed in the question. As others have previously observed, as the law stands it means that there will never be any liability providing there was a less than 50 per cent chance of survival, regardless of the manner of the negligence.[6]

The majority judgment in ***Gregg*** held that the claimant had not shown on a balance of probabilities that the negligence had affected the course of Mr Gregg's illness or his prospects of survival. Furthermore, they argued that loss of a chance of a more favourable outcome should not be introduced into a personal injury claim. Hoffman LJ states that to compensate all those claimants where a defendant may have caused injury and increased the likelihood of injury would 'involve abandoning a good deal of authority'. Baroness Hale was similarly like-minded arguing that if the law were reformulated then it would effectively mean that 'almost any claim for loss of an outcome could be reformulated as a claim for loss of a chance of that outcome'.

[4] Charles Foster writes of the decision in *Gregg* that many think it was intuitively unjust – see Foster (2005).

[5] It is not always essential to quote from a case but in *Gregg* where the judgments are so diverse it helps to illustrate the depth of judicial debate.

[6] Lord Nicholls himself quotes Dore J in *Herskovits v Group Health Cooperative of Puget Sound* (1983) 664 P 2d 474, 477: 'To decide otherwise would be a blanket release from liability for doctors and hospitals any time there was less than a 50% per cent chance of survival, regardless of how flagrant the negligence.'

It is noteworthy that there was little or no attempt to put forward a plausible argument why clinical negligence should be dealt with differently from other tort cases. Furthermore, although there is something to be said for maintaining legal certainty and applying black letter law, ***Gregg*** does not sit happily with the decisions in ***Fairchild* v *Glenhaven Funeral Services Ltd*** [2002] UKHL 22 and ***Chester* v *Afshar*** [2004] UKHL 41 which adopted a more creative approach.[7] However, it seems that the Australian judiciary are also not minded to be more creative; the decision in ***Tabet* v *Gett (2010)*** 84 ALJR 292 firmly rejected the loss of chance claim. For the present, claimants must be content with an award for damages for loss of life expectancy (***JD* v *Mather*** [2012] EWHC 3063 (QB)), an alternative to the loss of a chance claim and one that had been previously been suggested by Baroness Hale in ***Gregg***.[8]

[7] Here the answer demonstrates to the examiner that you are aware of other decisions where policy factors influenced the eventual outcome.

[8] Not essential but again by quoting cases from other jurisdictions the answer demonstrates wider reading.

The decision in ***Gregg*** may be taken as an example of legal certainty triumphing over judicial creativity, in contrast to the decisions in ***Fairchild*** and ***Chester***. What is apparent, however, is that, as Mr Gregg himself demonstrated by surviving beyond his predicted life expectancy, relying on statistical evidence is inherently unreliable. As Bean J, referring to ***Gregg*** in ***JD* v *Mather*** acknowledged: 'There is a difficulty about applying such statistics to show an individual cancer patient's prognosis for the purposes of a trial of causation.'[9] Unlike in contract or tort actions, a clinical negligence loss of a chance claim has seemingly little hope of success and for some that is 'rough justice' indeed.

[9] The conclusion again refers to the problems with relying on statistical evidence linking to the earlier discussion.

✓ Make your answer stand out

- A thorough knowledge of the case law in this area is essential. Not only should you be familiar with the House of Lords' judgments in *Hotson* v *East Berks AHA* and *Gregg* v *Scott* but you should be able to refer to the first instance and/or the Court of Appeal's judgments in both cases where it adds to your argument.
- It is important that you demonstrate how the courts deal with the loss of chance claim in non-clinical negligence claims, thereby illustrating how this differs to the approach in clinical negligence claims.
- The question is not simply about the loss of a chance claim. You must be alert to the policy issues involved here and this should be evident in your answer by quoting the parts of the key judgments and, if relevant, other decisions which have policy overtones.

- There is extensive academic commentary and de
claim. You could refer to Maskrey, S. and Edis, W
Scott: mixed messages for lawyers. *Journal of Pe*
(2005) *Gregg* v *Scott*: loss of a chance, chance c
11(2): 166; or Foster, C. (2005) Last chance for
Lords). *New Law Journal*, 18(2): 248.

! Don't be tempted to . . .

- Give a narrative of all aspects of causation – the question is focused on the loss of a chance claim only.
- Simply write a case review of *Gregg* v *Scott*. The majority of the marks are allocated for critical analysis.
- Be too one-sided – you should put forward the reasons why the court eventually ruled against Mr Gregg even if you yourself do not agree with the decision!

Question 2

'The patient's right to be appropriately warned is an important right, which few doctors in the current legal and social climate would consciously or deliberately violate.' (per Lord Bingham *Chester* v *Afshar* [2004] UKHL 41)

Critically analyse the development of the courts' approach to this 'important right' in clinical negligence cases for non-disclosure of risk.

Answer plan

→ Explain what the risk disclosure claim is and why it is distinct from other clinical negligence claims.

→ Identify the two parts to the question – standard of care and causation.

→ Set out the courts' approach to standard of care with reference to *Bolam* and *Sidaway*.

→ With reference to case law critically analyse if the courts' approach has changed.

→ Causation – explain the test before *Chester*.

→ Evaluate the significance of *Chester*.

→ Discuss the significance of *Montgomery*.

→ Conclude – are risk disclosure cases treated differently?

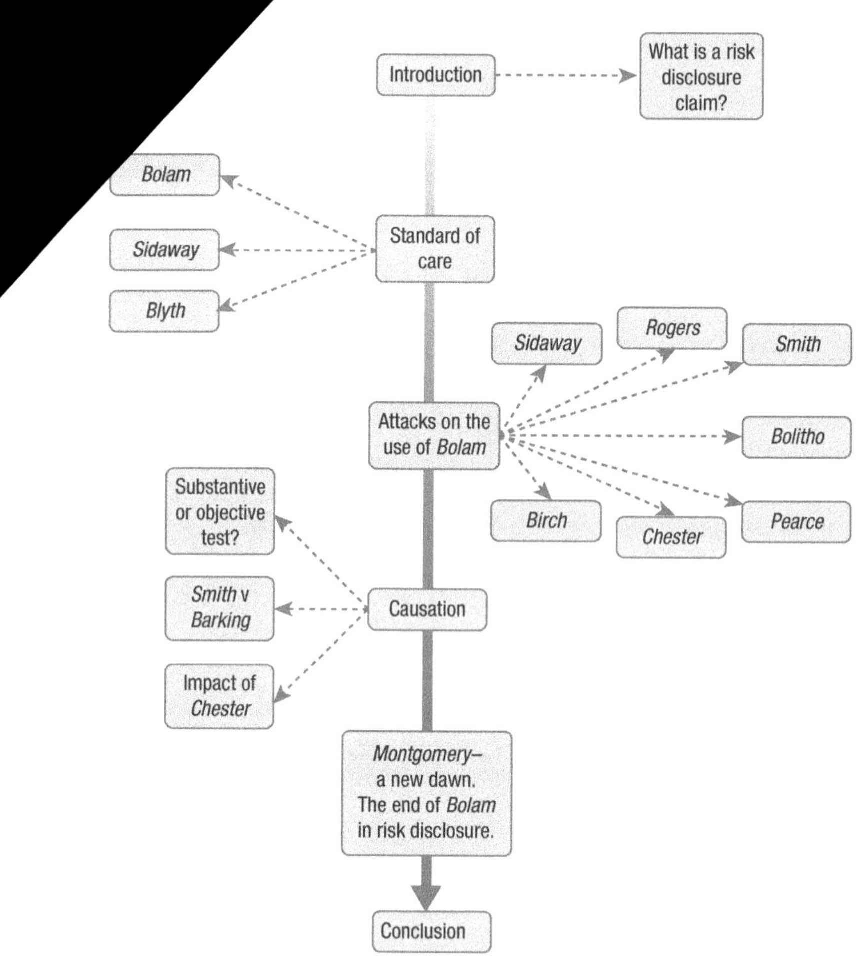

A printable version of this diagram plan is available from **www.pearsoned.co.uk/lawexpressqa**

Answer

A risk disclosure claim arises when a claimant alleges that, had they been informed of the risks associated with treatment, they would not have undergone the treatment, or would have delayed it. This is distinct from other clinical negligence claims; deciding what information to disclose to a patient involves no clinical skill.[1]

[1]Show that you are aware of what makes a risk disclosure claim distinct.

With the shift away from medical paternalism towards patient autonomy, academics such as Brazier and Miola have argued for a different approach to the ***Bolam*** test (***Bolam* v *Friern Hospital Management Committee*** [1957] 2 All ER 118) in risk disclosure claims.[2] The requirement that a claimant must establish that, had they known of the risk(s), they would have declined the procedure has been seen as unjustified. This essay examines the courts' change in approach to risk disclosure claims.

[2] By referring to academic opinion the answer demonstrates that it is aware information disclosure is topical and controversial.

In ***Bolam***, the claimant argued that he should have been informed of the risk of bone fractures while receiving ECT treatment. Justice McNair applied what has become known as the ***Bolam*** test which states there will be no negligence if the defendant has 'acted in accordance with a practice accepted as proper by a responsible body of medical men skilled in that particular art'. It does not matter if other doctors would have acted differently to the defendant – 'a doctor is not negligent, if he is acting in accordance with such a practice, merely because there is a body of opinion that takes a contrary view'.

The flaws with the ***Bolam*** test are well versed, but significantly in risk disclosure cases ***Bolam*** seemingly gave doctors free rein to decide what information to disclose.[3]

[3] The answer must explain *Bolam* but always refer to the test in the context of a risk disclosure claim.

In ***Sidaway* v *Board of Governors of the Bethlem Royal Hospital*** [1985] AC 871 the House of Lords considered information disclosure. While the claimant failed to convince the court she should have been informed of a 1–2 per cent risk and the ***Bolam*** test was followed, the House of Lords deliberated on whether ***Bolam*** should apply to risk disclosure cases.

Lord Scarman, dissenting, argued that the court should ask 'what a reasonably prudent patient' would want to know subject only to 'therapeutic privilege'. He described the patient's right to make his own decision as a basic human right. Lord Bridge, although favouring ***Bolam***, opined that 'disclosure of a particular risk was so obviously necessary to an informed choice on the part of the patient that no reasonably prudent medical man would fail to make it.'[4]

[4] An essay on risk disclosure must discuss *Sidaway*. It is desirable if you can quote from the case demonstrating that you are aware of the marked differences in the judgments.

In Sidaway the judiciary recognised the right of a patient to make his own decision. Yet change was slow, see ***Gold* v *Haringey HA*** [1988] QB 481 and ***Blyth* v *Bloomsbury HA*** [1993] 4 Med LR 151 (even if a patient asked questions, ***Bolam*** applied).[5] The lower

[5] Note how the essay is following a chronological approach thereby charting the development of the law in risk disclosure claims.

courts did challenge the application of ***Bolam*** in risk disclosure cases (see ***Smith* v *Tunbridge Wells HA*** [1994] 5 Med LR 334). But these instances were rare – the English courts lagged behind the approach taken in other jurisdictions. In ***Rogers* v *Whitaker*** (1993) 4 Med LR 79, in finding the defendant negligent for failing to disclose a 1/14,000 risk, the Australian court deemed that evidence of accepted practice is useful but the courts must 'adjudicate on what is the appropriate standard of care after giving weight to the paramount consideration that a person is entitled to make his own decisions about his life'.[6]

[6] Referring to case law from other jurisdictions is useful but only if it is relevant to the question. The significance of the decision in *Rogers* v *Whitaker* cannot be overstated.

In ***Bolitho* v *City and Hackney HA*** [1997] 4 All ER 771 ***Bolam*** was scrutinised again. Lord Browne-Wilkinson stressed that the accepted practice must be logical and the experts must have reached a 'defensible conclusion'. However, he added it will be a 'rare case' for a court to find a practice unreasonable.

Bolitho only referred to cases of diagnosis and treatment and it was not until ***Pearce* v *United Bristol Healthcare NHS Trust*** [1999] PIQR P53 that ***Bolitho*** was applied in a risk disclosure case. Mrs Pearce gave birth to a stillborn child. She claimed her consultant should have advised her of the increased risk of stillbirth (0.1–0.2 per cent) associated with non-intervention. Lord Woolf, commenting on the legal duty of doctors, said: 'if there is a significant risk which would affect the judgment of a reasonable patient . . . it is the responsibility of a doctor to inform the patient of that significant risk.'[7]

[7] *Pearce* is again extremely significant for the comments made by Lord Woolf and for its application of *Bolitho.*

Pearce applied ***Bolitho*** to risk disclosure claims and declared information disclosure should be decided with reference to the patient and not accepted medical practice.

This sentiment was echoed in ***Chester* v *Afshar*** when remarkably the House of Lords created an exception to the rules of causation in risk disclosure claims. Following ***Chester*** claimants can recover damages even if they are unable to prove that, if the warning had been given, they would not have had the treatment. Acknowledging that the decision was one of policy, Lord Steyn said: 'This result is in accord with one of the basic aspirations of the law, namely to right wrongs.'

The judgment in ***Chester*** was influenced by the Australian decision in ***Chappel* v *Hart*** [1998] HCA 55 and has attracted academic criticism for the courts disregard of causation law. However, ***Chester*** is a decision maximising patient autonomy and a definitive . a failure to recognise a patient's right to make an informed d. will attract liability, notwithstanding that that failure has not cau. the patient harm.[8]

[8] *Chester* should be discussed in detail for both its comments on policy and patient autonomy and for its unique approach to causation in risk disclosure actions.

In ***Birch* v *University Hospital NHS Foundation Trust*** [2008] EWHC 2237 (QB) the court held that there was a duty to disclose the comparative risks between two procedures. This approach has recently been endorsed by the Supreme Court in ***Montgomery* v *Lanarkshire Health Board*** [2015] UKSC 11, approving the judgment of Lord Scarman in ***Sidaway***.[9] Nadine Montgomery argued that her consultant had negligently failed to disclose a 9–10 per cent risk of shoulder dystocia (which eventuated) associated with a vaginal delivery and failed to discuss with her the alternative of a caesarean section. In finding for the claimant Lords Kerr and Reed stated the doctor's duty is to 'take reasonable care to ensure that the patient is aware of any material risks involved in any recommended treatment, and of any reasonable alternative or variant treatments.' Commenting on what is a material risk, the court said it is whether in the particular circumstances, 'a reasonable person in the patient's position would be likely to attach significance to the risk, or the doctor is or should reasonably be aware that the particular patient would be likely to attach significance to it.'

[9] *Montgomery* is a momentous decision; it pronounces the majority decision in *Sidaway* unsatisfactory and effectively the end of the application of *Bolam* in risk disclosure cases. Therefore the answer must explain the facts and refer to the key judgments in appropriate detail.

Sidaway is no more. In tandem with changes introduced by the medical profession, ***Montgomery*** has now pronounced that risk disclosure is patient-centred. In ***Chester*** Lord Hope declared 'paternalism no longer rules and a patient has a . . . right to be informed . . . of a small, but well established risk.' With the Montgomery ruling, the courts have at last afforded this important right the protection it deserves.[10]

[10] Always conclude with reference to the question– now with the *Montgomery* decision a clear view can be reached.

✓ Make your answer stand out

- As for all essays you should be familiar with the case law in this area. This is a question on risk disclosure and as such you must use case law relevant to risk disclosure claims.
- It is important that you consider both standard of care and causation; both areas of law have attracted debate and controversy.

→

chance claim, the question again features policy issues and you need quoting relevant parts of key judgments and referring to academic ropriate.

cademic commentary in this area, both on the law relating to d causation. See, for example, Miola, J. (2009) On the materiality of risk – paper tigers and panaceas. *Medical Law Review*, 17: 76–108; Brazier, M. and Miola, J. (2000) Bye bye *Bolam*: a medical litigation revolution? *Medical Law Review*, 8(1): 84–115; Shaw, M. (2004) Sick pay. *Solicitors Journal*, 29(10): 1228; Foster, C. (2004) It should be, therefore it is. *New Law Journal*, 5(11): 1644. A good answer will refer to a number of academic sources.

! Don't be tempted to . . .

- Give a narrative of all aspects of standard of care or causation – the question is focused on the risk disclosure chance claim only and hence you must be selective on the case law.
- Only refer to *Chester* v *Afshar*; the question involves far more than that.
- Spend too much time looking at the ethics and why patient autonomy should be favoured over medical paternalism. The question requires you to look at the courts approach to risk disclosure claims and how it has developed.

? Question 3

In July 2010, Victoria, aged 46, who was experiencing abdominal pains and menstrual bleeding, saw her General Practitioner (GP), Dr Spring, at the Eldon Practice. Dr Spring conducted a brief examination and advised Victoria that her symptoms were due to the onset of the menopause. In September, with increasing pains, Victoria saw Dr Lake, a locum who was covering for Dr Spring. Victoria explained her symptoms and, after looking at Victoria's medical records, Dr Lake concluded that Victoria was suffering from menopausal symptoms. She prescribed paracetemol to help with the pain.

Victoria, experiencing increasingly severe pains, saw Dr Pond, another GP in the practice in November. Dr Pond referred Victoria to Oceanton NHS Trust Hospital for immediate investigation of her symptoms. There was a waiting list and it was eight weeks before Victoria saw a consultant gynaecologist, Mr Well. On his advice Victoria underwent an ultrasound examination. This revealed a mass in her abdominal cavity which was then diagnosed as a malignant tumour. Victoria underwent an abdominal hysterectomy and, as an unavoidable consequence of the surgery, sustained an injury to her bowel.

Following the operation, Mr Well said if Victoria had been referred earlier he could have treated the tumour less aggressively, without such invasive surgery. Victoria, however, was so elated to have the tumour removed that she did not listen to what was being said. Several months later when Victoria was attending a follow-up appointment Mr Well informed her that her bowel problems would not improve.

It is now January 2015 and Victoria wants compensation for her injuries.

Discuss:

(i) the prospects of establishing breach of the duty of care by any of the parties; and

(ii) the main procedural problem with this claim.

Answer plan

→ Identify the defendants and whether a duty is owed.

→ Apply *Bolam/Bolitho* tests re breach of the standard of care.

→ Apply sections 14(1), (3), 33 Limitation Act 1980 identifying the date of knowledge.

Diagram plan

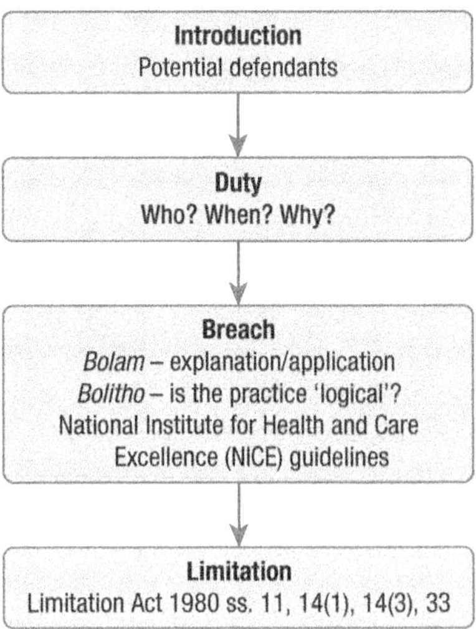

A printable version of this diagram plan is available from **www.pearsoned.co.uk/lawexpressqa**

Answer

Victoria may have a claim against any of the GPs who may be sued individually or she may sue the Eldon Practice directly as all partners are jointly and severally liable.[1] The locum, Dr Lake, is not an employee of the practice but is an independent contractor and should be sued personally unless it is established there were errors in his recruitment. Victoria may also have a claim against the Oceanton NHS Trust: first, as it is vicariously liable for the negligence of its employees; and, second, they may be directly liable for the eight-week delay.[2]

Victoria is owed a duty of care by all the health workers.[3] She is owed a duty of care by the GPs as she is a patient on their list, by Mr Well as she receives treatment from him, and by the trust to provide competent staff and safe working practices. The duty of care begins when treatment commences and ends when treatment is completed, or the patient dies.

Dr Spring diagnoses that Victoria is suffering from the onset of menopause. Would other GPs also have performed a brief examination and arrived at the same conclusion as Dr Spring?

There will be no negligence if Dr Spring has 'acted in accordance with a practice accepted as proper by a responsible body of medical men skilled in that particular art',[4] (***Bolam* v *Friern Hospital Management Committee*** [1957] 2 All ER 118 at 122, 'the ***Bolam*** test'). It doesn't matter if some other GPs would have acted differently, as 'a doctor is not negligent, if he is acting in accordance with such a practice, merely because there is a body of opinion that takes a contrary view' (***Bolam***).[5] An error in diagnosis is not negligent (***Whitehouse* v *Jordan*** [1980] 1 All ER 650). Providing that a body of other GPs would have acted similarly and diagnosed menopausal symptoms, she will not be in breach of the standard of care.[6]

We would need to establish whether current medical practice was being followed (***Roe* v *Minister of Health*** [1954] 2 QB 66) and whether any National Institute for Health and Care Excellence guidelines (NICE) are applicable.[7] The practice must also be adopted by at least two other GPs (***Defreitas* v *O'Brien*** [1995] 6 Med LR 108) and is capable of 'withstanding logical analysis' (***Bolitho* v *City and Hackney HA*** [1997] 4 All ER 771).

[1] In the opening paragraph identify all the potential defendants.

[2] Demonstrate that you are aware that the trust may be both potentially vicariously and directly liable which will be discussed in detail later.

[3] Explain who owes a duty of care and why.

[4] You should quote the *Bolam* test given that it is the legal test for the standard of care.

[5] The *Bolam* test must be explained and applied to the present scenario.

[6] Note how the answer constantly speculates on what is the approved practice.

[7] The answer continues to define what is accepted practice as per *Bolam* and also refers to guidelines which are of increasing importance in evidence-based medicine.

On the facts available, particularly noting Victoria's age and symptoms and that this is the first occasion she has visited a GP with these symptoms, Dr Spring may not be found in breach of the standard of care.[8]

[8] It is appropriate to come to a conclusion for each party with the caveat that you should state what further information you need should you not be able to arrive at a definitive conclusion.

Similarly, Dr Lake will have to satisfy the ***Bolam*** test.[9] Dr Lake consults Victoria's medical records before making the same diagnosis as Dr Spring. Victoria is presenting with the same symptoms several weeks after seeing Dr Spring, therefore Dr Lake may be at fault for failing to review the diagnosis[10] (***Stacey* v *Chiddy*** [1993] 4 Med LR 216) or refer Victoria to a specialist (***Judge* v *Huntingdon HA*** [1995] 6 Med LR 223). Dr Lake may contend that other GPs would have acted similarly (***Bolam***) but given the increased severity of the symptoms, the practice may be illogical (***Bolitho***). No conclusions may be reached without further information on accepted practice and any relevant guidelines.

[9] The answer continues applying the *Bolam*/*Bolitho* tests for each potential tortfeasor.

[10] Remember to apply the tests with reference to the particular facts, here the failure to review the initial diagnosis.

Dr Pond refers Victoria to the trust for further investigation. His actions seem reasonable, however it is eight weeks before she sees Mr Well. We would need to ascertain what information Dr Pond included in the referral letter, for example was the letter ambiguous or did it make clear that Victoria needed to be seen on an urgent basis.[11] Again the ***Bolam*** and ***Bolitho*** tests will apply. The requisite information to be included will be what other GPs would have stated, however if Victoria is to be seen on an urgent basis and it is not customary practice (***Bolam***) to include this in the letter then the court may find the practice illogical (***Bolitho***).

[11] Here the answer speculates on the reasons for the eight-week delay and who may be responsible.

At present we don't know the cause of the delay. It may be due to the trust not having a reasonable system in place for scheduling appointments (***Bull* v *Devon AHA*** [1993] 4 Med LR 117) and/or for failing to recognise that Victoria should be seen urgently. It is improbable that the trust could argue that an eight-week delay is accepted practice. Even if this is ***Bolam*** compliant, it is likely to be ***Bolitho*** illogical. Thus the trust may find itself directly liable for the delay in scheduling an appointment and also vicariously liable for the negligence of its employees.[12]

[12] The paragraph concludes by discussing direct and vicarious liability which was referred to in the introduction.

The actions of Mr Well appear to be those of a reasonably competent surgeon as the facts state Victoria's injuries were 'unavoidable'. He is not in breach of the standard of care and thus not negligent.

Even if Victoria were to establish that any of the potential tortfeasors were in breach and this was causative of her injuries, then she will be unable to pursue her claim if it is outside the limitation period.

A claim for personal injuries must be commenced three years from the date when the cause of action accrues or the date of the claimant's knowledge, whichever is the later (s. 11 Limitation Act 1980). We need to ascertain whether Victoria has either actual or constructive knowledge (s. 14(1)), (s. 14(3)).

Victoria need not know of the specific act or omission which caused her injury or that the defendant was negligent, but she must have knowledge that the defendant's acts might have caused her injuries.[13]

It is unlikely that Victoria will be deemed to have knowledge before the surgery as she was unaware that her tumour may have been treated differently had it been diagnosed earlier. However, when Mr Well informs her that surgery may have been avoidable (***Dobbie* v *Medway HA*** [1994] 5 Med LR 160) she may be fixed with actual knowledge. If Victoria is deemed not to have actual knowledge, it can be argued that Mr Well's comments should have led her to make further enquiry and she will be fixed with constructive knowledge[14] (***Whiston* v *London Strategic HA*** [2010] EWCA Civ 195). Victoria may find it difficult to argue that she does not have actual knowledge when Mr Well sees her for a second time. From the facts we must assume that this is sometime in 2011 and thus her claim may be statute barred. Victoria can request the court to exercise its section 33 discretion and disapply the limitation period, though the court must be satisfied that there are cogent reasons for not bringing the claim within the limitation period, and here Victoria may struggle.

[13] It is useful to generally state what Victoria need have knowledge of so explaining how the Limitation Act is applied.

[14] After examining whether Victoria has actual knowledge, the answer must then go on to consider constructive knowledge as time will begin to run if she is fixed with either actual or constructive knowledge.

Make your answer stand out

- Adopt a chronological approach and deal with each party as they arise in the scenario.
- Quote directly from *Bolam* v *Friern Hospital Management Committee* and *Bolitho* v *City & Hackney HA* – these cases are essential when discussing breach of the standard of care.
- Explain and apply the *Bolam* and *Bolitho* tests to the facts in the question – do the facts indicate that the defendant may have not been *Bolam*/*Bolitho* compliant?
- Apply other case law which is relevant to the particular facts in the question, e.g. an error in diagnosis (see *Whitehouse* v *Jordan* [1980] 1 All ER 650).
- Speculate on what further information you need to arrive at any definite conclusion.

! Don't be tempted to . . .

- Discuss anything other than duty, breach and limitation.
- Critically analyse the *Bolam/Bolitho* tests – this would be suitable for an essay question but not a problem question.
- Simply state the *Bolam/Bolitho* tests apply and go no further in the discussion. The question requires you to apply the tests not simply recite them.
- Refer extensively to academic commentary. Again the place for this is an essay question.

? Question 4

In March 2014 Ted, aged 29, went to his GP's practice complaining of persistent headaches. His GP, Dr Rock, advised him that perhaps he needed new spectacles and that he make an appointment with his optician. Ted did change his spectacles but the headaches persisted.

In May 2014, still suffering from headaches, Ted went back to see Dr Rock. Dr Rock was on holiday and Ted was examined by Dr Stone. Prior to making a diagnosis Dr Stone consulted Ted's medical records and noted the last entry said: 'March – headaches – stress – holiday?' Dr Stone, having examined Ted, advised rest and painkillers.

In June 2014 Ted collapsed at work with blinding headaches. Dr Stone visited Ted at home and suggested that Ted may have contracted the flu bug. Ted asked Dr Stone if he could be seen by a specialist but was told 'he would be wasting his time'.

Two months later, Ted was attending the local hospital after standing on a nail. While there he complained to the Accident and Emergency (A&E) doctor, Dr Pebble, of the persistent headaches and dizzy spells. Dr Pebble said that Ted was probably suffering from the after-effects of the accident; however, he agreed to X-rays being taken and said he would forward the results to Ted's GP.

Two months later Ted received an urgent phone call from the practice asking him to make an immediate appointment. When he attended the practice he learnt that the X-ray results had been available for some time but the practice's receptionist had simply filed them away. Ted was now told that the X-rays revealed he had a tumour on the brain which had become inoperable.

Advise Ted if he may have a claim in clinical negligence.

Answer plan

→ Identify potential defendants.

→ Work through the problem chronologically, identifying duty and potential breach of the standard of care and applying the legal tests.

→ Discuss and apply the relevant legal rules for causation.

→ Conclude – advise Ted.

Diagram plan

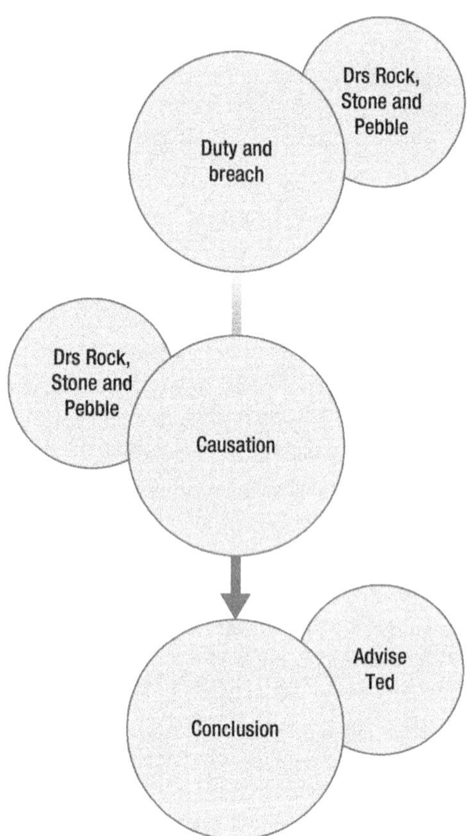

A printable version of this diagram plan is available from **www.pearsoned.co.uk/lawexpressqa**

Answer

Ted may have a claim against any of the GPs either individually or he may elect to sue the GP practice. The practice is vicariously liable for the actions of their employees; here the conduct of the receptionist is questionable. Ted may sue his local hospital if Dr Pebble is in breach of the standard of care.[1]

[1] Introduce the parties who may be liable in your opening paragraph.

Ted is owed a duty of care by all the health carers.[2] The GPs owe Ted a duty as he is a patient on their list; Dr Pebble and the local hospital as Ted was admitted for treatment. The duty of care begins when

[2] Deal with duty succinctly as this is not an issue in this case.

treatment commences and ends when treatment is completed or the patient dies.

Dr Rock attributes Ted's headaches to poor vision. Dr Rock will not be negligent 'if he has acted in accordance with a practice accepted as proper by a responsible body of medical men skilled in that particular art'.[3] (***Bolam* v *Friern Hospital Management Committee*** [1957] 2 All ER 118, 'the ***Bolam*** test'). Dr Rock must have followed a practice adopted by other GPs, like is compared with like. It does not matter if other GPs would have acted differently: 'A doctor is not negligent, if he is acting in accordance with such a practice, merely because there is a body of opinion that takes a contrary view' (***Bolam***). If other GPs would have made a similar diagnosis, then he is unlikely to be in breach. However, Dr Rock cannot adopt any medical practice; the practice must be a current practice (***Roe* v *Minister of Health*** [1954] 2 QB 66). We need to confirm if National Institute for Health and Care Excellence guidelines apply; although not legally binding they are indicative of current practice. The practice must also be adopted by at least two other GPs (***Defreitas* v *O'Brien*** [1995] 6 Med LR 108) and must be capable of 'withstanding logical analysis' (***Bolitho* v *City and Hackney HA*** [1997] 4 All ER 771). In summary the practice must be ***Bolam*** and ***Bolitho*** compatible.[4]

[3] *Bolam* is introduced and then the paragraph continues to explain the *Bolam* test and apply it.

[4] It is important that you consider whether the practice is not only *Bolam* but *Bolitho* compliant.

Given Ted's young age, notwithstanding ***Bolam***, then applying ***Bolitho*** it may be illogical not to ask Ted to revisit the surgery if the headaches continue or send him for further tests.[5] However, without expert medical evidence on the accepted practice we cannot arrive at a definitive conclusion. Dr Stone must act as a responsible GP (***Bolam***). He consulted Ted's medical records before making a diagnosis. Dr Rock has a duty to write accurate medical records but the medical records omit to mention his view that Ted's vision may be impaired. Dr Stone is under a duty to review Ted's diagnosis (***Hutton* v *East Dyfed HA*** [1998] 1 Lloyd's Rep Med 335) particularly as Ted continues to suffer from his original symptoms. Dr Stone could have referred Ted to a specialist or scheduled a follow-up appointment (***Judge* v *Huntingdon HA*** [1995] 6 Med LR 223). There is a duty to refer or seek further advice when a doctor is unable to diagnose or treat a patient (***Macdonald* v *York County Hospital*** (1973) 41 DLR (3d) 321). All of these factors may indicate that despite being ***Bolam*** compatible, the practice may be ***Bolitho*** illogical. Further information is required on accepted practice and any clinical guidelines covering Ted's scenario.[6]

[5] It is acceptable after considering whether Dr Rock is in breach to then come to a conclusion with reference to the available facts.

[6] After applying case law that is relevant to this factual scenario the paragraph concludes again with reference to the *Bolam*/*Bolitho* tests and noting that further information is required.

Dr Stone's actions will be judged according to the ***Bolam*** and ***Bolitho*** tests. There is a more convincing case that Dr Stone may be in breach for not referring Ted to a specialist; Ted requests a referral and this is the third occasion he has been seen by the GP practice with the same symptoms. As discussed above there is a duty to review a diagnosis, so although Dr Stone may contend he followed accepted practice; Ted may argue that although the practice is ***Bolam*** acceptable it is not ***Bolitho*** compatible.

Dr Pebble agrees that Ted has an X-ray, although attributing Ted's headaches to his minor accident. He has acted as a responsible A&E doctor (***Bolam***). What is not clear from the facts is what happened to the X-ray results. Were these forwarded to the GP without review? This would not seem logical (***Bolitho***). If the X-rays were reviewed was it evident that Ted had a serious condition; and why was Ted not informed? If Dr Pebble reviewed the X-rays then he cannot argue that he mis-diagnosed due to inexperience (***Wilsher* v *Essex AHA*** [1986] 3 All ER 801). He will, however, escape liability if he asked the advice of a more senior colleague (***Wilsher***).[7]

The GP practice is vicariously liable for the actions of the receptionist. They are also under a direct duty to have safe procedures in place (***Bull* v *Devon*** [1993] 4 Med LR 117). Filing X-rays without review raises questions about the practice's procedures and it could be both directly and vicariously liable.

On the assumption that any of the parties have breached their duty of care[8] Ted must establish on the balance of probabilities that the negligence caused his injuries, in this case the failure to make a prompt diagnosis resulted in his brain tumour becoming inoperable. The GPs cannot avoid liability by asserting that had they not been in breach the damage would still have occurred because of the hospital's subsequent negligence (***Wright* v *Cambridge Medical Group*** [2011] EWCA Civ 669).

As there are potentially a number of defendants, applying the 'but for' test (***Barnett* v *Chelsea and Kensington Hospital Management Committee*** [1969] 1 QB 428) will not produce a definitive answer.[9] Instead Ted may argue that the GPs and Dr Pebble materially contributed to the delay (***Bonnington Castings* v *Wardlaw*** [1956] AC 613).[10] Ted cannot point to a breach of duty being the sole cause of the delay, but he may contend that the GPs' cumulative acts all made a material contribution to his brain tumour now being inoperable. He

[7] This paragraph probably poses more questions than answers, simply as it can only speculate on what did actually happen. However, it is acceptable to discuss the range of possibilities.

[8] The answer points out that causation is discussed on the assumption the defendants are found in breach of the standard of care and reminds the examiner that no firm conclusions are possible on the information provided in the question.

[9] Always begin with the 'but for' test even if you eventually conclude it is not applicable.

[10] The paragraph continues by stating the relevant tests for causation and critically applying the law to the facts.

may also argue that because of the delay he was denied the chance of making a full recovery (***Gregg* v *Scott*** [2004] UKHL 2). He must prove that because of the defendant's negligence he lost a chance in excess of 50 per cent of making a complete recovery. Clearly his chances must diminish as the scenario progresses.

Dr Rock may be negligent for not instructing Ted to return to the surgery if the headaches persisted. Dr Stone may be in breach for not reviewing his diagnosis, Dr Pebble for not reviewing the X-ray. The practice may be liable for the actions of the receptionist and/or Dr Stone. Ted, however, will only succeed if he can establish that the delays resulted in his brain tumour becoming inoperable which we cannot know without medical evidence.[11]

[11] The answer summarises the potential outcomes and reiterates that no definitive conclusion may be drawn.

✓ Make your answer stand out

- Structure is all important; discuss duty and breach for each party before moving on to discuss causation as it is argued that all the parties have contributed to the delay.
- Weave the *Bolam* v *Friern Hospital Management Committee* and *Bolitho* v *City & Hackney HA* tests throughout the section on breach – you must constantly apply the legal tests to each potential party.
- Use similar case law decisions to the facts in question, for example case law on failure to review a diagnosis.
- State that there may be a range of outcomes/possibilities, e.g. what happened following the X-rays. It demonstrates that you are considering the facts and not simply stating the legal tests.
- Methodically work through the tests for causation always beginning with 'but for' and then moving on. It demonstrates that you understand the relationship between the various tests and that more than one test may be relevant.

! Don't be tempted to

- Discuss duty, breach and causation separately for each party; you will get into a muddle.
- Simply recite the legal tests without applying them to the facts in the question.
- Side-step causation. It is definitely more complex than standard of care but you must discuss it in your answer.

Question 5

Mick, aged 22, was assaulted and suffered a blow to his head. On arrival at the Accident & Emergency Department (A&E) at Oldcastle NHS Trust Hospital, the ambulance crew informed the nurse that Mick had received a blow to his head that had rendered him unconscious. The nurse assessed Mick's condition as non-urgent and recorded that Mick 'has drunk at least six pints of beer, collapsed . . . vomited a lot of stale beer, and there are no signs of injury to the head'. She telephoned the doctor on call, Dr Bone, and informed him of Mick's condition. Dr Bone failed to attend Mick.

By 11.30pm, Mick's dad arrived at the hospital to take him home. The nurse told Mick that he should go and 'sleep it off'.

During the night Mick was frequently sick. At 8 a.m. Doris, Mick's mother, telephoned Mick's GP. She described Mick's condition but the GP said that he was suffering from a hangover and should rest. When Mick had not woken up by 8 p.m., Doris rang 999 and Mick was rushed to Oldcastle Neurosurgical Unit.

On admission Mick had a brain scan which revealed a blood clot causing brain compression. The consultant surgeon operated to remove the clot and reduce the pressure in Mick's brain. While recovering, Mick developed an infection which was not due to the negligence of any of the hospital staff, and suffered further bleeding in his brain.

Mick now has brain damage.

The hospital and GP practice have admitted negligence but deny it was causative of Mick's injuries. Medical evidence indicates that the longer compression continues in the brain the greater the chance of brain damage. Had surgery been carried out earlier, there is a 75 per cent chance that Mick would have avoided injury.

Discuss whether causation may be proven against any of the parties above.

Answer plan

- → Identify defendants.
- → Introduce the tests for causation.
- → Apply the tests, identifying what further information is required.
- → Conclude.

Diagram plan

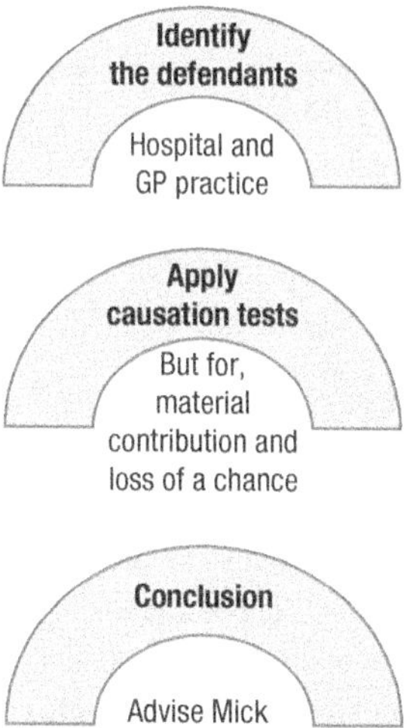

A printable version of this diagram plan is available from **www.pearsoned.co.uk/lawexpressqa**

Answer

We are told that the hospital and GP practice have admitted negligence. Therefore we may assume that the nurse, Dr Bone, and the GP have not met the requisite standard of care required of a medical practitioner, i.e. the ***Bolam*** standard (***Bolam* v *Friern Hospital Management Committee*** [1957] 2 All ER 118). Their actions, or inactions, have led to a delay in Mick's surgery which it is alleged has resulted in Mick sustaining brain damage. As a preliminary point any claim will be against Oldcastle NHS Trust as it is vicariously liable for Dr Bone and the nurse, and/or the GP or the GP practice.[1]

[1] In your introduction identify briefly who the defendants are but that is all. Do not discuss breach – the question requires you to discuss causation only.

It is not sufficient to establish that the parties have breached the standard of care, rather we must prove on a balance of probabilities that their negligence is causative of Mick's injuries. As there is more than one potential tortfeasor, the 'but for test' will not give a definitive answer (see ***Barnett* v *Chelsea and Kensington Hospital Management Committee*** [1969] 1 QB 428). Therefore we must either establish that the negligence materially contributed to the delay resulting in increased bleeding in the brain, or argue that the delay has deprived him of the chance of making a full recovery. We shall discuss each of these in turn.[2]

[2] This paragraph identifies the relevant legal tests and also sets out the structure for what the answer will discuss.

[3] It is perfectly acceptable to state what arguments/tests will not apply. This demonstrates to the examiner, first that you understand the law, and second that in stating that not all tests are relevant you know how to apply the legal rules to any given facts.

At the outset note that Dr Bone and the nurse cannot escape liability by establishing that, had they not breached the standard of care, the damage would have occurred in any event because subsequently the GP was negligent (***Wright* v *Cambridge Medical Group*** [2011] EWCA Civ 669).[3] It is also improbable that Dr Bone and the nurse could maintain that the GP's failure constituted a *novus actus interveniens* (a break in the chain of causation). It was reasonably foreseeable that, if they attributed Mick's condition to a severe bout of drinking, that others would rely on their diagnosis.

As we cannot establish which of the tortfeasors have caused his injury, then we must contend that each breach of duty has materially contributed to the damage, i.e. the bleeding in Mick's brain. It is submitted that the consecutive failures to promptly diagnose, attend and refer Mick have all contributed to the delay in surgery which has ultimately led to his injury. Any contribution to the injury must be more than *de minimus* (***Bonnington Castings* v *Wardlaw*** [1956] AC 613). It is likely that each of the negligent acts and omissions would satisfy this requirement. Although medical evidence may be inconclusive as to which failure contributed more to Mick's injuries, all tortfeasors will be liable as all have cumulatively contributed to the delay. This differs from the situation in ***Wilsher* v *Essex AHA*** [1988] AC 1074 where all of the potential causes were independent of each other and therefore causation could not be established.[4] It is unlikely however that we can maintain the negligence of the tortfeasors 'materially increased the risk' of Mick sustaining harm (***McGhee* v *NCB*** [1972] 3 All ER 1008). The House of Lords in ***Fairchild* v *Glenhaven Funeral Services Ltd*** [2002] UKHL 22 specified that the test will apply only in specific instances. To date the test has not been successfully introduced in a clinical negligence action, principally on policy grounds. The courts are instinctively reluctant to extend any potential liability for fear of the impact this will likely have on the NHS budget.[5]

[4] The answer explains and applies the material contribution test. In so doing it discusses the important distinction between cumulative and discrete causes.

[5] The answer explains why some legal tests will not apply, here materially increasing the risk. Furthermore, the answer also uses the opportunity to demonstrate an awareness of the courts' different approach in non-clinical negligence cases and the influence that policy may have on the eventual outcome.

We are informed the longer the compression remains in the brain the greater the chance of brain damage. Therefore we may suppose that when Doris rang the GP the damage had already occurred and the GP's lack of referral made no difference to the eventual outcome. However, without further medical evidence we cannot assume this and therefore we must conclude that all parties have contributed to the delay and the resulting injury.

Unfortunately for Mick, even though the operation reduces the compression in his brain he contracts an infection causing further bleeding in the brain. In ***Bailey* v *Ministry of Defence*** [2008] EWCA Civ 883 the Court of Appeal held causation will be established if the risk of injury was enhanced by negligence which had a significant, albeit unquantifiable, effect on the claimant's general condition. We cannot definitively establish that Mick would not have suffered further bleeding in the absence of negligence. However, there is a strong indication that, as in ***Bailey***, both the negligent cause (the delay in receiving treatment) and the non-negligent cause (the infection) contributed to his eventual condition.[6]

[6] *Bailey* is a 'difficult' case on causation. As such it is acceptable to state that it may apply in this scenario but more facts are required.

We may also contend that the delay in treatment has lost Mick the chance of making a successful recovery.[7] In ***Hotson* v *East Berkshire AHA*** [1987] AC 750 the House of Lords held that the claimant must establish that as a result of the negligence he had been deprived of a greater than 50 per cent chance of avoiding the harm. This decision was upheld in ***Gregg* v *Scott*** [2005] UKHL 2. We are told that Mick would have had a 75 per cent chance of avoiding brain damage so we may claim that he has been deprived of a loss of chance of a successful recovery. However, we can only speculate as to how much earlier the surgery should have been performed for Mick to still have had the possibility of making an effective recovery. It is probable that as the delay continues, at some point in the timeline set out in the question Mick's prospects are reduced from the original 75 per cent to below the 50 per cent threshold. Therefore a loss of a chance claim is more likely to succeed against Dr Bone and the nurse for we must assume that at the beginning of the scenario Mick's prospects of survival were above 50 per cent.[8]

[7] The answer introduces the second main route mentioned earlier for causation to be proven, namely loss of a chance.

[8] Not only does the answer explain the legal rules but it applies the loss of a chance test and identifies that as time progresses Mick's chance of avoiding injury diminishes.

Consequently it would seem that causation may be established against all tortfeasors for materially contributing to the delay which resulted in surgery and led to additional complications.[9] The loss of a chance argument is perhaps only sustainable against Dr Bone and the nurse as Mick's chance of a successful recovery will, in all probability, have fallen below the 50 per cent threshold as the scenario progresses.

[9] A reasoned conclusion should be stated even if it is inconclusive, it reminds the examiner that you have considered and applied the law.

Make your answer stand out

- At the outset make clear the causation tests which you will discuss.
- Deal with any preliminary issues first; i.e. here the parties are identified and additionally potential defence arguments are dismissed.
- Crucially you must know the case law; for example you cannot successfully apply *Bailey v Ministry of Defence* if you are not aware of the factual background and that there were two causes, one negligent and the other non-negligent.
- Don't be afraid to speculate, for example that Mick's chance of recovery must have diminished as the scenario progressed.

! Don't be tempted to

- Discuss duty and breach – the question is on causation only!
- Write down everything you know about causation; you must be selective.
- Discuss each causation authority in depth; you simply do not have the time.

www.pearsoned.co.uk/lawexpressqa

Go online to access more revision support including additional essay and problem questions with diagram plans, You be the marker questions, and download all diagrams from the book.

4 Consent to treatment

How this topic may come up in exams

The legal framework applicable to consent to (or refusal of) treatment is fundamental to medical law. It may present as a question that just focuses on key consent principles in essay or problem form (particularly in problem form) or combined with other areas. The principles extend across many medical law topics. The legal framework comprises a mix of common law and statutory provision with an understanding of the application and effect of the Mental Capacity Act 2005 being essential. Other statutory provisions, such as the Mental Health Act 1983 and Human Rights Act 1998, also play an important part in the overall legal framework.

Before you begin

It's a good idea to consider the following key themes of consent to treatment before tackling a question on this topic.

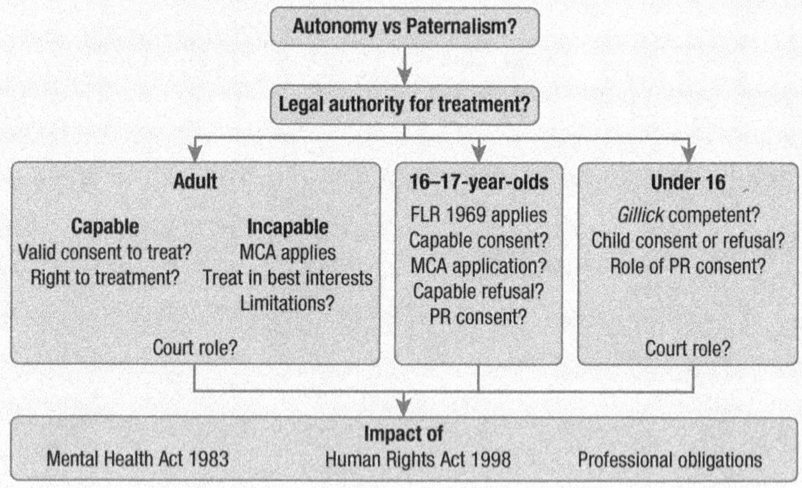

A printable version of this diagram is available from **www.pearsoned.co.uk/lawexpressqa**

Question 1

Annie, aged 78, suffers from a mental illness, dementia. Her condition fluctuates and frequently causes her to be confused.

Annie has fallen at home and may have broken her hip. She is in considerable pain and distress. Her daughter Poppy has called for an ambulance and the paramedics have arrived. They decide that Annie needs to be taken to hospital for treatment and that Annie may need surgery on her hip. They want to give Annie an injection of medication to alleviate her pain.

Annie is very distressed and insists that she does not want to go to hospital because she thinks she 'will die there'. She insists she wants to stay at home where Fred, her husband, can look after her. She will not let the paramedics touch her to carry out any necessary checks, including taking her blood pressure and screams at them when they try to.

Fred is also very distressed and does not want Annie to be 'forced into anything'. Poppy says Fred is too upset to make any decisions and that Annie 'does not know what she is saying'. Poppy is insistent that Annie be taken to hospital immediately and given something to 'take away her pain'.

Advise the paramedics whether Annie can be treated by them and taken to hospital.

Answer plan

- Identify the legal framework that applies to Annie.
- Consider Annie's capacity to make each of the relevant decisions in question and apply the Mental Capacity Act (MCA) principles and capacity assessment in sections 1, 2 and 3 MCA.
- Identify the legal position if the conclusion is that Annie has capacity and is refusing treatment, even if the decision is 'unwise'.
- Detail the position if Annie lacks capacity, considering any duty to treat Annie in her 'best interests' and how these are assessed, drawing conclusions as appropriate.
- Describe the effect of section 5 and how this applies to provide 'authority' to treat Annie.
- Identify the limitations on the application of section 5 and how they may apply to this scenario.

Diagram plan

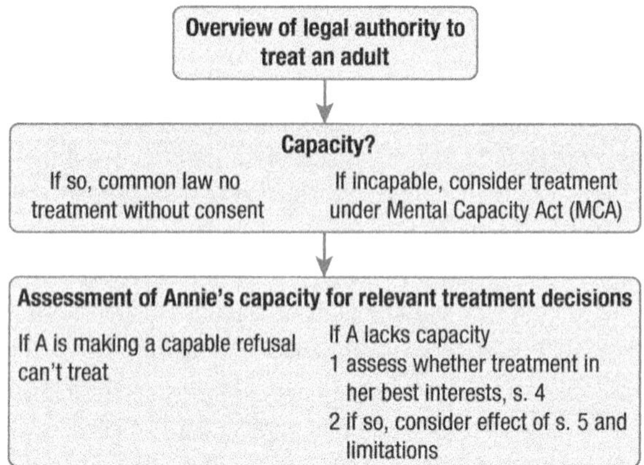

A printable version of this diagram plan is available from **www.pearsoned.co.uk/lawexpressqa**

Answer

The overall legal framework which provides authority for care and treatment of an adult needs to be considered. In particular, we will need to assess whether Annie is making a binding capable refusal of treatment, or whether she lacks capacity in respect of the proposed treatments, in which case the Mental Capacity Act 2005 (the MCA) will apply and may provide the necessary legal authority for the care and treatment, even if Annie objects.

1. Legal framework[1]

Where an adult has 'capacity', case law has confirmed that the adult has the right to consent to or refuse treatment. See for example ***Re T (Adult: Refusal of Treatment)*** [1993] Fam 95, where the Court of Appeal confirmed the capable adult's right to choose 'exists notwithstanding that the reasons for making the choice are rational, irrational, unknown or even non-existent'. Thus, if Annie is 'capable' she has the right to refuse the proposed treatment.

[1] It may be useful to break your answer into clearly structured parts using subheadings. It is particularly important with essay questions to ensure you have a clear structure to your answer and that you plan it out in advance.

If, however, Annie lacks capacity, then the MCA may provide authority for the treatment in her 'best interests' subject to the limitations set out by the MCA.

2. Capacity

If Annie has capacity she can consent to or refuse treatment. The paramedics will need Annie's valid consent for each of the interventions proposed.[2] It does not appear that Annie is prepared to consent, although paramedics may try to persuade her.[3] If Annie will not consent the proposed interventions cannot be carried out even though this may result in serious deterioration or injury to Annie (***Re T***).

The paramedics will need to assess Annie's capacity in accordance with the MCA.[4]

The starting point is to presume that Annie has capacity (s. 1 MCA) and that she will not be incapable just because she makes an unwise decision, and any stereotypical assumptions must not influence the capacity assessment. All reasonably practicable steps would need to be taken to assist Annie to make the decision.

Capacity is decision specific, so capacity will need to be assessed for the relevant decision at the relevant time.

The two-part capacity assessment is set out in sections 2 and 3 of the MCA.[5] Is Annie unable to make the relevant decision because of 'an impairment of, or disturbance in the functioning of, the mind or brain' (s. 2)?[6] If Annie does have such an impairment or disturbance in functioning, her ability to make a decision is assessed in accordance with section 3, by considering whether Annie is able to understand relevant information, retain it, use or weigh up the information and communicate the decision. If she is unable to do any of these then she will lack capacity for that decision.

The decisions in question here are the decisions to refuse the initial checks, pain relief and transportation to hospital.[7] Although the starting point is to presume Annie is capable, however, we are told that Annie has dementia. Dementia is a disturbance or impairment of functioning of mind, so we will need to assess whether this has the effect of rendering her incapable of making the relevant decisions.

[2] You may include some detail here as to what constitutes a valid consent, i.e. that it has to be a capable consent, based on sufficient information and that there is no requirement as to format in this context. The main focus of this question, however, is on Annie refusing treatment so take care not to go into too much detail where time is limited.

[3] You may refer to the fact that an agreement given under duress will not be a valid consent, though again you need to take care to stay focused on key issues.

[4] You may refer to the assessment process originating in the common law cases such as *Re C* [1994] 1 WLR 290 but it is important to demonstrate you understand the effect and application of the MCA.

[5] It is important that you are sufficiently detailed and precise when applying/referring to these key provisions of the MCA.

[6] You may wish to note that this this is what is known as the 'diagnostic' element, with the section 3 assessment being the 'functional element'.

[7] You need to take care to clearly identify the particular decisions in respect of which capacity is assessed and attempt to apply the law to the facts drawing conclusions where you can and identifying what further information may be required as appropriate.

We are told that Annie is confused and disorientated at times with very poor short-term memory, and that she is distressed and in pain. This may affect her ability to understand, retain or weigh up the relevant information provided by the paramedics.[8]

They will need to assess whether Annie is capable for each decision.[9] If they decide she is, then they cannot treat. If they have a reasonable belief that she lacks capacity for the particular decision then they may treat (s. 5 MCA) in her best interests (s. 4 MCA).

[8] If time allows, you can include details of relevant cases, such as *Re C* [1994] 1 WLR 290, to illustrate this.

[9] You may wish to note that the paramedics will need to take the necessary steps so far as is practicable in the circumstances.

3. Best interests

If Annie lacks capacity, consideration will have to be given to whether it is in her best interests to be given the particular treatment in accordance with section 4. This requires considering the 'checklist', which will include taking into account Annie's wishes and feelings, the views of relatives/carers as to what is in her best interests and whether she is likely to regain capacity to decide for herself. Annie is objecting to the treatment, Fred is also against it, however Poppy is in favour of it.[10] It seems likely that all of the proposed treatment is in her best interests, to relieve her pain and treat her hip to prevent further pain and deterioration. The level of resistance Annie demonstrates will be relevant, particularly if restraint will be required. So long as the paramedics have a 'reasonable belief' that the treatment is in her best interests then there may be authority to carry it out under section 5.

[10] You may wish to note in your answer that the views of relatives are not 'binding' (unless they have a lasting power of attorney (LPA)) but will be taken into account for section 4 purposes and it is their view as to what is in Annie's best interests that is relevant.

4. Section 5 Legal authority

Section 5 effectively provides legal authority[11] for an act in connection with care or treatment to be carried out in a person's best interests where the 'actor' has a reasonable belief that the person lacks capacity and a reasonable belief that the act is in their best interests.[12] In this case the acts in question are clearly acts in connection with care or treatment. So long as the paramedics can show they have assessed capacity and best interests and have the requisite reasonable belief that Annie lacks capacity and the acts are in her best interests then they can provide the necessary treatment. The legal authority provided by section 5 may, however, be limited. Legal limitations on relying on section 5 may be because there is an advance decision (s. 24 and s. 25 MCA), a Lasting Power of Attorney (LPA)

[11] You may wish to note that section 5 is actually a defence, in the same way as the common law doctrine of necessity, rather than a legal authority, to what otherwise would be unlawful touching of the person, however it may be easier to explain the effect of section 5 by reference to it as an 'authority'.

[12] Your answer should make clear that this can probably only be achieved by considering the section 4 checklist and other relevant factors. It does not require a 'right' answer.

(s. 9 MCA), where restraint is to be used (s. 6 MCA) or where there is a deprivation of liberty. There is no indication that Annie has made an advance decision or LPA.[13] Restraint is defined in section 6 and includes the use or threat to use force to do an act the person resists or a restriction of their liberty. In this scenario it may be that restraint will be necessary. If that is the case, restraint can only be carried out where there is a reasonable belief that it is necessary to prevent harm to that person and is a proportionate response. The paramedics would have to be satisfied these criteria were made out before any restraint could be used to carry out the necessary treatment. If the treatment, in particular the conveyance of Annie to hospital, amounts to a deprivation of liberty[14] then this could not be carried out without authorisation from the Court of Protection.

[13] You could give more detail explaining these and their effect, but only where there is sufficient time/word limit to do so. Otherwise they do not appear to be relevant here so focus on the more obviously relevant aspects.

[14] The concept of deprivation of liberty is notoriously difficult, but you may wish to expand on this in your answer. It is unlikely that transporting someone to hospital would constitute such a deprivation, see the Code of Practice to supplement the main Mental Capacity Act 2005 Code of Practice, Paragraph 2.14.

Make your answer stand out

- Familiarise yourself with Code of Practice guidance and relevant case law pre- and post-MCA which you may refer to in relation to assessment of capacity and best interests, though making it clear that each case is fact specific.
- Demonstrate a detailed understanding of the nature of the capacity and best interests assessments.
- Make sure you identify with sufficient precision and detail the key aspects of the MCA and their application to the facts and understand the ethos and principles of the Act.
- Demonstrate you understand the effect and application of the limitations in section 6 and the concept of deprivation of liberty.

! Don't be tempted to . . .

- Simply recite the key provisions of the MCA without applying it to the scenario.
- Make assumptions, such as that Annie lacks capacity, without justifying them by applying the law to the facts.
- Introduce cases which are of limited or no relevance to the actual scenario (in particular pre-MCA cases).
- Jump to conclusions which are not supported by the information given.

Question 2

Ben, aged 54, has been diagnosed as suffering from early onset dementia, a deteriorating mental illness. He has periods of confusion and impaired short-term memory. As a solicitor, Ben is finding that his illness has affected his ability to work and has had to give up his job. Ben has always been fiercely independent and is particularly concerned that as his illness progresses he will lose capacity and, unable to make any choices for himself, may end up being cared for in a way he wouldn't want. He says he could not bear to go into a nursing home, be unable to recognise his family or to look after himself and 'would rather die' than be in that position. He and his wife Emma want to make plans now, for his future care, rather than leaving care and treatment decisions for the doctors to make.

Advise Ben as to what steps, if any, he could take legally to ensure his care and treatment wishes are followed in the future, once he loses capacity.

Answer plan

- Identify the legal framework that applies to care and treatment of an adult who lacks capacity.
- Consider what options may be available to Ben now.
- Identify the legal effect of those options, including any limitations.
- Analyse to what extent these options may provide Ben with what he wants.
- Conclude your advice to Ben.

Diagram plan

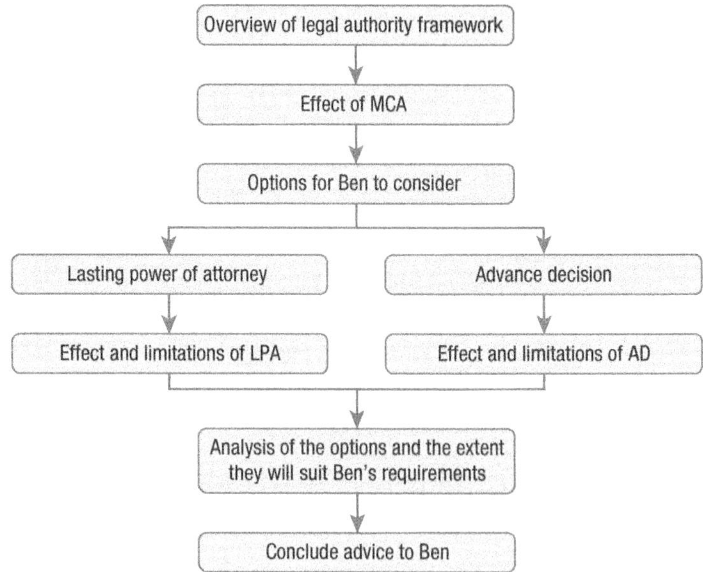

A printable version of this diagram plan is available from **www.pearsoned.co.uk/lawexpressqa**

Answer

The overall legal framework which provides authority for care and treatment of an adult needs to be considered. In particular, we need to assess Ben's capacity to make care and treatment decisions, identify what options may be available for him making decisions for future care and treatment under the Mental Capacity Act 2005 (the MCA) and assess the potential impact of any options, advising Ben.

1. Legal framework

Ben is an adult, so if he has 'capacity' case law has confirmed that he has the right to consent to or refuse treatment (see, for example, ***Re T (Adult: Refusal of Treatment)*** [1993] Fam 95). While Ben is 'capable' he has the right to determine what care or treatment he has, in that he may refuse proposed care or treatment. He does not, however, have the right to 'demand' care or treatment[1] (see the

[1] You may wish to expand on this important distinction and the effective limit on Ben's 'control' over treatment that an advance decision can convey. However, just because any request for treatment or preference may not be legally binding as a refusal would be, this does not render it ineffective, rather it will be an important part of the assessment of Ben's best interests.

Court of Appeal in ***R (Burke)* v *General Medical Council*** [2005] EWCA Civ 1003).

If Ben loses (or lacks) capacity to make such decisions, then the MCA may provide authority for treatment in his 'best interests', subject to the limitations set out by the MCA (s. 6 MCA). This could mean decisions about his treatment could be taken about what is seen to be objectively in his best interests[2] in accordance with section 4 MCA, even though it might be treatment that Ben would not have wanted.

[2] Although the section 4 best interests is a more subjective focus, arguably, than at common law, nevertheless it is still not a 'substituted judgement' test. Make sure this is clearly reflected in your answer.

The MCA does provide two options Ben could consider in relation to his future care/treatment which would allow him some element of 'control', namely an advance decision and/or a lasting power of attorney (LPA), assuming he still has the capacity to do so.

2. Advance decision

The relevant provisions are set out in sections 24, 25 and 26 of the MCA.[3]

[3] This replaces the common law position developed in cases such as *Re C* [1994] 1 WLR 290. If you have time/word count to do so, you may wish to include details of *Re C* and other common law developments to illustrate how the law applies.

An advance decision (AD) would enable Ben to make a legally binding refusal[4] of treatment[5] which would be binding in the future once he has lost capacity. There are generally no procedural requirements to making an AD unless the refusal is of life-sustaining treatment. If it is then the AD must be in writing, signed by Ben and witnessed (ss. 25(5) and (6)).

[4] Which can't be overridden by the court or anyone acting under section 5 – make sure this is clear.

[5] Note, this is a refusal of treatment not care, see the Code of Practice at Paragraph 9.28. You may wish to expand on this and reference extracts from the Code.

To be binding the AD must be 'valid' and 'applicable'. It will be valid if Ben has capacity when he makes the AD. His capacity is assessed in accordance with section 2 and section 3 of the MCA, although section 1 MCA sets out a presumption of capacity. We need to establish whether Ben has an impairment or disturbance of functioning of mind or brain (s. 2), which we are told he does.[6] We then need to establish whether this operates to such a degree so as to make him unable to understand relevant information, retain it, use or weigh it up to make a decision and communicate the decision. If Ben is unable to do any of these things then he would not be able to make an AD.

[6] We are told he has dementia so the 'diagnostic' element is satisfied. We now need to assess whether the effect of this, the 'functional' element, means he is unable to understand, retain, or weigh up the information. The two parts of the test need to be clearly set out in your answer.

If Ben does have capacity he can make an AD. He will have to ensure that he does not subsequently invalidate the AD by withdrawing it, or acting inconsistently with it or making an LPA covering the same treatment.

He will also have to be clear as to what treatment he is refusing and in what circumstances, to make sure it is clear what the AD applies to. Otherwise his AD may be held to be 'inapplicable' (s. 25(3)).[7]

[7] You should note that this is one of the difficulties with making a binding AD where future circumstances may be difficult to predict, leading to a risk the AD will be said to be not 'applicable'.

Ben can only refuse treatment and not care, so could not refuse being admitted to a care home for basic care, for example.

If Ben's AD is subsequently held not to be binding, it would be relevant in the assessment of his best interests for section 4 purposes.

3. Lasting power of attorney (LPA)

Ben could also consider making an LPA in relation to his health care and welfare (ss. 9 and 10 MCA). This would enable him to appoint someone else (the 'donee') to make his decisions for him, should he lose capacity. This could include refusal of life-sustaining treatment, if he expressly includes that in the LPA. The donee would then have the authority to make decisions on Ben's behalf, in his best interests. The donee's decisions could not be overridden by healthcare professionals (the 'authority'[8] set out in section 5 MCA being limited in such circumstances) without challenging the decision before the Court of Protection (CoP).

[8] You may find it easier to refer to section 5 as conferring an 'authority' to provide care or treatment, but in fact legally it is a defence.

The LPA has to be in the prescribed format and registered to be valid.[9]

[9] The LPA has to be registered with the Office of the Public Guardian. You should not spend too much of your answer on the procedural elements here, but you do need to summarise the effect of them.

Ben would have to be capable of making the LPA, which would be assessed in accordance with ss. 2 and 3.

Any donee has to act in Ben's best interests, so could make a decision contrary to what Ben would have wanted where the donee sees this as being in his best interests. The decisions made by an LPA can be challenged[10] in the Court of Protection (CoP).

[10] Your answer should clarify that this is one of the potential limitations of the LPA. It will not necessarily get Ben what he wants, even where the donee follows his wishes, since it is subject to his best interests, which ultimately is a court decision.

4. Advice summary

As outlined above, if Ben still has capacity to do so, he could make an AD refusing treatment and/or appoint Emma (or another) as his donee under an LPA.

The advantage of an AD would be that, if valid and applicable, he could not be treated contrary to it, even if such treatment were in his best interests.[11] If, however, he made Emma his donee, although she has to take Ben's views into account in deciding what is in his best

[11] Remember, if the AD is valid and applicable the court has no jurisdiction to intervene even if the AD is not in his best interests. You may wish to incorporate this.

interests, she would not be bound to follow any refusal of treatment by him, or any other decision.

It may practically be difficult to make an applicable AD unless Ben is clear what treatment he is likely to need and in what circumstances. The courts have demonstrated a reluctance to uphold ADs refusing life-sustaining treatment (see, for example, ***Re E (Medical Treatment: Anorexia)*** [2012] EWHC 1639 (COP)).[12] A doctor can treat a patient unless the doctor is 'satisfied' that the AD is valid and applicable (s. 26(2)). If Ben wishes to have 'control' over care as well as treatment, then the AD will not cover that.

[12] Note this case focused on capacity, but is still an interesting example of the arguable reluctance of the courts to allow people to refuse life-sustaining treatment and you may wish to include it.

The advantage of an LPA is that Ben can choose someone who he knows and trusts (Emma) to make decisions for him in his best interests. This can cover care and treatment[13] and choice of treatment options, rather than just focusing on refusal of treatment. Although the CoP could override Emma's decisions, if judged not to be in Ben's best interests, this would only occur where an application was made to the CoP and likely to be limited to situations where there is a real dispute about best interest, rather than just a difference of opinion.

[13] Potentially then the refusal to be admitted to a care home could be refused by the donee, however this may well be challenged on best interest grounds. You could expand on this point if time allows.

Ben could draw up an LPA giving Emma power to make decisions for him and an AD, to cover any treatment he does not want. He would have to take care that the creation of the LPA did not inadvertently invalidate the AD (s. 25(2)(b)). This would best protect his treatment preferences.

Make your answer stand out

- Familiarise yourself with Code of Practice guidance and approach of the Court of Protection to advance decisions and best interests in the context of previously expressed wishes.
- Demonstrate that you understand the effect of the MCA on 'forward planning' for care and treatment.
- Stay focused on the relevant aspects of the MCA and their legal effect in the context of Ben's requirements.
- Analyse the appropriateness of the legal options for Ben.

! Don't be tempted to . . .

- Simply recite the key provisions of the MCA without applying it to the scenario.
- Focus on the procedural elements rather than the legal effect.
- Describe the pre-MCA provisions and compare and contrast without identifying the relevance to the actual task of advising Ben.
- Introduce cases which are of limited or no relevance to the actual scenario and/or provide too much factual detail of cases.
- Forget the actual task set by the question.

? Question 3

Kerry, aged 22, is 32 weeks pregnant. She has a mild learning disability and she needs a lot of support to make decisions. She lives in a council property with her partner Richard, who also has a mild learning disability. They receive considerable support from Kerry's mum Sue and from their social worker Kay. Both Kerry and Richard have part-time jobs. They are very excited about the new baby and have already begun to prepare for the baby with help from Sue and Kay. Kerry starts to experience severe stomach pains and a worried Sue takes her to hospital, where Kerry is examined by Dr James. Dr James notes that there are complications with the pregnancy. He wants to admit Kerry for further tests and thinks it is likely that they may have to induce the baby. Kerry, who is now very frightened and in a lot of pain is insisting she wants to go home, that the baby can't be born yet, as it is too early and it will die. Dr James is concerned that if Kerry is not admitted and given the necessary treatment, her life and that of the baby will be at risk. Sue is begging Kerry to accept Dr James's advice and begging Dr James to save her daughter and grandchild.

Advise Dr James as to the legal position in treating Kerry.

Answer plan

→ Identify the legal framework that applies to care and treatment of an adult.

→ Consider what legal authority might be available to Dr James to carry out the treatment.

→ Consider how the identified legal authority might apply to the facts of Kerry's case.

→ Identify any additional information required or steps Dr James may need to take to enable him to legally treat Kerry.

→ Conclude your advice to Dr James.

Diagram plan

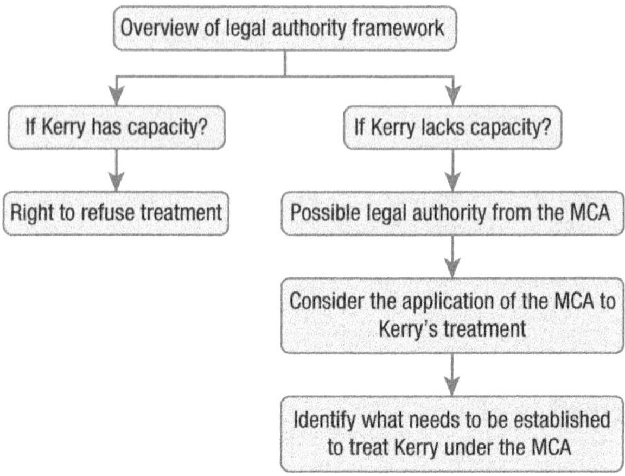

A printable version of this diagram plan is available from **www.pearsoned.co.uk/lawexpressqa**

Answer

We need to advise Dr James as to what the legal position is in relation to treating Kerry, an adult, without her consent. We also need to consider whether the Mental Capacity Act 2005 (the MCA) applies and if so advise Dr James whether Kerry can be treated under the MCA.

1. Legal framework

Kerry is an adult so, if she has 'capacity', case law has confirmed that she has the right to consent to or refuse treatment (***Re T (Adult: Refusal of Treatment)*** [1993] Fam 95). This is the case even though she or the foetus she carries may die as a result of her decision. This was confirmed in ***Re MB (An Adult: Medical Treatment)*** [1997] 2 FLR 426, which involved the refusal of medical treatment of a woman about to give birth.[1] It was also confirmed that the foetus, up to the moment of birth, has no independent rights.

Although Sue wants Kerry to accept the treatment she has no authority to provide a consent.[2] Only Kerry can do this, if she has capacity to do so. Kerry is currently refusing.

[1] The legal position in relation to pregnancy and treatment was also confirmed and applied in the *St George's NHS Healthcare* v *S* case, which you may also wish to refer to if time allows.

[2] Avoid being side-tracked by 'next of kin' or what would happen if Kerry was under 18, since this is not relevant to the actual question.

Kerry may lack capacity to make this decision in accordance with section 2 and section 3 of the MCA. If this is the case then Kerry could not give a valid consent even if she was persuaded to agree to treatment, and the legal authority would have to come from the MCA. This could provide authority to restrain Kerry and to treat her (ss. 5 and 6 MCA), in Kerry's best interests (s. 4 MCA). If the treatment results in a deprivation of liberty[3] of Kerry then this would require express legal authorisation (see s. 4A MCA).

[3] The level of detail you would need to consider the deprivation of liberty issue might depend on the extent this is covered in your course syllabus. In any event the question requires a focus on the legality of the actual treatment.

2. The MCA application

If Kerry lacks capacity, treatment may be authorised by the MCA or by court order.[4]

[4] It may be possible that Kerry is unable to consent to treatment, even though she has capacity, e.g. because she is under duress and so treatment could be authorised by the court under its inherent jurisdiction.

The starting point in assessing Kerry's capacity to make the particular decision under the MCA is to presume she has capacity (s. 1 MCA).

Kerry will not be incapable just because she makes an unwise decision, and any stereotypical assumptions must be avoided. All reasonably practicable steps need to be taken to assist Kerry to make the decision (s. 1 MCA).

The capacity assessment is set out in section 2 and section 3[5] of the MCA. Kerry has a learning disability which is 'an impairment of, or disturbance in the functioning of, the mind or brain' (s. 2). Dr James needs to assess whether this means Kerry is unable to make a decision in accordance with section 3. He will have to assess whether she is able to understand relevant information, retain it, use or weigh up the information and communicate the decision.[6]

[5] It is important that you are sufficiently detailed and precise when applying/referring to these key provisions of the MCA, even in exam conditions.

[6] You could include case details, such as *Re C* [1994] 1 WLR 290, to illustrate this.

If Dr James forms a reasonable belief that Kerry lacks capacity to make the decision then the treatment may be authorised under section 5 MCA in her best interests (s. 4 MCA), subject to limitations (s. 6, s. 4A).

Dr James needs to assess Kerry's best interests by reference to section 4 and the checklist of factors set out. He should consider the guidance set out in the Code of Practice to the MCA.[7] This will include taking into account her views, feelings and wishes, past and present and consultation with relevant carers and family members, so far as it is practicable to do this. Dr James must focus on Kerry's best interests not that of others, for example Sue or the foetus.

[7] Remember the Code is not legally binding but professionals working to the MCA need to have regard to its guidance. The Code is a useful basic guidance and explanation of the effect of the MCA and you may wish to include extracts in your answer.

If Dr James is of the view[8] the proposed treatment is in Kerry's best interests, then authority for the treatment would come from section 5 of the MCA.[9]

Section 6 of the MCA applies additional criteria that need to be met where the treatment will involve restraint.[10] Since it seems likely that it will, in which case Dr James also needs to be satisfied that the restraint is necessary to prevent harm to Kerry and is a proportionate step to take. This will involve the balancing of the likelihood of harm to Kerry if she does not have the treatment against the effect of being restrained and forcibly treated.

If it is likely that Kerry will be deprived of her liberty to provide her with the treatment, then this will require express legal authorisation (s. 4A MCA).[11]

3. Advice summary

Dr James needs to assess Kerry's capacity in accordance with sections 2 and 3 of the MCA, starting with a presumption of capacity. Kerry has a mild learning disability, however he needs to assess whether this means she is unable to make the decisions in question (s. 3).

This will involve a clinical assessment of her ability to understand, retain and weigh the information that is relevant to the treatment decision in question. Although Kerry needs considerable support, she lives independently and has a job. Kerry is insistent the baby can't be born early. She is in pain and frightened. The decision is one which may involve complex clinical information and have serious consequences. It may well be that Dr James decides she lacks capacity to make the necessary decision. Although he has to take reasonably practicable steps to try to assist her to understand, it may be that in the urgency of the case this is not feasible.

If Dr James does assess her as lacking capacity then he will need to assess best interests and the proportionality of any restraint. If Kerry needs the proposed treatment and there is a substantial risk to Kerry if she is not admitted and treated then it may well be that such treatment would be assessed as being in her best interests. Sue is clearly of the view it is and this would be taken into account. If there was time Dr James may also consult with Kay and Richard.[12]

[8] Your answer should make it clear that Dr James only needs to have a reasonable belief.

[9] You should note that section 5 is actually a legal defence to the offences that otherwise would be committed if Kerry were treated without her consent, rather than an authority to treat.

[10] Include appropriate details from the definition set out in section 6, that restraint is defined as the use or threat to use force to do an act the person resists or restriction of their liberty.

[11] This will need to be assessed on the facts of the case. You may wish to expand on this. Authorisation of any deprivation could be under the Deprivation of Liberty Safeguards (DoLs) set out in Schedule A1 to the MCA.

[12] You should demonstrate that you understand that the consultation is about taking their views as to what is in Kerry's best interests into account, not what they want to happen.

It seems likely that Kerry will be deprived of her liberty if it is decided she does need to be admitted and this must be authorised.

If Dr James is unable to decide whether Kerry has capacity, what is in her best interests or there are concerns that she will need to be restrained or given a caesarean section contrary to her wishes, then an application to court may be necessary.

If, following assessment, Dr James forms a reasonable belief Kerry lacks capacity and a reasonable belief the treatment is in her best interests in accordance with section 4 then she could be treated under section 5 of the MCA, provided any restraint meets the criteria of section 6.

✓ Make your answer stand out

- Demonstrate that you understand the impact of Kerry being deprived of her liberty in the context of being provided with treatment and the consequences of this.
- Stay focused throughout on the actual question and deal with more peripheral issues succinctly.
- Demonstrate an up-to-date knowledge of the role of the court and relevant case law.
- Show you have an in-depth knowledge of the MCA and its focus on the incapacitated person and how that applies in this practical scenario.

! Don't be tempted to . . .

- Simply recite the key provisions of the MCA without applying it to Kerry's case.
- Focus too much on the rights of the foetus and stray into ethical discussion in relation to this.
- Make assumptions as to Kerry's capacity because she has a learning disability.
- Place too much emphasis on the details of other pregnancy cases rather than the legal principles.
- Forget the actual task set by the question.

? Question 4

Sasha, aged 15, has a history of self-harming behaviour, following a traumatic incident when she was younger. She regularly cuts herself, when distressed, saying that this helps to relieve negative feelings and makes her feel better. Recently the level of self-harm has increased after Sasha was bullied at school. Sasha's mum Debbie and her partner Mike (who is not Sasha's dad) are increasingly worried about her. One day, while Debbie is away on a business trip, Mike finds Sasha cutting her arm with a knife. One of the cuts is very deep and she is bleeding heavily. Mike takes Sasha to A&E. While in the waiting area, Sasha becomes increasingly upset and says she just wants to go home. By the time she is seen by Dr Smith, she is very upset, refusing to let him examine her. The cut is still bleeding heavily and Sasha clearly needs stitches. She may even need further surgery to repair damage to the underlying tendons and to have a blood transfusion due to the amount of bleeding. Sasha becomes increasingly distressed and has to be restrained by nursing staff. She is refusing any treatment. Debbie and Mike are Jehovah's Witnesses and are against the receiving of blood or blood products. Dr Smith needs to begin treating Sasha but is worried whether legally he can.

Advise Dr Smith. Your advice should not include any consideration of the application of the Mental Health Act 1983.

Answer plan

- → Identify the overall legal framework that applies to the treatment of a 15-year-old.
- → Identify the ways in which legal authority may be obtained for Sasha's treatment.
- → Explain the effect of the *Gillick* case and consider its application to Sasha.
- → Consider who may have parental responsibility for Sasha and the implications of this.
- → Explain the role of the court and application of the common law doctrine of necessity.
- → Advise Dr Smith.

Diagram plan

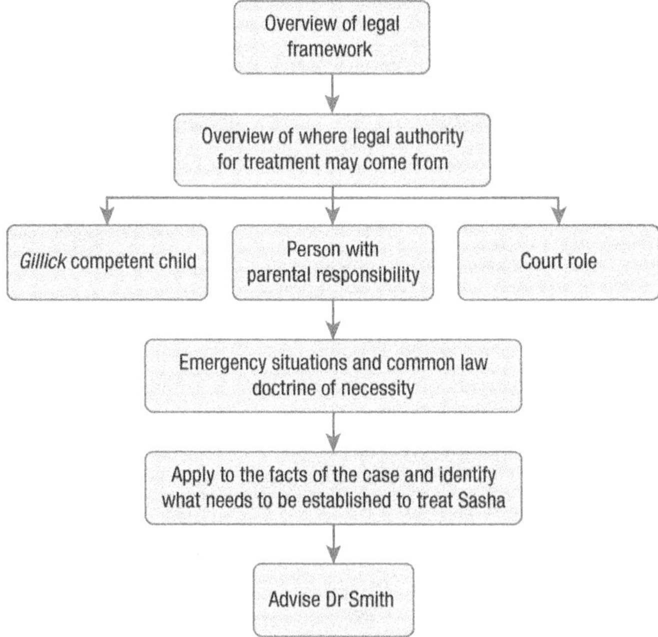

A printable version of this diagram plan is available from **www.pearsoned.co.uk/lawexpressqa**

Answer

We need to consider the legal framework that will apply to Sasha's treatment and identify who may be able to provide the necessary legal authority required to treat her. Given Sasha is 15, this will include a consideration of the ***Gillick*** case (***Gillick* v *West Norfolk and Wisbech AHA*** [1986] AC 112), the role of those with parental responsibility (PR), the role of the court and the position should the treatment become urgently required. The Mental Health Act will not be considered.[1]

[1] It is possible to argue that if Sasha falls into the definition of the Mental Health Act 1983 that the Act could be applied and treatment may fall as a treatment of symptoms or manifestations of the mental disorder. Because of time/word constraints, this question requires you to focus instead on the general legal framework covering treatment of a 15-year-old.

1. Legal framework

The professionals treating Sasha will need legal authority to be able to do so. The relevant legal framework is that which applies to the treatment of under 16s. This is a different legal framework to that which applies to an adult (18 and over) or young person aged 16 or 17.[2]

For an under 16 there is no statutory provision which provides for the child to give consent.[3] However, in the case of ***Gillick*** it was held that a child could consent where they were competent; this is known as '***Gillick*** competence'. Legal authority for treatment may also come from the consent of the parent, where they have parental responsibility (PR) for the child, from the court or in emergency circumstances from the common law doctrine of necessity. It is possible for there to be 'concurrent' consent providers.[4]

We need to consider if Sasha is ***Gillick*** competent and the implications if not. We need to identify who may have PR and whether they can provide the necessary authority. We need to consider a possible application to the High Court and the position should Sasha's treatment become urgent.

2. *Gillick* competence

Even though Sasha is refusing treatment at present, the question of whether she is ***Gillick*** competent still needs to be considered. The notion of ***Gillick*** competence is primarily derived from the judgments of Lord Frazer and Lord Scarman in the House of Lords' decision.[5] The concept is a developmental one, whether Sasha is sufficiently mature of understanding to be able to understand the purpose and effect of the proposed treatment and consequences of not having it. Increasingly the components of the MCA may be considered[6] to assess whether the child is able to understand, retain and use or weigh up the relevant information. There is no presumption of competence and the courts seem to set the bar high, particularly where the treatment may be life sustaining (see ***Re E (A Minor) (Wardship: Medical Treatment)*** [1993] 1 FLR 386).[7]

The court has held that ***Gillick*** competence is a developmental concept, not one gained then lost as mental health fluctuates (see ***Re R (A Minor)*** [1992] Fam 11). This makes it more difficult to apply where there is the potential for mental health issues to complicate the assessment.[8]

Although Sasha is 15, an age at which a child may be expected to be ***Gillick*** competent to consent to having a wound treated, she has a

[2] It is helpful to show the examiner that you know a different legal framework applies for adults and 16–18-year-olds, but it is enough to mention this in passing. You don't need to go into details, unless this is relevant to the actual question, for example if you are asked to consider how the position would change if Sasha was 16 or 18.

[3] For 16–17-year-olds the Family Law Reform Act does convey such provisions. Again, it is sufficient to mention this in passing.

[4] Remember, the Mental Capacity Act 2005 (MCA) does not apply to treatment of an under 16. You need to stay focused on the relevant legal regime that does apply.

[5] The *Gillick* case is a key case. Although detailed references may not be practicable in exam conditions, you need to be familiar with it and the key judgments.

[6] See, e.g. the suggested approach to capacity assessment of a child in the Code of Practice to the MHA, which you could incorporate into your answer.

[7] There are a number of cases you could include references to here if time allows – see *Re R* (also referred to above) and *Re L* [1998] 2 FLR 810.

[8] Make it clear in your answer that you are not assuming that Sasha lacks competence solely because she has self-harmed.

history of self-harming behaviour and is very distressed. It may well be that she would not be found to be ***Gillick*** competent of making the treatment decision.

3. Refusal of *Gillick* competent child

In any event, it appears that Sasha is not prepared to consent. Her competence may still be relevant, however, to the question as to whether her refusal could be overridden by someone with parental responsibility. In the case of ***Re R*** (referred to above) and ***Re W (A Minor)*** [1993] Fam 64), it was held that even where a child could give a valid consent to their treatment, this did not mean their decision to refuse was decisive. Instead such refusal may be overridden by the consent of someone with parental responsibility. It is suggested (see, for example, guidance in chapter 36 of the MHA Code of Practice) that it would be unwise to rely on such consent where the child were ***Gillick*** competent and refusing. The position has not been tested post-Human Rights Act 1998.[9]

[9] The lack of recent case law and commentary makes this a difficult legal area to provide clear authorities at times. It is helpful to acknowledge this in your answer.

4. Parental responsibility consent

In relation to a child there may be more than one 'consent giver'. A person with parental responsibility may provide a consent to treatment in the best interests of the child (Children Act 1989).[10] Here Debbie will have PR but it seems unlikely Mike will, so he cannot provide consent. If Debbie can be contacted she may consent to the treatment and in theory this could be provided. However, she may not be prepared to consent to Sasha having any blood products.

[10] Remember, this right is only one to act in the child's best interests. Only one consent is required. Make this clear in your answer.

5. Role of the court

The High Court has an inherent jurisdiction[11] that it may exercise in relation to a child to make decisions about whether a child should be treated, in particular where the child and/or parents disagree with healthcare professionals as to whether treatment should be given.[12] On a number of occasions the courts have been asked to determine whether a child should have blood products following the child and parents' refusal for religious reasons (see ***Re E*** and ***Re L (Medical Treatment: Gillick Competency)*** [1998] 2 FLR 810). The court tends to approach the decision on the basis that a child 'should not be allowed to martyr himself' (***Re E***) and to order the treatment be given.

[11] There are many examples and you will need to be familiar with the key cases, such as *Glass* v *UK*, so you can select relevant ones to support/illustrate your answer.

[12] You may wish to refer to the fact that applications may also be made under the Children Act 1989 to decide specific issues. However, don't try to include too much detail on the procedural elements.

6. Emergency

In an emergency, treatment could be given without consent under the common law doctrine of necessity (see ***Gillick***). There would have to be a genuine emergency. Where the treatment is contrary to the wishes of the child and those with parental responsibility an application to court should be made where there is time to do so (see ***Glass* v *UK*** (App. No. 61827/00)).

7. Summary of advice to Dr Smith

If Dr Smith cannot persuade Sasha to consent, and assesses her as being ***Gillick*** competent, then he will need to assess the urgency of the situation and need for treatment. He should consider whether there are any alternative treatments that Sasha may agree to. If, as seems likely, Sasha is not ***Gillick*** competent, then if Dr Smith can obtain Debbie's consent, he could proceed on that basis. If he cannot obtain a valid consent from Sasha and or Debbie, then if the situation is genuinely urgent Dr Smith could treat on the basis of the common law doctrine of necessity, and should do so if Sasha's life is at risk. Otherwise the safest legal option may be to make an application to the High Court for an order that it is lawful to treat. The court will balance the various considerations but is almost certainly going to conclude that a child should be given life-sustaining treatment even where parent and child objects.

Make your answer stand out

- Demonstrate throughout a clear focus on the applicable legal framework and actual question.
- Introduce key case references and quotations to support your arguments.
- Demonstrate clear understanding of how the legal components fit together and their practical application.
- Show you have an appreciation of the potential for challenge in this area from a human rights context.

! Don't be tempted to . . .

- Simply recite the overall legal framework for consent, including adults and 16–17-year-olds. Although some compare and contrast may be appropriate.
- Start your answer without a clear answer plan. This is a tricky legal area with overlapping and sometimes conflicting provisions. Failure to plan a sound structure from the start will lead to a confused rambling answer.
- Waste too much time (or word limit, if applicable) on the facts of the cases. Your answer will just read like a case summary.
- Get too 'bogged down' in the procedural aspects of the possible court applications.

Question 5

The introduction of the Mental Capacity Act 2005 and its application to 16- and 17-year-olds, highlights the need for a review and update of the legal framework which governs the medical treatment of young people aged 16 or 17. Discuss.

Answer plan

→ Introduce the relevant legal framework that applies to the treatment of 16–17-year-olds.

→ Consider the effect of the Family Law Reform Act, Parental Responsibility and *Gillick*.

→ Detail the application of the Mental Capacity Act 2005 (MCA).

→ Consider how this 'sits alongside' the surrounding legal framework.

→ Analyse to what extent this highlights the need for a review and update.

→ Conclude your answer.

Diagram plan

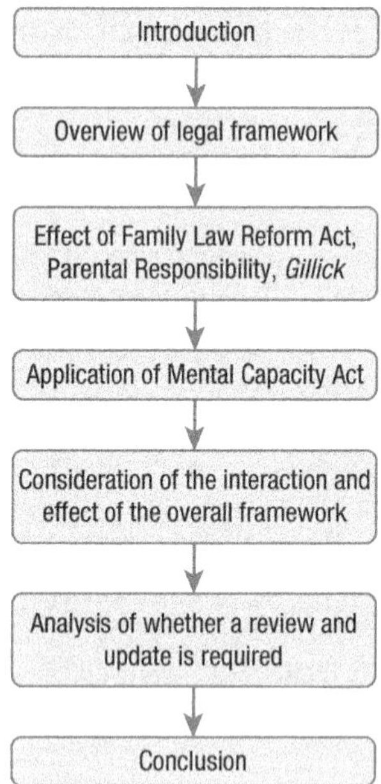

A printable version of this diagram plan is available from **www.pearsoned.co.uk/lawexpressqa**

Answer

It is suggested that the introduction of the Mental Capacity Act 2005 (the MCA) highlights the need for review and update of the legal framework relating to the medical treatment of young people aged 16 and 17 (referred to as young people). In order to determine to what extent this may be the case, we need to consider the overall legal framework, including the effect of the MCA, and analyse to what extent this has indeed highlighted such a need.[1]

[1] Remember to introduce your answer to the actual question.

1. Legal framework

As with a person of any age, any medical treatment needs to be 'legally authorised'. The overall legal framework is complex, with arguably overlapping and at times apparently inconsistent provisions. The framework is made up of the Family Law Reform Act 1969 (the FLR), Parental Responsibility (PR)[2] and more recently the MCA. The High Court has an inherent jurisdiction to authorise treatment. Where the

[2] You may wish to include more detail as to PR and relevant provisions of the Children Act 1989, but take care to stay focused on the treatment aspects.

young person requires treatment for mental disorder then the Mental Health Act 1983 may apply, although detailed consideration of this is outside the scope of this essay.[3]

Unlike an under 16,[4] a young person is statutorily able to provide consent for treatment by the FLR, which provides that the consent of a young person is as valid as if they were an adult. This is an age-based concept.[5]

The full effect of the FLR has been subject to considerable debate and was considered in the case of ***Gillick* v *West Norfolk and Wisbech AHA*** [1985] J All ER 402 and subsequently ***Re R (A Minor)*** [1992] Fam 11) and ***Re W*** [1993] Fam 64. The main issue raised is the question whether its effect is to confer exclusive authority to determine whether to have treatment[6] on the young person. It was ultimately held in the ***Re R*** and ***Re W*** cases that it did not, but that it simply permits the young person to provide their legal authority for the treatment. It does not impact on the authority of the person with PR, who has a 'concurrent' right to authorise the treatment. The validity of such a conclusion that a capable young person may consent but not refuse treatment has been much debated and criticised. In *Mason & McCall Smith's Law and Medical Ethics* it is suggested that the level of understanding required to refuse a treatment is not necessarily on a par with that required to consent to treatment (Mason, J.K. and Laurie, G.T. (2006) *Mason & McCall Smith's Law and Medical Ethics* 7th edn. Oxford: Oxford University Press, para. 10.52). However, many other commentators share John Harris's view that 'the idea that the child . . . might competently consent to a treatment but not be competent to refuse it is a palpable nonsense . . . ' (Harris, J. (2003) Consent and end of life decisions. *Journal of Medical Ethics*, 29: 10–15).

In certain circumstances the application of the FLR may be limited[7] in which case the case of ***Gillick*** may have an application to the young person, requiring an assessment of whether they are ***Gillick*** competent to consent to the proposed 'treatment'. Although the application and relevance of ***Gillick*** to a young person will not be considered in any detail here, the possibility of the decision falling outside the FLR adds a further complication.

The authority of the person with PR to consent to treatment on behalf of a young person is not removed by the FLR, but relying on PR consent where the young person is capable is controversial. Even where the young person lacks capacity relying on PR consent may no longer be necessary or justifiable since the introduction of the MCA.[8]

[3] The extent to which the MHA should be considered as part of your answer may depend upon the scope of the question and answer, the time and/or word limit and the extent to which it has formed part of the syllabus.

[4] Where *Gillick* applies. Take care not to deal in any detail with the position in relation to under 16s as this is not relevant to the question. Some comparisons between the different legal regimes may be appropriate.

[5] The law recognises that the young person is old enough to consent. This is in contrast to the MCA which is mental capacity based. You need to make sure your answer is clear on this point.

[6] In other words, be clear in your answer that this means whether to consent to and refuse treatment.

[7] You may wish to include an example, such as the young person consenting to being a blood donor.

[8] Try to keep the actual question in mind throughout your answer and refer back to it as appropriate throughout your answer.

This is highlighted by the concept of the 'zone of parental responsibility',[9] where it is recognised that certain decisions would be outside the scope of the parent in any event.

The High Court will always have an inherent jurisdiction to intervene in relation to issues relating to the treatment of a young person.[10] However, with the introduction of the MCA, issues relating to the capacity of the young person and whether treatment is in their best interests may be brought before the Court of Protection,[11] established by the MCA.

2. Application of the MCA

The MCA applies generally to young people.[12] It provides a legal framework for the authorisation of treatment in the best interests of the young person, a presumption of capacity (s. 1) a set of core principles (s. 1), a definition and assessment process of capacity (ss. 2 and 3) and a process for the assessment of best interests (s. 4). Where a clinician has a reasonable belief that the young person (P) lacks capacity and that the treatment is in her best interests then this may be 'authorised'[13] (s. 5) subject to limitations[14] (s. 6). The MCA provides this 'authority' to treat regardless of any PR consent or refusal[15] and effectively adds yet another 'layer' to the complex picture of where authority to treat may legally come from.

3. Analysis

With the introduction of the MCA, it is arguable that the role of PR becomes unnecessary and represents an out-of-date approach and simply serves to complicate matters. Where the young person is capable and able to consent for themselves then the role of PR is unnecessary. Where the young person lacks capacity the MCA provides a clear legal framework for authorising any treatment in best interests. Any assessment of best interests would usually involve consideration of the views of those with PR in any event, but with a clear statutory-based focus on the young person's best interests, rather than just what the parent may prefer. Again, the role of PR is unnecessary and may simply complicate matters where the parent confuses their role and conflates their wishes with the young person's best interests. The only 'gap' in the framework might be where the

[9] See for example the Code of Practice to MHA which explores this zone. The decision to deprive a child of their liberty falls outside this zone. You may wish to refer to this in your answer, if time allows.

[10] The court may also decide specific issue applications made under the Children Act.

[11] Note the distinction between the courts, which you might want to pick up on in your answer, though in reality the same judge may sit in both the High Court and the Court of Protection.

[12] If time allows you could detail the limitations of the application of the MCA to under 18s, such as the fact an advance decision or a lasting power of attorney cannot be made.

[13] Remember section 5 is actually legally a defence rather than a general authority, though it may be easier to refer to it and its effect that way.

[14] This includes additional criteria being met where restraint is necessary and an express legal authority for any deprivation of liberty. This detail could be included if you have time.

[15] Be clear as to the effect of PR views, these may be an important consideration in assessing best interests.

young person is capable and refuses treatment and where it may be argued that the role of PR is important here in providing the necessary legal authority. However, to rely on the consent of someone with PR in such circumstances would probably be legally unsound[16] and raise Human Rights considerations.[17] If the legality of reliance on it is so uncertain, surely this needs to be clarified and the cases of ***Re R*** and ***Re W*** consigned to history. In an emergency, treatment could be provided under the common law doctrine of necessity in any event (see ***Gillick***). Where the proper treatment is in dispute this could be (and usually is) resolved by the court.

[16] You may wish to conclude that it is likely any clinician would require a court order in such circumstances.

[17] You might want to explore the argument that post the HRA 1998 implementation, the reliance on PR consent to override the young person's refusal would breach key rights such as Articles 8 and 3. Though there is disagreement as to this view, see *Mason & McCall Smith's* text above.

The application and effect of the FLR could also be clarified, post-MCA introduction. Although it still has a role in providing that a young person may consent as an adult could, a clearer statement as to the effect of the FLR, its relationship with the role of PR and interaction with the MCA would assist clinicians for whom this is more than an academic debate.

4. Conclusion

Having reviewed the relevant legal framework, it can be concluded that this is unnecessarily complex and out of date in its approach to the autonomy of the young person and should now be reviewed and updated to provide a clearer picture more consistent with the rights of young people and society and the law's approach to their treatment.

Make your answer stand out

- Demonstrate that you are familiar with the various arguments advanced by commentators in this area.
- Ensure your structure is clear and ensures your answer remains focused on the question.
- Demonstrate an up-to-date knowledge of the issue of the 'zone of parental responsibility'.
- Make it clear where more peripheral aspects, which are still relevant to the question, are not considered in detail because of time/word constraints.

Don't be tempted to

- Simply recite all you know about the legal framework applicable to young people.
- Focus in too much detail on the legal framework applicable to adults or under 16s.
- Get 'bogged down' in the relevance and application of *Gillick*.
- Just provide your own opinions on whether and how young people should be treated.
- Recite in too much detail the provisions of the MCA.

Question 6

The Mental Capacity Act 2005 (MCA) ensures that the individual adult patient's views are always respected and upheld. Discuss.

Answer plan

→ Introduce and identify the scope of the question.

→ Identify the relevant provisions of the MCA.

→ Detail and analyse the best interest assessment under the MCA.

→ Consider the relevance and effect of the lasting power of attorney (LPA) and advance decision.

→ Analyse the extent to which the relevant provisions of the MCA ensure the patient's views are respected and the extent to which they are upheld.

→ Conclude your answer.

Diagram plan

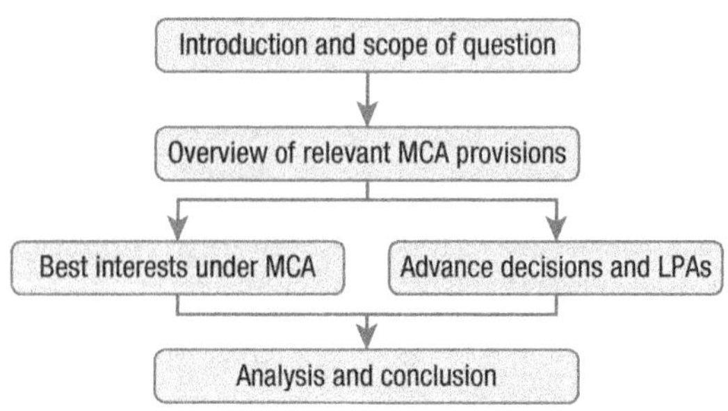

A printable version of this diagram plan is available from **www.pearsoned.co.uk/lawexpressqa**

Answer

This question raises the issue as to what extent the Mental Capacity Act 2005 (the MCA) ensures the patient's (P's) views are firstly respected and secondly upheld. To assess this we need to consider the relevant provisions of the MCA, the best interest assessment process and those provisions which allow P to determine decisions for some future time when P has lost capacity.

1. Legal framework

The MCA provides a framework to authorise the care and treatment of adults who lack capacity. It essentially replaces the common law doctrine of necessity[1] with a statutory framework that has largely the same effect. Although the courts have developed the notion of 'best interests' over a series of judgments, the MCA creates a process for assessment of best interests in section 4, in accordance with core principles (s. 1) and guidance given in the Code of Practice to the MCA.[2]

In addition to providing what is in effect a 'general authority' to provide treatment (s. 5),[3] the MCA introduces rights to make an advance refusal of treatment (s. 25) and to create lasting powers of attorney (LPAs) (s. 9) in relation to welfare matters.[4]

Since the MCA contains a presumption of capacity (s. 1), then this, in itself, provides a protection for the views and wishes of P, who is permitted to be as unwise as P likes (s. 1). The authority to intervene in P's decision making is only triggered by a decision that P lacks capacity in accordance with the definition and assessment process set out in sections 2 and 3 of the MCA.[5]

2. Best interests

The MCA sets out a process for assessment of best interests in section 4, and section 1 contains the core principles of the Act, which include a requirement that anything done under the MCA must be in P's best interests.[6]

Section 4 of the MCA sets out a 'checklist' of key factors which must be taken into account when assessing P's best interests,[7] placing P's

[1] See *Re F* [1989] 2 All ER 545. If time allows you could provide more detail of the common law developments here, but take care not to include too much background description.

[2] Remember to make it clear that this is not legally binding as such but professionals must 'have regard to it'.

[3] Remember, section 5 actually operates as a 'defence' in a similar way to the common law doctrine of necessity. You may wish to expand on this.

[4] LPAs can also be made to cover finances but they are not relevant to this question which focuses on treatment so take care not to waste time focusing on them.

[5] Make sure you are not filling your answer with unnecessary recital of the MCA provisions.

[6] You may wish to identify that the only exception to this is the decision made by the capable P by means of a valid advance decision.

[7] This is, of course, subject to practicability, so in an emergency there may be limited scope for considering the checklist factors and you may wish to explore this if time allows.

views at the heart of the process. In section 4(3) an assessment is required of whether P is likely to regain capacity and if so when. So, if the decision could be left to P to make once capable, then this may well be the least restrictive way (see s. 1) of proceeding.

P's participation must be permitted and encouraged, so far as practicable (s. 4(4)). Mary Donnelly argues that this requirement means 'it cannot be enough for a decision-maker simply to acknowledge the views of the person lacking capacity before reaching a decision which takes no account of these views' (Donnelly, M. (2009) Best interests, patient participation and the Mental Capacity Act 2005. *Medical Law Review,* 17: 1–29). Section 4(6) is particularly important in requiring any decision-maker[8] to consider, 'so far as is reasonably ascertainable' P's 'past and present wishes and feelings', P's 'beliefs and values that would be likely to influence his decision',[9] and 'any other factors he would be likely to consider'.[10]

Although P's views are central, this is not the same as a substituted decision-making process. The decision-maker is not required to identify what P would have done, then do it, but to form an objective assessment of P's best interests.[11]

Although this ensures that P's views are respected in the sense that they must be taken into account it does not mean they are respected[12] in the sense of always being upheld.[13]

The decision-maker only needs to form a 'reasonable belief' as to the best interests of P, so there is considerable scope for differences of opinion as to P's best interests and for the decision-maker's own notions of what is best for P to be influential,[14] particularly where P's life is at risk.

The courts may be more prepared to make riskier decisions[15] than an individual decision-maker. The court has raised the question what good does it do to protect P if that provides them with a life that makes them 'merely miserable' (***Re MM (An Adult)*** [2007] EWHC 2003 (Fam)). However, the court may only rarely be involved in decision-making.

3. Advance decisions

Advance decisions are put on a statutory footing in the MCA,[16] which provides a right (subject to certain criteria) to make a refusal of

[8] This is how the Code refers to the person carrying out the assessment and making the best interests decision.

[9] For a consideration of the relevance of altruistic motives see Herring and Foster (2012). You could consider expanding on this in your answer, if time allows.

[10] You need to be sufficiently detailed and precise when referring to key provisions of the MCA, even in closed book exam conditions.

[11] You may wish to refer to Munby J's guidance in *Re M* [2009] EWHC 2525 (Fam) which identifies that different weight will be placed on different aspects of the decision in accordance with the individual's circumstances.

[12] Take care to define what might be meant by respect here.

[13] Again, remember what the question is asking you to consider.

[14] Though, be clear that the focus must always be on P's best interests. See *Re MM* [2007] EWHC 2003 (Fam).

[15] Mr Justice Baker refers to the 'protection imperative', whereby the decision-maker should be overinfluenced by the need to protect P. You may wish to incorporate this into your answer.

[16] Set out in sections 24, 25 and 26 of the MCA.

future treatment. In fact ***Re C*** (***(Adult: Refusal of Treatment)*** [1994] 1 WLR 290) provided the legal authority at common law and again, the MCA largely takes the common law position and places it on a statutory footing.

This provides a key way for a capable P to refuse treatment at some future time. Where the treatment refused is 'life-sustaining' then procedural requirements apply (s. 25(5)).[17] This requirement was never part of the common law (see ***Re C***).

To be binding the refusal has to be a capable one and 'applicable' to the treatment (s. 25(1)) and P must not have acted in a way inconsistent with it (s. 25(2)).[18] In reality, it may be difficult to create a decision which satisfies these requirements, particularly where P's life is at risk if P is not treated. See, for example, the case of ***Re E*** [2012] EWHC 1639 COP.[19]

A clinician is not bound by an advance decision where he is satisfied 'that a valid, applicable advance decision exists' (s. 26). This appears to allow the clinician considerable leeway to avoid being bound by the advance refusal.[20]

It may be that in fact P's ability to protect his advance wishes is not really furthered by the advance decision provisions in the MCA.

[17] The refusal must be in writing, witnessed and verified. Although you do not need to dwell too much on procedural aspects, you need to be familiar with the basic points.

[18] You may wish to note that this would invalidate it.

[19] This case is to be compared with the decision in the *Re L* case ([2012] EWHC 2741 COP). You could expand on this if time allows.

[20] See Alasdair Maclean's (2008) comments on the effect of this which he says 'provides patients with a trump that only works when healthcare professionals and/or the courts are comfortable with the patient's decision'. You could incorporate this into your answer.

4. Lasting power of attorney (LPA)

Another option introduced by the MCA is the LPA (s. 9). This was not an option at common law, so represents an important development in the options to ensure P's views are respected and upheld. The LPA can be created to convey decision-making powers on a chosen individual when P loses capacity. However, although P can choose who to appoint and what decisions that person can make, ultimately the attorney is not bound to do what P instructs, rather the attorney has to act in P's best interests (s. 9(4)). As seen above, this is an objective assessment of best interests. However, although the LPA may not mean P's wishes are always upheld, they will have to be respected in accordance with the best interests process and, of course, P may select an appropriately trusted person to make decisions for him, rather than an unknown clinician.

5. Conclusion

The MCA has largely replicated the common law provisions, and so may arguably not have advanced P's position much. However, it does provide a statutory mechanism for the respecting of the views and wishes of P, through the required s. 4 process, which applies to any decision-maker. It has also introduced the LPA which may be a further way P can protect his future wishes. However, it does not always provide that P's views will be upheld and, indeed, particularly where P may die if not treated, still provides considerable leeway for decision-makers to override an advance refusal of treatment.

✓ Make your answer stand out

- Demonstrate that you understand how the MCA differs from the common law position.
- Ensure you have a clear structure which keeps your answer focused throughout on what the question requires.
- Demonstrate an up-to-date knowledge of the MCA and relevant case law.
- Include references to relevant articles.

! Don't be tempted to . . .

- Simply recite chunks of the MCA.
- Be too general with references to the MCA.
- Confuse the common law position pre MCA with the post-MCA position.

www.pearsoned.co.uk/lawexpressqa

Go online to access more revision support including additional essay and problem questions with diagram plans, You be the marker questions, and download all diagrams from the book.

5 Medical confidentiality

How this topic may come up in exams

There are various sources of the duty of confidence including the common law, the Human Rights Act 1998, the Data Protection Act 1998, and professional and ethical obligations. The duty of confidence is not absolute. Difficulties often arise when deciding whether disclosure of confidential information can be justified and public interest issues are key here. Essay questions may focus on a particular aspect of this topic (e.g. how confidentiality is protected or how disclosure is permitted). A problem question may focus on difficult disclosure issues. Entitlement to access medical records also falls within this topic; this issue could appear within a problem question.

Before you begin

It's a good idea to consider the following key themes of medical confidentiality before tackling a question on this topic.

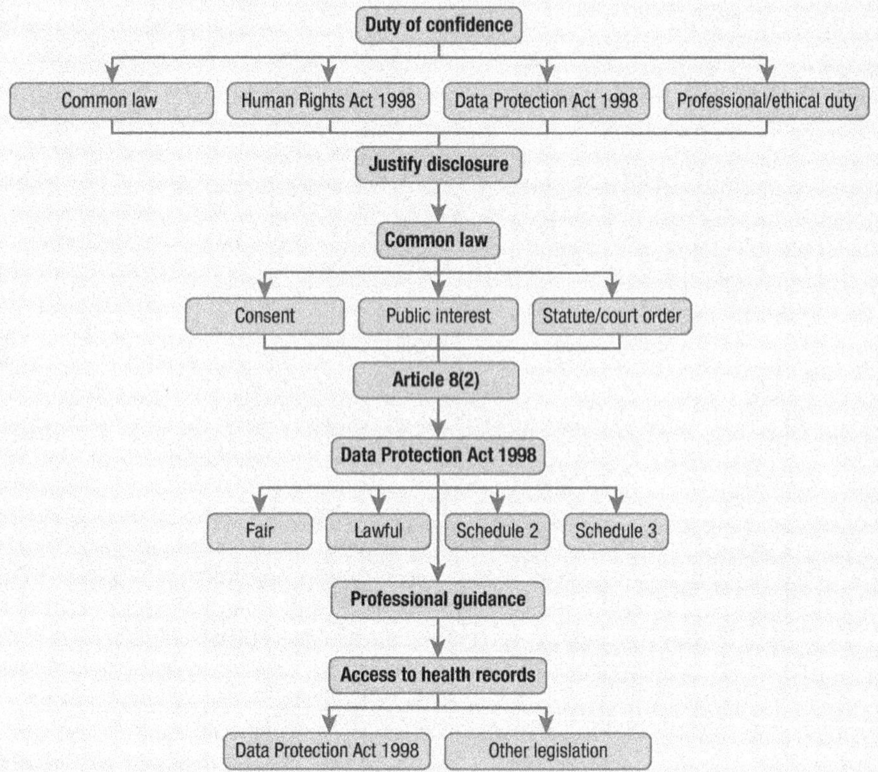

A printable version of this diagram is available from **www.pearsoned.co.uk/lawexpressqa**

Question 1

Eddie is a lorry driver and visits Dr Findlay, his General Practitioner (GP), as he has been experiencing unexplained dizziness. Eddie has various blood tests and is diagnosed with an illness which affects his coordination and balance. His condition will continue to deteriorate in the long term. Dr Findlay advises Eddie that he can no longer drive. Eddie explains he is unable to stop driving as he will lose his job and will be unable to afford his mortgage payments. Dr Findlay informs the DVLA of Eddie's condition. Eddie loses his driving licence and job.

Eddie begins to drink alcohol excessively. His drinking is affecting his existing health problems including his diabetes. Dr Findlay advises him of the long-term risks to his health and recommends counselling as Eddie says he won't talk about it with his family. Dr Findlay would like to discuss this with Eddie's wife Gail, as he believes she would be supportive. Due to Dr Findlay's assessment that Eddie has capacity, Dr Findlay has so far refused to discuss his condition or his drinking with Gail.

Discuss the confidentiality issues which arise in the scenario.

Answer plan

➜ Confirm whether a duty of confidentiality exists.

➜ Is disclosure to the DVLA justified?

- At common law
- Human Rights Act 1998
- Data Protection Act 1998
- Professional guidance

➜ Would disclosure to Gail be justified?

Diagram plan

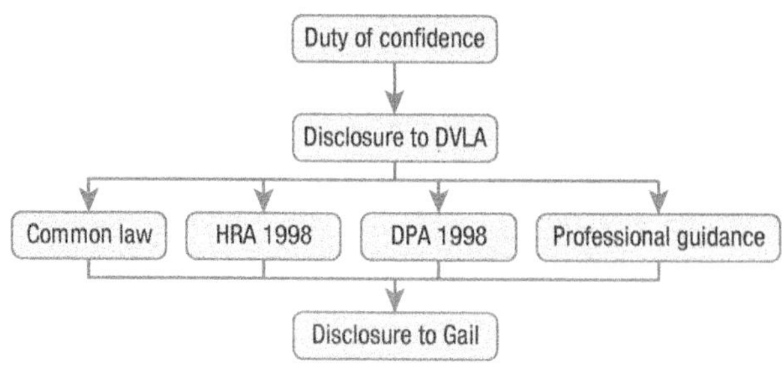

A printable version of this diagram plan is available from **www.pearsoned.co.uk/lawexpressqa**

Answer

[1] This acknowledges that there is more than one disclosure issue involved in the scenario.

A duty of confidentiality is easily established so disclosure to the DVLA and Gail must be justified.[1]

1. Duty of confidence

Information regarding Eddie's medical condition is protected by the common law duty of confidence. In ***A-G* v *Guardian Newspapers (No. 2)*** [1988] 3 All ER 545 it was held that a duty of confidence arises where confidential information is passed to a person in circumstances where it would be just and reasonable to impose an obligation not to disclose the information further. Medical information gained in the course of the doctor–patient relationship clearly meets these criteria. This information will also be protected under the Human Rights Act 1998 by relying upon Article 8(1) which protects the right to respect for his private and family life. Information regarding Eddie's 'physical or mental health or condition' will be protected as 'sensitive personal data' (s. 2(e) Data Protection Act 1998). Dr Findlay additionally has a professional obligation of confidence and must comply with the General Medical Council's *Confidentiality* guidance. The duty of confidence, however, is not absolute.

2. Disclosure to DVLA

[2] You should still take the opportunity to comment on the significance of consent in relation to disclosure (as consent would be Dr Findlay's starting point when contemplating disclosure) and the scenario does not expressly state whether consent had been sought and refused.

Was disclosure to the DVLA justified? We are not expressly told whether Eddie gave or withheld consent to this disclosure.[2] If Eddie had consented this would have provided a justification at common law and there would not have been a breach of the Human Rights Act 1998 either, as there would only be an infringement of Article 8 if there was no consent. As this was sensitive personal data a condition from Schedule 2 and a condition from Schedule 3 of the DPA 1998 would need to be met. Eddie's consent would have satisfied conditions in both Schedules (condition 1, Sch. 2 and condition 1, Sch. 3). Consent is also recognised as a justification in the GMC's *Confidentiality* guidance (see paras. 33 and 34).

Given Eddie's reluctance to stop driving it may be that Eddie had not consented to this disclosure so an alternative justification is needed. The public interest justification arises where there is a strong public interest in disclosure which may outweigh the public interest in maintaining confidentiality (***A-G* v *Guardian Newspapers (No. 2)***). Dr Findlay should have engaged in a balancing exercise to weigh the competing public interests. Where there is a risk of serious harm to a third party, this is a public interest issue which can justify disclosure. In ***W* v *Egdell*** [1990] 1 All ER 835 a psychiatrist had been instructed by W's solicitors to prepare a report regarding W in preparation for an application for discharge from a secure hospital. W had previously killed several people. The psychiatrist thought that W remained a risk and the solicitors withdrew the application (and so the report was not disclosed). The psychiatrist still disclosed the report. The Court of Appeal held that disclosure could be justified where there was 'a real risk of consequent danger' to a third party. Admittedly, this was an extreme case which involved a risk of serious violence. In this scenario, although Eddie would not inflict violent injury himself, his condition could cause an accident which could result in grave harm or death to other road users or passengers, so the principles could still apply here.[3] Disclosure would be permitted in this situation.[4]

[3] This sets out application of the principles in *W* v *Egdell* to this scenario.

[4] Use of the word 'permitted' here is important. The current legal position is that the public interest justification would *permit* the doctor to disclose rather than *require* him to do so.

To be protected by the public interest defence it is not enough to simply show a sufficient reason, there are further requirements too. Disclosure must be made to the 'responsible authorities' (***W* v *Egdell***). Here information is disclosed to the DVLA, so this requirement is satisfied. Dr Findlay must also disclose the minimum necessary to achieve his aim. We will presume that Dr Findlay only disclosed information about the condition which affected his driving and not further sensitive clinical information.[5]

[5] It is important not to focus solely on the 'reason' for disclosure. You need to address the further requirements to comply with to be protected by the public interest defence.

Disclosure should also be permitted by Article 8(2)[6] as this allows interference with Eddie's Article 8(1) right 'for the protection of health or morals, or for the protection of the rights and freedoms of others'. The disclosure is to protect those persons who could be injured by Eddie. The interference must also be 'in accordance with the law' and 'necessary in a democratic society'. Proportionality is key here, and this adds strength to the earlier assertion that disclosure should be the minimum necessary to the appropriate body.

[6] As medical information is protected under Article 8(1) you should also refer to the need to satisfy Article 8(2).

To comply with the Data Protection Act 1998 (DPA) 'processing' must be 'fair' and 'lawful' and a condition from both Schedule 2 and Schedule 3 must be satisfied (Sch. 1). In the absence of consent Dr Findlay may rely on condition 4 to show he complied with Schedule

2 which allows data to be processed where it is necessary to protect the vital interests of the data subject (here disclosure could have protected Eddie from injury). A condition from Schedule 3 must also be met as this is 'sensitive personal data'. Condition 3b seems to apply as this permits processing if necessary where consent has been 'unreasonably withheld' to protect the 'vital interests' of another person. Arguably, Eddie's refusal to allow disclosure was unreasonable and disclosure was *necessary* to protect third parties from the harm that could result from a road traffic accident.[7] Although this is not defined in the Act, the Information Commissioner has indicated 'vital interests' relate to 'matters of life and death'[8] (Information Commissioner's Office (2014) Human Tissue Authority Code of Practice 2 (Donation of solid organs for transplantation), *Guide to Data Protection*. London.

[7] It is important to stress the requirement that it is 'necessary' here. This term frequently appears in the DPA 1998. It must be shown that processing (i.e. disclosing) the information is the only way the intended outcome can be achieved.

[8] It is a good idea to try to identify how key terms have been described, i.e. have they been interpreted broadly or narrowly.

Professional guidance also allows disclosure to protect third parties. The GMC's *Confidentiality* guidance (para. 53) permits disclosure if others may be exposed to 'a risk of death or serious harm.' There is supplementary guidance regarding reporting concerns to the DVLA.[9] This provides (at para. 7) that a doctor 'should' contact the DVLA if the patient will not stop driving. It also seems that the patient should be told this information will be disclosed.

[9] The examiner will be impressed if you are able to refer to professional guidance in relation to the specific issue involved.

3. Disclosure to Gail

If Dr Findlay wishes to discuss Eddie's conditions with Gail, he needs Eddie's consent. The importance of consent is explained above.[10] If consent is refused Dr Findlay would struggle to justify disclosure based on public interest.[11] Risk of harm to third parties can justify disclosure (see ***W* v *Egdell***), however, Dr Findlay has already addressed this risk as he has disclosed to the DVLA and Eddie can no longer drive. Public interest allows disclosure to protect third parties rather than to protect the patient (where the patient has capacity[12]). Dr Findlay cannot discuss Eddie's condition with Gail even though Gail may offer Eddie help and support.

[10] There is no need to repeat consent coverage here as the same principles are applicable.

[11] This would show your understanding of the limits of the public interest defence.

[12] We are told Dr Findlay has drawn the conclusion that Eddie has capacity so you do not need to speculate how the position would differ if he lacked capacity.

4. Conclusion

In summary, it is likely that Dr Findlay's disclosure to the DVLA was justified, however disclosure to Gail in the absence of consent would not be justified *if* it is only Eddie himself who is at risk of harm.

Make your answer stand out

- Make sure you address the different sources of the obligation of confidence, both when confirming a duty exists and also when justifying disclosure.
- Familiarise yourself with GMC guidance which may help in difficult situations. The GMC's *Confidentiality* guidance contains supplementary guidance which deals with common problems. Here, we relied on the supplementary guidance regarding disclosure to the DVLA, there is other specific guidance too. This is particularly important as professional guidance will provide an indication of what the law will demand (*W* v *Egdell*).

! Don't be tempted to . . .

- Simply introduce cases regarding public interest without commenting on how they apply to the scenario. For example, here we are dealing with a different type of situation to that in *W* v *Egdell,* but it was important to explain how the principles in that case could apply.
- Forget there was more than one disclosure issue here. After spending time dealing with the DVLA issue, ensure you also address the problem regarding whether information can be passed to Eddie's wife Gail as separate issues are raised.

Question 2

The duty of confidence must always be breached by a doctor where he is aware that his patient poses a risk which could result in physical harm to a third party. Discuss.

Answer plan

→ Introduce the basis of the duty of confidence.

→ Critically discuss issues regarding the common law public interest justification, to include:
  - competing public interests;
  - case law regarding protecting third parties;
  - difficulties in application.

→ Comment on the relevance of the Human Rights Act 1998 and Data Protection Act 1998.

→ Refer to professional guidance.

→ Discuss the distinction between a power and a duty to disclose.

Diagram plan

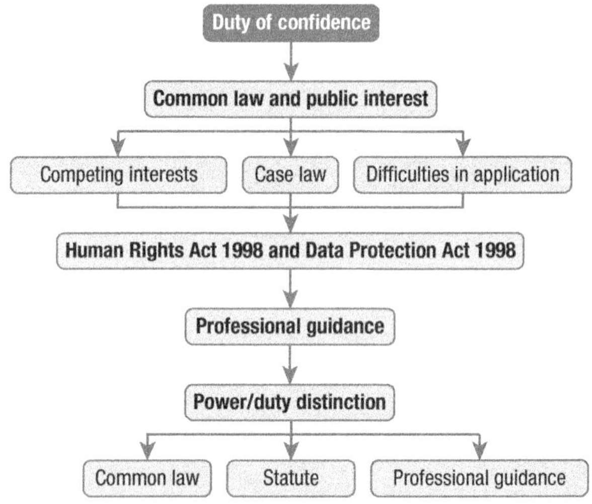

A printable version of this diagram plan is available from **www.pearsoned.co.uk/lawexpressqa**

Answer

Can disclosure be justified where a doctor possesses information about a patient which shows a third party is at risk of physical harm? If justifications for disclosure exist we need to explore whether the duty of confidence 'must' be breached. Would a doctor have an *obligation* to pass this information on, or does the doctor simply have a *power* to do so?[1]

[1] This shows focus on the question. Note the question asks you to consider whether the duty '*must* always be breached'. This means the question extends beyond simply looking at the scope of the *power* to disclose.

There are various different sources of the obligation of confidence. A common law duty of confidence will arise in respect of information shared in the doctor–patient relationship (***X* v *Y*** [1988] 2 All ER 648). The patient is also protected by the Human Rights Act 1998 (HRA) using Article 8(1) with regard to respect for his private and family life. Also, the Data Protection Act 1998 (DPA) will protect clinical information as 'sensitive personal data' under section 2(e). Ethical and professional obligations also exist.[2]

[2] Although this question focuses on justifying disclosure, it is still important to introduce the nature of the duty. If there was no duty, there would be no need to justify disclosure.

The common law 'public interest' defence is potentially applicable if a patient refuses to consent to disclosure. This defence acknowledges that although there is a strong public interest in maintaining confidentiality (otherwise a patient may not confide sensitive personal information), this can be outweighed by a countervailing public interest (***A-G* v *Guardian Newspapers (No. 2)*** [1988] 3 All ER 545).

There is no definition of what particular circumstances fall within the 'public interest' to justify disclosure. From the limited case law we have it is apparent that where there is a risk of harm to a third party, disclosure may be justified. It is not the case that a risk of *any* harm is sufficient, rather the case law suggests that *serious* harm would be required.[3] Consider ***W* v *Egdell*** [1990] 1 All ER 835 where W was detained in a secure hospital having killed several people. A psychiatrist prepared a report, as instructed by W's solicitors, in relation to the patient's application for discharge. The report referred to the ongoing risk he posed. The solicitors withdrew the application and therefore the report was not disclosed. The psychiatrist was concerned that the information in his report was relevant due to the continued risk W posed, so he disclosed the report. It was held this was justified because there was a 'real risk of consequent danger' if information was not disclosed. It must be noted that this was an extreme case which could have involved extremely serious harm to third parties.[4] This case does little to help us assess where the line is to be drawn in terms of the degree and likelihood of harm which justify disclosure.[5]

It should also be stressed that for the public interest defence to succeed disclosure must be made to the apt person. In ***W* v *Egdell*** it was key that disclosure was to the 'responsible authorities', namely the Secretary of State and the hospital. Also, the minimum amount of information necessary should be disclosed. So even if a public interest reason exists, the defence would not be available if the doctor disclosed too much information to the wrong person.[6]

Public interest is not only relevant in cases involving risks of physical violence, it may also apply where a patient's illness could result in infection and subsequent harm to a third party. Mason and Laurie (2013) consider public interest could permit disclosure of a patient's HIV status where the patient refuses to tell his/her sexual partner of the risk[7] (see Mason, J.K. and Laurie, G.T. (2013) *Mason & McCall Smith's Law and Medical Ethics* (9th edn). Oxford: Oxford University Press.)

Article 8(2) allows interference with the Article 8(1) right to protect the rights and freedoms of others. Even if there is a legitimate aim the disclosure must still be proportionate to aim to be achieved (***Z* v *Finland*** (1997) 25 EHRR 371) echoing the common law requirements. The DPA

[3] This helps to breakdown the very broad statement in the question which refers to 'a risk' of 'physical harm'. It is important to acknowledge that the seriousness and likelihood of the harm will be key in terms of whether disclosure can be justified.

[4] You could bring in reference to further case law too, for instance *R* v *Crozier* (1990) 8 BMLR 128 (another 'extreme' violence case).

[5] Engage in commentary on the case law to address the question, avoid simply summarising the cases.

[6] Develops the proposition in the question, although *serious* harm may justify disclosure, there are 'extra' requirements to comply with to be protected by the public interest defence.

[7] Existing case law regarding confidentiality and HIV cases (e.g. *X* v *Y* [1988] 2 All ER 648) has centred on press freedom to report on the HIV status of medical practitioners. You could still refer to this case law to confirm the importance of confidentiality in relation to HIV status.

[8] Remember the question is not confined to the common law public interest position.

[9] If you cannot remember lengthy direct extracts from statute, try to set out key phrases.

1998 provides that Schedule 2 and Schedule 3 to the Act must be met when 'processing' sensitive personal data.[8] Schedule 3 contains the more onerous requirements. Condition 3b of Schedule 3 applies where the 'vital interests of another person' are at risk where consent has been 'unreasonably withheld'.[9] Although not defined in the Act, 'vital interests' are considered by the Information Commissioner (Information Commissioner's Office (2014) Human Tissue Authority Code of Practice 2 (Donation of solid organs for transplantation), *Guide to Data Protection*. London. to involve 'matters of life and death', thus a high level of threat is needed. The GMC also permits disclosure if non-disclosure 'may expose others to a risk of death or serious harm' (para. 53 *Confidentiality* guidance). There is still a lack of clarity regarding what constitutes serious harm.

[10] This demonstrates an intention to focus on a key angle of the question.

Although a risk of serious harm to a third party *permits* disclosure we must consider whether confidentiality 'must always be breached' where such risk exists.[10] This proposition goes too far. It seems that a doctor would have the power to disclose information, but would not be required to do so. The US case of ***Tarasoff* v *Regents of the University of California*** (1996) 131 Cal Rptr 14 highlights a different approach. In this case a male student made specific threats against a particular female student during a therapy session. The therapist did not inform the girl of the threats and she was killed. It was held that a duty could exist where there was an identifiable victim and a risk of serious harm.

We do not yet have a case which has succeeded on this basis here. A victim harmed by a third party would have to establish the doctor owed the victim a duty of care. Using the three stage ***Caparo Industries plc* v *Dickman*** [1990] 1 All ER 568 test it may be that the requirements of reasonable foreseeability and proximity could be satisfied, but a case may struggle on the third limb, namely whether it is fair, just and reasonable to impose a duty.[11] On this point it is argued a duty would have resource implications and would create a difficult conflict in duties owed to the different parties (***Selwood* v *Durham County Council*** [2012] EWCA Civ 979).

[11] Refer to your general 'duty of care' knowledge here.

[12] It is important to confirm that a duty to share information may be imposed in professional guidance, although it is equally important to stress the limited nature of this.

The HRA 1998 and DPA 1998 authorise disclosure rather than create an obligation. Professional guidance generally simply permits disclosure, although there are limited situations where a duty is imposed, for example in the child protection context (e.g. para. 63 GMC *Confidentiality* guidance).[12] Legislation may also impose a duty, for example the Health Protection (Notification) Regulations 2010 require doctors to notify the local authority if it is suspected a patient has a 'notifiable disease' such as measles.

To conclude, not all harm will justify disclosure, the likelihood and gravity of harm must be considered. The boundaries when determining serious harm are unclear. Although a real risk of serious harm to a third party will permit disclosure, there is a reluctance to impose a legal duty on the doctor to disclose. However, limited circumstances exist (for instance in relation to child protection) where information must be shared.

✓ Make your answer stand out

- Refer to further source material such as *Confidentiality: NHS Code of Practice Supplementary Guidance: Public Interest Disclosures* (Department of Health (2010) *Confidentiality: NHS Code of Practice Supplementary Guidance: Public Interest Disclosures*. London: DoH.). Also consider *A Guide to Confidentiality in Health and Social Care* published in 2013 by the Health and Social Care Information Centre.
- Consider the professional guidance in more detail. For instance, the GMC's *Confidentiality* guidance contains supplemental guidance in relation to particular problems such as 'serious communicable diseases'.
- Consider the moral and ethical positions. For a consideration of how utilitarian reasoning may support disclosure and how this compares with a rights-based approach see Pattinson, S.D. (2014) *Medical Law and Ethics* (4th edn). London: Sweet and Maxwell.
- Evaluate the arguments for and against the imposition of a duty – see for example Jones, C. (2003) Tightropes and tragedies: 25 years of Tarasoff. *Medicine, Science and the Law*, 43(1): 13–22.
- Develop coverage of case law further to support your points. *Selwood* v *Durham Council* [2012] EWCA Civ 979 could be considered further in relation to the difficulties in establishing a duty of care.

! Don't be tempted to . . .

- Simply summarise key cases such as *W* v *Egdell*, you would need to ensure you tailor your commentary to the angle of the question.
- Consider *all* the justifications for disclosure. The question has focused upon 'physical harm' and this is where your focus should lie. So, if you incorporate reference to guidance (e.g. the NHS Code of Practice) regarding 'crime' make sure you focus on crimes against the person rather than theft offences.

Question 3

Arthur is in the early stages of dementia. He lives with his eldest son Ben. Arthur has a serious lung infection and has been prescribed a strong course of antibiotics by his General Practitioner (GP), Dr Davis. Arthur's daughter, Carol, attends Dr Davis's surgery and asks for access to all of Arthur's medical records as she thinks he is losing weight and believes Ben is not looking after him properly. She asks whether Arthur is suffering from any particular illness at present which would explain the weight loss. Dr Davis is also concerned about Arthur's health and is worried that he may be forgetting to take his medication. Dr Davis has already passed his concerns on to the district nurse who will visit Arthur at home later in the week.

Consider the issues regarding whether Dr Davis is able to provide Carole with the information she requires and whether he was justified in telling the nurse about his concerns.

Diagram plan

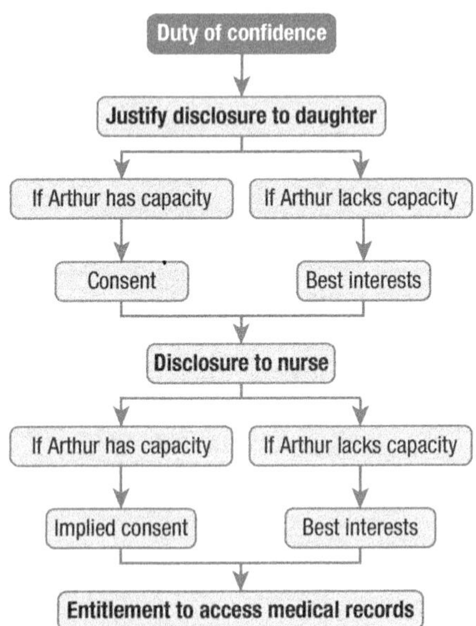

A printable version of this diagram plan is available from **www.pearsoned.co.uk/lawexpressqa**

Answer plan

- → Confirm whether Arthur is owed a duty of confidence.
- → Consider whether disclosure of Arthur's medical conditions could be justified:
  - – if he has capacity;
  - – if he lacks capacity.
- → Discuss whether a doctor can justify passing information to another member of the health-care team.
- → Identify whether a relative is able to access a patient's medical records.

Answer

We must consider whether Dr Davis can inform Carol about Arthur's medical conditions and provide access to his medical records. We must also confirm how disclosure to the nurse is justified.[1]

Arthur is owed a duty of confidence by Dr Davis.[2] ***A-G* v *Guardian Newspapers (No. 2)*** [1988] 3 All ER 545 held that a duty of confidence will arise when confidential information is given to a person in circumstances where he is aware that the information is confidential and it would be just and reasonable to impose an obligation. We are told that Arthur is in the early stages of dementia. Even if he lacks capacity, he is still owed a duty of confidence and any disclosures made must still be justified (***R (Stevens)* v *Plymouth City Council*** [2002] EWCA Civ 388). The information will also be protected under the Human Rights Act 1998 (HRA) by relying upon Article 8(1) which provides that 'everyone has the right to respect for his private and family life'. Arthur's medical records would also be protected under the Data Protection Act 1998 (DPA) as 'sensitive personal data' which is defined under section 2(e) of the 1998 Act as including personal data relating to 'physical or mental health or condition'. There is also a clear professional obligation of confidence (General Medical Council (2009) *Confidentiality*. London: GMC.).

The first consideration when looking at whether disclosure can be justified is whether the patient has given his consent to the disclosure. To rely on Arthur's consent, he must have capacity to make the decision in question. We are given insufficient information to determine the capacity issue; we only know that he 'is in the early stages of dementia'. We must consider the different possibilities.[3]

[1] It is important to identify the different disclosure issues in the scenario. Whether disclosure can be justified will depend on a variety of factors including who the information is being disclosed to and why.

[2] It is surprising how often students forget to confirm the basis of the duty of confidence and leap ahead to disclosure issues. The existence of a duty should be established first.

[3] The alternative positions should be considered as we cannot make assumptions about capacity.

1. If Arthur has capacity

There is a presumption of capacity (s. 1(2) Mental Capacity Act 2005 (MCA 2005)) and assumptions cannot be made based on someone's age (s. 2(3)(a)). Dr Davis would need to apply sections 2 and 3 of the MCA 2005 to determine whether he has capacity.[4] He must consider whether there is an impairment of or a disturbance in the functioning of the mind or brain and whether this impacts on Arthur's ability to make decisions (s. 2). Arthur will be unable to make a decision if he is unable to understand the information, retain it, use and weigh it or communicate his decision (s. 3).

If he has capacity Dr Davis would need permission from Arthur before passing any confidential information to Carol. If Arthur refuses consent Dr Davis will have to respect this. Public interest would not be available as a justification to disclose information here as the only person who would be affected would be Arthur himself and not a third party.[5] The common law public interest exception in ***W* v *Egdell*** [1990] 1 All ER 835 is not available as there is no risk of danger to a third party. The GMC also recognises that you should comply with a patient's refusal to disclose '. . . even if their decision leaves them, but nobody else, at risk of serious harm' (General Medical Council (2009) *Confidentiality*. London: GMC, para. 53).[6] There would be no justifications under HRA 1998 or DPA 1998 to allow disclosure in the face of a refusal of consent where no third party would be affected.

To justify disclosure to the nurse Dr Davis may rely on 'implied consent'.[7] Implied consent can be used to permit disclosure among the healthcare team. Paragraphs 25–29 of the GMC *Confidentiality* guidance are relevant. Patients should be informed that personal information will be shared within the healthcare team (unless they object to this).[8] If the GP practice has made such information available and Arthur has not objected to disclosure to others supporting his care in the practice, then Dr Davis can rely on implied consent. It is likely that disclosure to the nurse is also permitted under the DPA 1998. One condition from Schedule 2 and one condition from Schedule 3 must be met as this is sensitive personal data. Perhaps condition 4 of Schedule 2 ('the processing is necessary in order to protect the vital interests of the data subject') could be applied here. Condition 8 of Schedule 3 also seems applicable, as this would allow disclosure if 'necessary for medical purposes'.[9]

[4] As it is unclear whether Arthur has capacity you should identify the relevant test which will be used to determine this.

[5] This clearly identifies the limits of the public interest defence.

[6] This reinforces the point and confirms the GMC guidance reflects the common law position here.

[7] It is important to separate the different disclosure issues. Here, implied consent can be used to authorise disclosure to the nurse (whereas it would not have applied to justify disclosure to Carol).

[8] It is acceptable to paraphrase rather than quote directly from GMC guidance here.

[9] When covering the DPA 1998 conditions you should make sure you refer to the use of the word 'necessary'. It is key that processing (i.e. disclosure) must be 'necessary' to achieve the particular outcome in the condition.

2. If Arthur lacks capacity

If Arthur lacks capacity, any steps taken by Dr Davis must be justified under the MCA 2005. Section 4 must be considered to determine whether it is in Arthur's best interests for Carol to be informed. For instance section 4(6) highlights the need to consider Arthur's wishes and feelings.[10] So if, for example, Dr Davis understood that Carol and Arthur had a troubled relationship, disclosure may not be appropriate. If Dr Davis is concerned regarding the level of care at home a referral to social services may be justified. Section 5 permits acts in connection with the care and treatment of the patient lacking capacity and this should protect Dr Davis in terms of disclosure to the apt people and agencies. It would certainly appear that disclosure to the nurse to enable her to undertake a home visit was justified. The DPA 1998 has probably also been complied with in this situation too (see commentary above). The GMC *Confidentiality* guidance (para. 61) also acknowledges that where a patient lacks capacity, disclosures can take place, provided this is in the person's best interests.

[10] The examiner will be impressed if you draw upon your knowledge of other topics, i.e. how best interests is determined under the MCA 2005.

3. Entitlement to access medical records

Only the data subject has a *right* of access to records under section 7 DPA 1998, so Carol would not have a 'right' of access. Where a patient lacks capacity it is possible to allow access to records if this is in the best interests of the patient, but it would be highly unlikely that access to the whole of the records could be justified. Even if Carol was acting under a lasting power of attorney (LPA), the MCA Code of Practice chapter 16.14[11] makes it clear that the donee of the LPA is only entitled to the information that would help him or her to make the decision necessary (so she would only be entitled to have access to records relating to current conditions).

[11] It is good to show you have conducted wider reading and the examiner would be impressed that you have identified relevant material from the MCA Code of Practice.

4. Conclusion

In summary, the issue of whether any disclosure to Carol can be justified depends on whether Arthur has capacity. Dr Davis would need Arthur's consent to disclose to Carol (if Arthur has capacity) but could disclose to Carol if this would be in Arthur's 'best interests' (if he lacks capacity). Regarding disclosure to the nurse, the possible 'defence' of implied consent arises (if Arthur has capacity) and 'best interests' would apply (if he lacks capacity).

Make your answer stand out

- You would always try to seek consent before disclosing information as a starting point, therefore it is important to raise any issues regarding capacity to make a decision regarding disclosure. You will impress the examiner by drawing upon your knowledge of consent and capacity.
- Use headings to help break down your commentary as this will help to create a clear division of issues which are contingent upon whether the patient has capacity.
- Refer to the Mental Capacity Act 2005 Code of Practice further. Chapter 16 of the Code 'What rules govern access to information about a person' is relevant here.

! Don't be tempted to . . .

- Make assumptions about capacity unless the scenario gives you a clear indication (e.g. if the patient is unconscious). You need to consider the alternative positions, namely what are the confidentiality issues if he has capacity or if he lacks capacity.
- Fail to address different disclosure decisions to be made, so don't assume because disclosure of one issue may be justified that disclosure of a different issue will also be justified.

Question 4

Where genetic testing reveals a patient has a genetic disorder, disclosure of the relevant information to the patient's relatives can easily be justified. Discuss.

Answer plan

→ Introduce the significance of genetic information.

→ Outline the Human Rights Act 1998 and Data Protection Act 1998 issues regarding genetic information.

→ Introduce the common law duty of confidence and the public interest justification to disclose.

→ Critically discuss how public interest applies in the context of genetic information.

→ Highlight that harm may arise from disclosure.

→ Discuss the difficult ethical issues which arise.

→ Refer to professional guidance on the issue.

Diagram plan

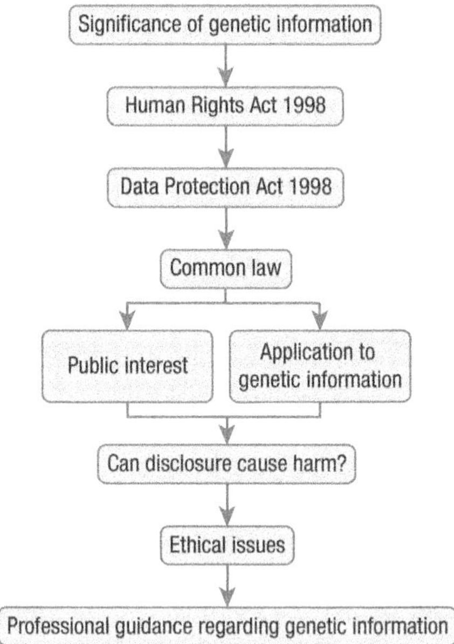

A printable version of this diagram plan is available from **www.pearsoned.co.uk/lawexpressqa**

Answer

Genetic information poses unique problems as it is not only relevant to the patient. It may have implications for the patients' relatives; it may indicate they could also suffer from a particular genetic condition or may be a carrier. Given the importance of the duty of confidence owed to the patient, any legal justifications for disclosure and possible ethical difficulties must be carefully discussed.

[1] The question does not focus only on the common law justifications for disclosure so it is apt to introduce other sources of the obligation too (e.g. Article 8).

A patient's medical information is protected under the Human Rights Act 1998 (HRA), relying on Article 8(1) 'the right to respect for private and family life'.[1] Article 8(1) may be interfered with under Article 8(2) where the interference is 'necessary in a democratic society . . . for the protection of health . . . or for the protection of the rights and freedoms of others'. Disclosure may be justified if this would allow a relative to seek early treatment. Genetic information is 'sensitive personal data' under section 2(e) Data Protection Act 1998 (DPA) as it relates to the patient's 'physical or mental health or condition'.[2] A condition in both Schedule 2 and Schedule 3 of the DPA 1998 must be shown to justify disclosure. Schedule 3 is viewed as setting more onerous conditions. Condition 8 of Schedule 3 may be satisfied as this permits disclosure for 'medical purposes' which include 'the purposes of preventative medicine, medical diagnosis . . . the provision of care and treatment'. Disclosure must be 'fair' and 'lawful' (Sch. 1, DPA 1998). If disclosure did not comply with the HRA 1998 or the common law, it would also not be lawful under the DPA 1998.

[2] You should demonstrate your awareness that genetic information will raise DPA 1998 issues.

The common law duty of confidence regarding medical information is well established (***X* v *Y*** [1988] 2 All ER 648). If patient consent is withheld, an alternative justification is required. It is appropriate to focus on the availability of the public interest defence[3] to justify disclosure of genetic information to relatives as its use in this context has been the subject of debate. A balancing exercise would take place. Although a strong public interest in maintaining confidentiality exists, this can be outweighed by a competing public interest. Disclosure to prevent harm to others may be permitted,[4] however case law in this area tends to focus on situations involving a likelihood of serious harm. In ***W* v *Egdell*** [1990] 1 All ER 835 the need for a 'real risk of consequent danger' was identified. At the outset we see how the current case law may not 'fit' well with the particular issues posed by genetic information. For instance, a relative may already be affected by the particular condition, so it is difficult to argue the disclosure will 'prevent' harm.

[3] As the use of public interest in this context has been extensively considered, you should balance your coverage accordingly. There is scope to develop sound critical analysis here.

[4] It is important to first introduce the nature of the public interest defence before applying it in the context of genetic information.

Laurie (1996) states 'the probability of manifestation and the severity of the condition' is significant[5] (see Laurie, G.T. (1996) The most personal information of all: an appraisal of genetic privacy in the shadow of the human genome project. *International Journal of Law, Policy* and *the Family*, 10(1): 74–101). The reality is that genetic testing may not provide clear predictions of risk and the risks for a relative in a particular case may be low. It may not be possible to predict when or the extent to which the relative would be affected. Skene (2001) questions the adequacy of the public interest justification in this context, given that it appears the risk should be 'serious and imminent' which is often not the case in relation to genetic risks (see Skene, L. (2001) Genetic secrets and the family: a response to Bell and Bennett. *Medical Law Review*, 9(2): 162).

[5] The examiner will be impressed if you refer to leading academics in this area.

The availability of therapies or cures for the relevant condition is also identified as a key issue. If, for instance, there is no cure for a particular condition we need to identify what disclosure would achieve. There are, however, conditions that may be prevented if the relative has knowledge of the risks they face and is able to make key lifestyle choices or take other steps to prevent onset of a particular condition.

Laurie also considers it is important to ascertain whether the relative will be 'directly affected' by the condition or whether they are simply a carrier of the condition. Even if a relative is only a carrier of a condition (such that their own health is not affected), knowledge of this may still benefit the relative. This may inform their decisions regarding having children or they may investigate the possibility of preimplantation genetic diagnosis. However, Ngwena and Chadwick (1993) suggest it may be difficult to argue that confidentiality can be breached on the basis of a relative's entitlement to 'informed reproductive decision making' (see Ngwena, C. and Chadwick, R. (1993) Genetic diagnostic information and the duty of confidentiality: ethics and law. *Medical Law International*, 73). It is difficult to identify the necessary serious harm; the person who ultimately will be affected is the child who would be born. If this argument carries weight it is also doubtful whether disclosure to the patient's partner[6] would be permissible to allow him/her to make an informed choice as to whether to have children with the patient.

[6] The question asks whether disclosure to the patient's *relatives* can be justified. It is appropriate to consider the related issue of whether disclosure beyond the patient's *blood* relatives, i.e. to the patient's husband/wife/partner can also be justified.

So far we have assumed that such disclosure would always benefit the relative and the only potential 'harm' caused by the disclosure is to the person whose confidentiality is sacrificed. This may be too simplistic an approach and these assumptions can be challenged.[7] If, for example, the relative did not want to know that they were at risk of a particular condition (for instance if there was no available cure), disclosure itself could result in psychological harm.

[7] The examiner will be impressed if you challenge the assumption that seems to underlie the question.

Even if we can construct an argument that disclosure in this context can 'fit' within the legal public interest model, difficult ethical and moral issues remain.[8] Maintaining confidentiality serves to promote and protect patient autonomy, so how do we justify interference? Sommerville and English, V. (1999) suggest that we should not concentrate solely on individual rights and autonomy given the 'complex and interwoven interests' that arise regarding genetic information (see Sommerville, A. and English (1999) Genetic privacy: orthodoxy or oxymoron? *Journal of Medical Ethics*, 25: 144–150). They comment on the significance of communitarianism here as a focus on mutuality and responsibility for others seems appropriate but the risk of an extreme approach is

[8] The question also encompasses the ethical/moral issues that arise.

acknowledged (as this may undermine personal liberty). They purport that autonomy interests could be combined with a modified version of communitarianism to recognise that 'an individual cannot have rights without also accepting that he or she has certain duties'.

This conflict between the different interests at play is also reflected in professional guidance.[9] General Medical Council (2009) *Confidentiality* guidance provides that where consent to disclosure of genetic information is refused the doctor is advised to balance his/her duty to the patient against the duty to protect the other person from serious harm (para. 69).[10] Again, we see the need to engage in a balancing exercise and it does seem that only 'serious harm' will suffice.

It is clear that disclosure of genetic information to relatives is *potentially* (rather than easily) justified.[11] The specific factors in each case must be considered including the likelihood and seriousness of the condition (and whether this can even be prevented). This information may not even benefit the relative and indeed may cause unintended harm.

[9] Professional guidance is also relevant here. A doctor will want to be sure he is not in breach of his professional obligations.

[10] It is fine to paraphrase the professional guidance providing you capture the essence of it.

[11] This conclusion demonstrates a focus on the particular angle of the question.

Make your answer stand out

- Refer to other source material – the Joint Committee on Medical Ethics of the Royal Colleges of Physicians and Pathologists publish guidance regarding genetic information (see the committee's second report: Royal College of Physicians, Royal College of Pathologists and British Society for Human Genetics (2011) *Consent and confidentiality in clinical genetic practice: guidance on genetic testing and sharing genetic information*, 2nd edn, Report of the Joint Committee on Medical Genetics, London: Royal College of Physicians, Royal College of Pathologists.
- Develop coverage of the difficulties in determining the likelihood and severity of the risk with reference to the range of different types of genetic disorders. Provide examples and refer to particular conditions, e.g. Huntington's disease which is a late onset disease with no cure.
- Consider articles in non-legal journals regarding the ethical issues involved. For instance Sommerville, A. and English, V. (1999) Genetic privacy: orthodoxy or oxymoron? *Journal of Medical Ethics*, 25: 144–150 was referred to in this answer.
- Develop consideration of the possible disadvantages of such disclosures (to challenge the assumption that disclosure would always benefit the relative). Consider Laurie, G.T. (1996) The most personal information of all: an appraisal of genetic privacy in the shadow of the Human Genome Project. *International Journal of Law, Policy* and *the Family*, 10(1): 74–101. He argues that the relative may have 'a right not to know' and that disclosure could infringe the relative's privacy.

! Don't be tempted to . . .

- Leave out the ethical difficulties which arise. The question does not restrict you to only consider legal issues.
- Stray too far from the focus of the question. Although 'blood' relatives are clearly more likely to be directly affected, the reference to 'relative' in the question allows you to also consider the patient's husband/wife/partner. This does not mean that you should consider the full range of issues generated by genetic information, for instance, an analysis of whether such information can be used for medical research purposes would stray too far.

www.pearsoned.co.uk/lawexpressqa

Go online to access more revision support including additional essay and problem questions with diagram plans, You be the marker questions, and download all diagrams from the book.

6 Children: consent and confidentiality

How this topic may come up in exams

Remember that any question referring to a child under 18 is going to involve different issues to adults (such as *Gillick* and the Family Law Reform Act 1969), although there are also overlaps. The Mental Capacity Act 2005, for example, is relevant to all people aged over 16. Examiners are keen on the following topics: the longstanding arguments as to whether children should have the right to refuse medical treatment; what is *Gillick* competence?; and to what extent should parents have the right to make treatment decisions on their children's behalf?

Before you begin

It's a good idea to consider the following key themes of children: consent and confidentiality before tackling a question on this topic.

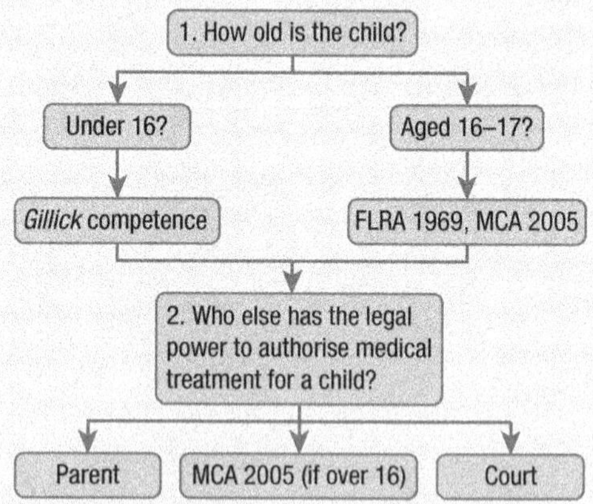

A printable version of this diagram is available from **www.pearsoned.co.uk/lawexpressqa**

Question 1

When considering medical treatment, to what extent does a child have the right to make a 'wrong' decision? Ignore the rights of others to consent on a child's behalf.

Answer plan

- → Explain who is a 'child' under English law.
- → Recognise that the right to make a 'wrong' decision suggests a refusal of medical treatment and that a capable adult can legally refuse.
- → Explain that different rules apply to the assessment of capacity for 16–17-year-olds – the Mental Capacity Act 2005; and for under 16s – *Gillick* competence.
- → Consider whether a child will be considered capable/competent if they are refusing medical treatment.

Diagram plan

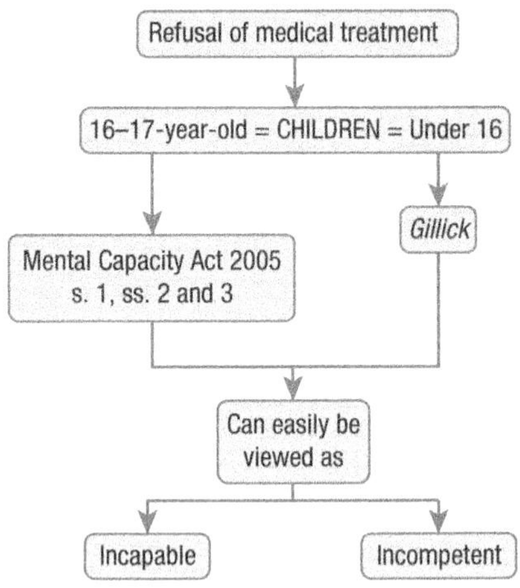

A printable version of this diagram plan is available from **www.pearsoned.co.uk/lawexpressqa**

Answer

Under English law, section 105(1) of the Children Act 1989 defines a 'child' as any person aged under 18, and this is echoed by the United Nations Convention on the Rights of the Child, which was ratified by the UK government in 1991. Any adult person under English law has the right to refuse medical treatment and to therefore make a 'wrong' decision[1] as long as they are not judged to be incapable of making that particular decision (see ***Re C (Adult: Refusal of Treatment)*** [1994] 1 WLR 290[2]), but I would argue that the same rights are not accorded to those aged under 18.

The key question as to whether a child will be seen as having the 'right to make a "wrong" decision' is whether the child in question has the capacity to make a decision at all. Different legal tests apply to the assessment of capacity to younger and older children.

1. 16–17-year-olds

The Mental Capacity Act 2005 (MCA) applies to all persons aged over 16. It contains in section 1 a set of 'guiding principles' including a general presumption of capacity[3] and the important statement that 'A person is not to be treated as unable to make a decision merely because he makes an unwise decision'.[4] This would suggest that a 16–17-year-old would therefore be assumed to have capacity to make a decision refusing medical treatment even if other people thought this to be unwise or 'wrong'.[5] However, the presumption of capacity can be overturned if a lack of capacity to make a particular decision can be established in accordance with sections 2 and 3 of the MCA.[6]

A 16–17-year-old would be deemed incapable under the MCA if they are unable to understand or retain the information relevant[7] to the decision (which means the 'reasonably foreseeable consequences of deciding one way or the other or failing to make the decision' (s. 3(4) MCA), or are unable to weigh up that information as part of making a decision, or are unable to communicate their decision. Any such inability has to be the result of 'an impairment of, or disturbance in the functioning of, the mind or brain' as set out in section 2 MCA, and this can be either permanent, or temporary, such as unconsciousness or the effects of alcohol or drugs.

The abilities to understand and weigh relevant information in the balance are therefore likely to be key considerations as to whether a 16–17-year-old will be judged to have capacity to make a 'wrong' decision, such as to refuse medical treatment. It is suggested that

1 This is the point of the question. Making a 'wrong' decision as regards medical treatment will generally be a decision against medical opinion, i.e. a refusal of the treatment suggested.

2 Although this is a question about children, your material and argument will make more sense if you contrast it to the position for adults, so don't ignore this – but equally, don't spend ages explaining this in detail.

3 Always use the term 'capacity' when referring to persons aged over 16.

4 See section 1(4) Mental Capacity Act 2005. Given the wording of the question as to 'wrong' decisions, you would lose marks if you didn't include and comment upon this.

5 Take your opportunity in each section to refer back to the question – then you won't lose focus.

6 When explaining the MCA, it is important for you to remember the various section numbers (note: sections 1–6 are the most important).

7 Because 'relevant information' must include the consequences for the young person.

the more 'wrong' the decision of a 16–17-year-old seems, the more likely it will be that the person assessing capacity (often the doctor proposing the treatment) will judge that the child is unable to fully understand to weigh up the information needed.

2. Under 16s

The MCA does not apply to those persons aged under 16,[8] and the common law is used to decide whether a child of that age is 'competent'[9] to make decisions. The most important case in this area is that of ***Gillick* v *West Norfolk and Wisbech AHA*** [1986] AC 112. In this House of Lords decision, it was stated by Lord Scarman (as part of the majority) that a child aged under 16 is competent to make decisions regarding medical treatment if they have achieved 'a sufficient understanding and intelligence to enable him or her to understand fully what is proposed', and thus to make up his/her own mind. This would suggest at first reading that a child aged under 16, if mature and intelligent enough, can make a decision regarding medical treatment, even if it is a 'wrong' decision. However, as Emily Jackson (2013) points out, Lord Scarman went on to say that the reason for establishing a child's competence was to recognise that some children aged under 16 are able to make 'sensible decisions' and to exercise 'wise choices in their own interests' and she suggests therefore that the ***Gillick*** decision supports a child's right to be seen as competent to make a 'right' decision, but is less conclusive about whether a child aged under 16 can be seen as competent to make a 'wrong' decision such as the refusal of medical treatment (see Jackson, E. (2013) *Medical Law: Texts, Cases and Materials* (3rd edn). Oxford: Oxford University Press).

[8] This is why it makes sense for you to deal with 16–17-year-olds first – you can easily explain now that there is no statute dealing with under 16s.

[9] Always use the term 'competent' when referring to persons aged under 16.

In the leading judgment in the ***Gillick*** case,[10] Lord Fraser suggested that the treatment which a competent child could consent to must be in their 'best interests'. These comments by Lords Fraser and Scarman would therefore suggest that a child's right to decide on medical treatment will only be supported when they are making a decision which is seen as 'sensible', 'wise' and 'in their best interests', i.e. not a decision which others would see as 'wrong'. This view is supported by the many cases in which a child who is refusing medical treatment is considered to be incompetent to make that decision.

[10] Don't worry about the fact that you are only referring to the *Gillick* case here. If you are short of time, then this is *the* case that you *must* refer to when discussing medical treatment for children aged under 16 – but make sure that you refer to the judgments and not the facts. While it may be tempting to explain the facts at length (because they are easy to remember) they are not relevant to the question that you are being asked. Apply your knowledge, don't just regurgitate it.

3. Conclusion

Article 8 of the European Convention on Human Rights has been interpreted to support the right 'to respect for private and family life' as including a right for a person to decide what is done to them in the form of medical treatment. Article 14 of the Convention states that this right is not limited to adults only, but, whether a child or an adult, the law is clear that a 'wrong' decision regarding medical treatment will only be respected if it is as a result of a capable/competent decision.

As I have explained above, although the common law and the MCA both suggest at first sight that a competent/capable decision will be respected, the focus on understanding and weighing (in MCA terms) – or the understanding, intelligence and maturity in ***Gillick*** terms – can allow for a clear perception that a 'wrong' decision is therefore one which has not 'weighed' the information sufficiently well, or which has not been 'maturely' considered – in which case the child's decision can be disregarded under English law. This may be a classic pragmatic response by English law to the extreme arguments that either a child should have equal rights to an adult, or that any person classed legally as a child should be fully protected by the law, and not able to choose to put themselves at risk. As Herring (2012) comments: 'We will respect your right to autonomy but only if you give the right answer!'[11] (see Herring, J. (2012) *Medical Law and Ethics* (4th edn). Oxford: Oxford University Press).

[11] This is a great quotation to conclude this particular essay, as it directly references the question itself and is a snappy ending.

Make your answer stand out

- Use subheadings. Where a question can be neatly subdivided into different areas, the use of subheadings helps you focus and allocate your time better.
- Be strict in using the term 'capacity' for 16–17-year-olds, and 'competence' for under 16s. This shows that you understand that these are different legal tests, and *not* interchangeable terms.
- Include the views of academic commentators in this field – see, for example, John Eekelaar's views on how to balance a child's autonomous decision with risks to his/her welfare (Eekelaar, J. (2006) *Family Law and Personal Life*. Oxford: Oxford University Press), or Jane Fortin's (Fortin, J. (2009) *Children's Rights and the Developing Law* (3rd edn). Cambridge: Cambridge University Press).

! Don't be tempted to . . .

- Forget to explain that the law treats 16–17-year-olds differently to under 16s.
- Concentrate just on under 16-year-olds and *Gillick* competence. This question is carefully phrased to include *all* children, and you can therefore expect that around half the marks will be allocated to 16–17-year-olds.
- Discuss cases referring to a parent's (i.e. *Re R* [1992] 1 FLR 190 or *Re W* [1992] 4 All ER 627) or the court's (i.e. *Re E* [1993] 1 FLR 386) legal ability to give consent to medical treatment despite a child's refusal. You are specifically told here to ignore the rights of any other person/body to give consent to medical treatment on a child's behalf.

Question 2

Where a child is very ill but too young to express his own wishes, to what extent legally are decisions to medically treat him left in the hands of his parents?

Answer plan

→ Recognise that this child is going to be too young to be *Gillick* competent.

→ Set out that parents or the court can make decisions on behalf of non-*Gillick* competent children.

→ Discuss issue of parental responsibility – not all 'parents' have the same rights.

→ Make clear that ultimately, the court can make decisions, overriding parents – using either section 8, Children Act 1989 or inherent jurisdiction.

→ Also deal with emergencies when there is no time to get agreement from parents or court. A doctor can treat in best interests but this might be a breach of Article 8 – see *Glass* v *UK*.

Diagram plan

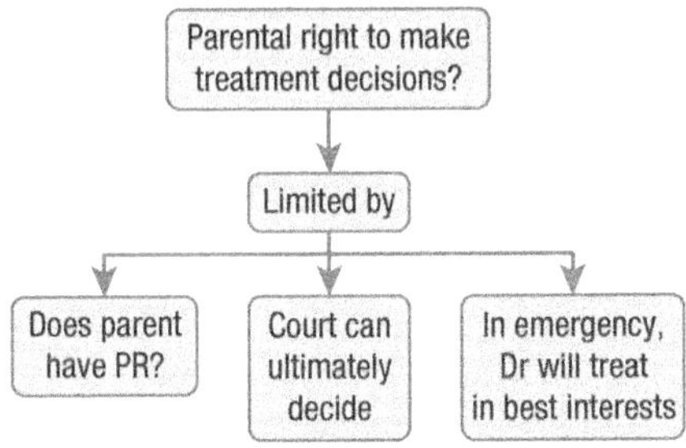

A printable version of this diagram plan is available from **www.pearsoned.co.uk/lawexpressqa**

Answer

Some children are too young to be able to express their own decision as to whether to have medical treatment. They are not going to be considered to be sufficiently mature, or in the words of Lord Scarman in the case of ***Gillick v West Norfolk and Wisbech AHA*** [1986] AC 112, to have 'sufficient understanding and intelligence' to be judged able to make their own decision as to the treatment that they need.[1] In these cases, it is naturally the child's parents who will be regarded as the decision-makers.

However, English law does not entirely 'leave' these difficult and emotional decisions 'in the hands of his parents'[2] – there is a legal limitation on which 'parents' can make decisions, caused by the operation of parental responsibility, and parents will anyway never be the absolute arbiters of such decisions – the court can ultimately make a determinative order. Emergency medical treatment needs special consideration too.

1. Which parents can legally make decisions as to medical treatment?

Section 3(1) of the Children Act 1989 (CA) sets out that 'all of the rights, duties, powers, responsibility and authority' held by a parent over a child, including the right to decide whether the child should have medical treatment, are defined as 'parental responsibility' (PR), but the CA also defines who has PR for any child. Briefly, all parents who are married, or who jointly registered their child's birth after 1 December 2003 will have PR, as will all mothers of children; however, for unmarried fathers who have not registered the birth, they can only acquire PR as a result of court proceedings, with the mother's formal agreement or by subsequently marrying the child's mother.

If a father does not have PR,[3] he will be unable to legally authorise his child's medical treatment, and without PR, such a father will therefore be excluded from being able to make these important decisions.

If there are a number of people with PR, then generally[4] the positive decision of any one person with PR to give consent is enough to provide a doctor with a legal 'flak jacket' (see Lord Donaldson MR in ***Re W (A Minor) (Medical Treatment: Court's Jurisdiction)*** [1993] 3 WLR 758) to go ahead with medical treatment on the child.

[1] You have been specifically told this is a very young child – so the *Gillick*/Fraser guidelines won't apply.

[2] Good second paragraph – you are referring back to the question, and using it as a springboard to briefly set out the key legal parameters to the issue. Now go on to explain and develop these points further.

[3] It would be legally incorrect to talk about a mother not having 'PR' – a mother can only lose PR if the child is adopted, in which case she is no longer seen as the child's mother legally.

[4] There have been some cases which have decided that a decision as to medical treatment can only be made by *all* people who have PR – see *Re J (Specific Issue Orders)* [2000] 1 FLR 571 (male circumcision for religious reasons), and *Re C (Immunisation: Parental Rights)* [2003] EWCA Civ 1148 (the MMR vaccination).

2. Powers of the court to make a decision

If, however, the doctor cannot gain the valid consent[5] from a person with PR, then an application to the court can be made for the authorisation of medical treatment on a child's behalf. An application can be made either under section 8 of the CA for either a specific issue or prohibited steps order; or the courts also can make orders using their inherent jurisdiction. However the case gets there, the court has to apply section 1(1) of the CA, which states that the child's welfare is 'paramount'. When considering this, the court uses the welfare checklist set out in section 1(3) of the CA – interestingly, this does not include any consideration given to the wishes of the child's parents. Once the matter of a child's medical treatment reaches the court, it is the court's decision alone. There have been many instances when the courts have overridden strong parental views as to whether a child should be treated or not.[6]

[5] When you are talking about consent, make the point that it has to be valid – of course, if sufficient information has not been given, or the person asked for consent is incapable, or is being coerced, etc., a consent will not be a valid one.

[6] You should include here any up-to-date cases that you have learned about in your course, where the courts have authorised medical treatment against parental wishes.

Emergency situations

Where an ill child needs treatment urgently,[7] it might be argued by a hospital that there is insufficient time for parents with PR to come to a decision, and the doctors will decide whether to treat or not, using their own conclusions as to what is in the child's best interests. It is important to recognise that any decision regarding whether an ill child should receive medical treatment will engage the Article 8 ECHR rights of both the children and his parents, whether the parent has PR or not – as this is the right for 'a person's private and family life' to be respected. In the case of ***Glass* v *United Kingdom* (2004)** 39 EHRR 341,[8] Article 8 was used to support a finding that if the parents did object to treatment, doctors should not proceed except in the most urgent cases when there was not enough time to refer the matter to a court.

[7] While the question does not specifically ask about emergencies, this is another example when decisions won't (or can't) be left to parents, so worthwhile including.

[8] For another perspective, see also the case of *Re OT* [2009] EWHC 633 (Fam) where the parents argued (unsuccessfully) that the NHS trust's bringing of an emergency application to court breached their Article 8 rights as they had insufficient time to properly contest this.

4. Conclusion

The CA appears at first instance to state that if a parent has PR, he/she does have full decision-making powers for their children, yet the court clearly retains overall power to authorise medical treatment in the face of opposition by a parent, and in extreme emergencies decisions to treat will be taken by doctors without regard to parental wishes. It is therefore incorrect to state that a medical treatment decision for a very ill and very young child will be left entirely in the hands of his 'parents' – particularly given the need under English law for a parent to have PR in the first place.

✓ Make your answer stand out

- Refer to the 'zone of parental control'. This contentious concept, introduced in the Mental Health Act Code of Practice (see chapter 36, paras. 36.9–15), suggests that decisions by a parent with PR will only be lawful in respect of a child's medical treatment for mental disorder if they fall within the 'zone'. This suggestion that a parent with PR power to authorise medical treatment is now limited is considered by Hewitt, D. (2008) Too young to decide? *Solicitors Journal*, 30(9).
- Recognise that a father without PR may still be able to have decisions as to medical treatment respected in certain situations – if PR has been 'delegated' to him (see s. 2(9) Children Act 1989), or if he has care of the child, he may 'do what is reasonable in all the circumstances . . . for the purposes of safeguarding or promoting the child's welfare' (see s. 3(5)).

! Don't be tempted to . . .

- Consider that the children referred to in this question are *Gillick* competent. You are specifically told that the child is too young to express an opinion, and that should warn you that the children here will not therefore be considered to have 'sufficient understanding and intelligence' (per Lord Scarman in *Gillick*).
- Equally, don't refer to the Mental Capacity Act 2005 – that only applies to over 16s.
- Spend too much time discussing who does and doesn't have parental responsibility – while relevant, it is not the main point of the question.

? Question 3

Jack Smith, aged 16½, has a learning disability and autism. He lives at home with his married parents, Bob and Sally Smith. Jack cannot speak as a result of his difficulties, but can communicate a 'yes' or 'no' by making gestures in response to simple questions. Jack has never been very good at cleaning his teeth, and recently has resisted all attempts by Bob and Sally to help him with this. He has a decayed molar tooth and his dentist has warned Sally that the tooth may need to be extracted. This would normally involve the need for anaesthetic to be injected and then the tooth to be removed while the patient cooperated with this.

Jack is used to going to see this dentist for check-ups, and usually sits happily in the chair for these but Sally and Bob are both concerned that Jack will be frightened of a needle and will react badly to any more intrusive dental work. Bob feels that the 'upset' caused by any tooth extraction will be too much for Jack and does not agree with it; Sally is uncertain herself but worried about the possible consequences if the tooth is not removed. The dentist is recommending that the treatment go ahead and feels that there will be long-term risks of future infections and pain for Jack if it does not.

Explain the legal position as to how the possible extraction could proceed.

Answer plan

➜ Set out that as Jack is aged over 16 but still a child, there are various legal authorities for his medical treatment.

➜ Detail the sources of legal authority, that is:

- consent from Jack himself under the Family Law Reform Act (if he is capable in the MCA sense);
- consent from one of Jack's parents – each can provide a 'flak jacket';
- the dentist can have a statutory defence under section 5 Mental Capacity Act 2005 – if reasonable belief Jack lacks capacity and in his best interests. (The test of capacity = ss. 2 and 3, best interests = s. 4.) NB – consider whether restraint will be necessary and the MCA implications;
- ultimately, the court can give permission for dental treatment.

Diagram plan

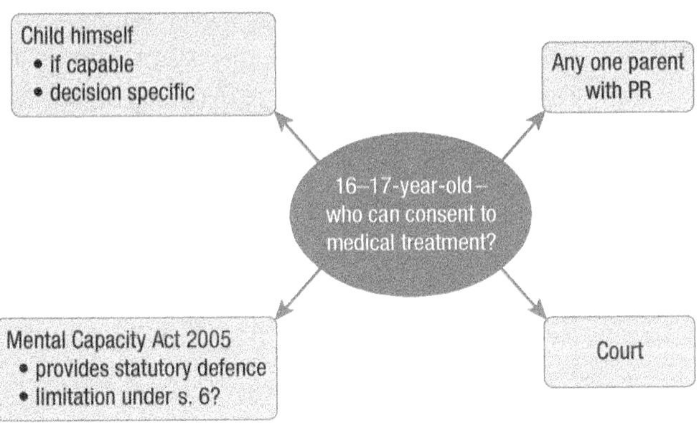

A printable version of this diagram plan is available from **www.pearsoned.co.uk/lawexpressqa**

Answer

Jack is aged 16½,[1] and is facing the possible extraction of a tooth.[2] This dental treatment can be authorised in a number of different ways.

1. Jack's consent

As Jack is over 16, under section 8 of the Family Law Reform Act 1969 (FLRA), he is able to give consent to dental treatment, including any diagnostic procedure and the use of anaesthetic[3] if necessary. Dental treatment is specifically covered in section 8(1).

However, Jack can only legally consent to this treatment if he is judged capable of being able to do so. This is decision-specific – Jack may be able to decide on the matter of whether to visit the dentist for a check-up, as he is familiar with this, but not be able to give a valid consent to the more complex issue of whether he should have his tooth removed. If there is any doubt as to his capacity to give a valid consent (which should be judged according to the criteria in the Mental Capacity Act 2005 (MCA) – see below[4]), then Jack's consent cannot be used as legal authority.

2. Consent of Bob or Sally

As Jack is aged under 18, he is still a minor, and therefore anyone who has parental responsibility (PR) can consent to any medical treatment for him. Both Bob and Sally have PR,[5] and section 2(7) of the Children Act 1989 sets out that any person with PR can act alone to authorise any medical treatment proposed. This was confirmed in the case of ***Re W*** [1992] 4 All ER 627 when Lord Donaldson MR said that either parent's consent would act as a 'flak jacket' to a claim that a doctor (or in this scenario, a dentist) did not have the legal right to proceed with treatment. It is uncertain that either Sally or Bob would consent to the tooth extraction and the necessary anaesthetic, particularly given Jack's fear of needles.

3. Statutory defence under the MCA 2005

It appears from the above that it may not be possible to obtain a valid consent from either Jack or his parents for the extraction of the tooth. However, the dentist may still be able to proceed with this if he can rely upon section 5 of the MCA.

[1] Key issue 1 – Jack's age. If he is over 16, the FLRA and MCA will apply and *Gillick* won't.

[2] Key issue 2 – what exactly is the medical treatment proposed? The question makes this simple for you – the removal of a tooth. Your answer needs to consider how the invasiveness and complexity of this proposed treatment may affect the legal authorities available.

[3] Diagnostic procedures (i.e. an examination) and ancillary procedures (i.e. anaesthetic) are specifically covered by section 8(2).

[4] If you have planned your answer out in advance, you will know that you are going to be referring to the MCA section 5 defence further on – don't waste words by repeating yourself now. Your examiner will appreciate this.

[5] Both Bob and Sally have PR here because they are married – if they were not, Sally would have PR but Bob might not – see Children Act 1989 section 2 and section 4 as to how an unmarried father may acquire this.

This provides that for any action in connection with Jack's 'care or treatment' (such as the tooth extraction and all of the ancillary work, including the use of injectable anaesthetic), the dentist will be able to proceed as if he did have a valid consent if he has taken reasonable steps to establish Jack lacks capacity for this intervention,[6] and also reasonably believes that Jack 'lacks capacity in relation to the matter, and it will be in [Jack's] best interests for the act to be done' – see section 5 MCA.

[6] Please don't forget this part of section 5. Students often forget that this is also a necessary precedent for the use of the section 5 defence.

Under sections 2 and 3 of the MCA, Jack will be said to not have capacity if he is unable to understand and retain necessary information, weigh it in the balance and communicate his decision because of an impairment of, or a disturbance in the functioning of, his mind or brain. In this situation, the necessary information[7] will include the reasons why the extraction might be necessary, the risks if Jack doesn't go ahead, the procedure that will be taking place including the use of a needle, and whether it will hurt.

[7] By listing these, you are demonstrating that you understand what is the 'information relevant to the decision' (see s. 3 MCA) on the facts that you are given.

The dentist will then have to consider whether the extraction will be in Jack's best interests by applying section 4 of the MCA, which includes the need to consider Jack's wishes and feelings, and also the views of Bob and Sally.[8]

[8] But of course although the dentist will have to consider these as part of the section 4 best interests consideration, neither Jack's nor his parents' views will themselves be determinative of whether the dentist concludes it is in Jack's best interests to proceed.

The issue of restraint must also be considered here,[9] as this may be necessary given Jack's likely frightened response to the injection; he also may need to be held down if he doesn't understand the treatment or resists this. Section 6 of the MCA will only allow the dentist to restrain Jack for the extraction and anaesthetic if he 'reasonably believes it is necessary to do so to prevent harm to' Jack, and doing so is a 'proportionate' response to the likelihood of Jack suffering harm, and the seriousness of the harm. The dentist will therefore have to weigh up how much restraint is going to be necessary to carry out the whole of the treatment, balancing that to the risks there may be of Jack getting repeated infections and pain from a rotting tooth.

[9] Please don't forget that section 5 can only be used if there is no restriction on this – so any use of restraint has to be considered, as does whether there is any conflicting decision made by a donee or deputy – see s. 6 MCA.

4. Authority of the court

If a valid consent cannot be obtained from Jack, Bob or Sally, and the dentist is unwilling to rely on section 5 of the MCA, then ultimately, the courts retain the ultimate power to grant legal authority for the dental procedure,[10] governed by the 'paramount consideration' of what is in Jack's welfare – see section 1(1) Children Act 1989.

[10] You can neatly wrap up your conclusion into the final discussion point, as I have done here.

✓ Make your answer stand out

- When discussing the use of restraint and section 5 of the MCA, consider whether Jack is going to be deprived of his liberty during this procedure – see the 'acid test' of Lady Hale in *P* v *Cheshire West* [2014] UKSC 19 – that is, will Jack be free to leave and be continuously under care and supervision during treatment? If so, section 5 cannot be used to authorise a 'deprivation of liberty' and separate authority from the court is going to be necessary.
- Contemplate how the ECHR might apply here. As well as the Article 5 deprivation of liberty issue, consider Article 3 – will this procedure amount to 'inhuman and degrading treatment' for Jack? Note, however, that if the treatment is considered to be a 'therapeutic necessity' (see *Herczegfalvy* v *Austria* (1992) 15 EHRR 437) Article 3 is not going to be engaged. Remember that Article 8 is also relevant as respect for an individual's 'private and family rights' has been held to include respect for his bodily integrity.

! Don't be tempted to . . .

- Just cover the FLRA 1969 when talking about a 16–17-year-old's agreement to treatment. Remember that the consent still has to be valid, i.e. capable in MCA 2005 terms.
- Set out that a donee of a lasting power of attorney or deputy appointed by the Court of Protection can also limit the use of the section 5 MCA defence – that is *not* relevant to the facts of this question.
- Try to give equal coverage to all of the four options – here, you are going to need to spend more time explaining the MCA 2005 option than the others, simply because it is more complicated.

? Question 4

Marcie is aged 14. She is an intelligent and sensible child, and has always previously visited the GP with her mother, Sue. Marcie's father and Sue were not married; he left the family home before her birth, and Marcie has had no further contact with him. She and Sue live together by themselves and have always appeared to be close. Today, Marcie has made her own appointment with her GP, Dr Smith, and came to see him alone. She tells Dr Smith that she is now in a serious relationship with her boyfriend, and doesn't want to get pregnant. They are using condoms but Marcie has heard that they are not 100 per cent reliable. Marcie has learned at school that a GP can fit a contraceptive implant into her arm, and it will be effective for up to three years. She tells Dr Smith that she would like to have the implant as soon as possible; the reason that she does not want contraceptive tablets is because she is worried about Sue's reaction if she found them. Marcie begs Dr Smith not to tell her mother.

Explain the legal position regarding the proposed medical treatment and Marcie's request to Dr Smith to keep this matter confidential.

Answer plan

- Discuss *Gillick* competence to consent to the medical implant as Marcie is under 16 – use Fraser guidelines.
- Consider disclosure of information to Sue – consider difference between Marcie being competent and being able to insist the information is not disclosed to Sue; but if she is not *Gillick* competent to consent to the treatment, does Marcie still have right to confidentiality?
- Make clear that all patients, including children, are entitled to confidentiality of their medical matters.
- Explain that Dr Smith can only disclose confidential information with Marcie's consent, if in the public interest or because of legal obligations. There is a possible safeguarding concern here given her age.
- Discuss the *Axon* case, weighing up the competing Article 8 rights of Sue and Marcie.

Diagram plan

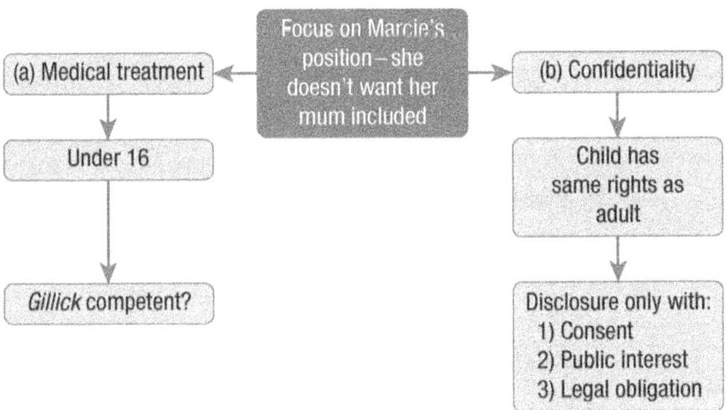

A printable version of this diagram plan is available from **www.pearsoned.co.uk/lawexpressqa**

Answer

Marcie is aged 14 and is asking Dr Smith to place a contraceptive implant into her arm, so that she cannot get pregnant when having sex with her boyfriend. Dr Smith needs to be confident that Marcie can validly consent to this medical treatment if he is to do this without letting Sue know – otherwise, he would need Sue's consent to authorise the treatment as she is the only parent with parental responsibility for Marcie.

In the House of Lords decision of ***Gillick* v *West Norfolk and Wisbech Area Health Authority*** [1986] AC 112, Lord Fraser set out guidelines which Dr Smith should follow in deciding whether Marcie is competent to give a valid consent to this contraceptive treatment, and he can go ahead without Sue's knowledge. The Fraser guidelines are:[1]

[1] To answer this question well, you need to be confident that you have a good understanding of the Fraser guidelines, and then as here, apply them to the facts.

1 Does Marcie understand his advice regarding contraception?
2 Has Dr Smith been unable to persuade Marcie to involve Sue in this decision?
3 Is Marcie very likely to continue having sex whether she has the implant or not?
4 Without the implant, is Marcie's physical or mental health likely to suffer?
5 Does Dr Smith believe that it is in Marcie's best interests to insert the implant without Sue's knowledge?

When considering the first question, Dr Smith needs to consider whether Marcie has 'sufficient understanding and intelligence'[2] to be competent to agree to the implant herself. Marcie is described as 'intelligent and sensible' and she obviously has a good understanding already of the various forms of contraception and their reliability. She doesn't want to get pregnant, and therefore it is likely that without the implant she will be very anxious, but she and her boyfriend are already having sex, so the likelihood is that this will continue. Marcie has already decided that she doesn't want Sue to be involved, and Dr Smith will therefore have to weigh up whether he thinks it is in Marcie's best interests[3] to go ahead without Sue's knowledge. As long as Dr Smith can answer 'yes' to all of Lord Fraser's questions, he can go ahead with this treatment without Sue being told.

[2] Lord Scarman's definition of competence in the *Gillick* case.

[3] There is guidance available to doctors on the General Medical Council website as to what they should consider when assessing the best interests of a child.

However, if Dr Smith judges Marcie not to be ***Gillick***/Fraser competent to make a decision about whether to have the contraceptive implant, but she is still keen to go ahead with this, he cannot do so on the basis of her consent. The only way Marcie could get such treatment is if her mother consents (there is also the option of obtaining consent from a court but Sue would inevitably find out about any such proceedings), and Sue will only be able to give a consent if she is told about the proposed medical treatment. There is no statutory provision or common law authority which states that a doctor should breach his patient's (i.e. the child's) confidentiality if a non-***Gillick*** competent child requests this. Herring (2012) endorses the view that in such a case, the child still has privacy rights, and there should be a separate assessment of the child's competence to decide if his/her parents should be informed (see Herring, J. (2012) *Medical Law and Ethics* (4th edn). Oxford: Oxford University Press).

In any event, I would suggest that regardless of whether Marcie is judged competent, and even if he does not go ahead with the implant, Dr Smith owes Marcie a duty of confidentiality in relation to her medical information, just as if she had been an adult. In the case of ***Venables* v *News Group Newspapers*** [2001] 2 WLR 1038, Butler-Sloss LJ confirmed that children are entitled to have their medical information kept confidential.[4] Doctors are under ethical and professional duties[5] to keep their patient's medical information entirely confidential, and it can usually only be disclosed to someone else (even the child's mother) if the child consents to this (and Marcie would need to be judged to be ***Gillick*** competent to give such a consent); or if Dr Smith considers disclosure to be in the public interest; or if there is some court order requiring the breach of confidentiality.

[4] Her exact words were 'Children, like adults, are entitled to confidentiality in respect of certain areas of information. Medical records are the obvious example.'

[5] That is, to the General Medical Council who have very specific guidance on doctors' professional obligations in respect of confidentiality.

Dr Smith may be concerned as to the possibility of a clash between the competing Article 8 ECHR rights of Marcie (who wants medical treatment to prevent a pregnancy, and to keep that private) and Sue (who may argue that as the mother of a 14-year-old, her right to respect for family life should acknowledge her right to know that her daughter is having this form of medical treatment). However, a similar such claim by a mother was explicitly rejected in the case of ***R (Axon)* v *Secretary of State for Health*** [2006] EWHC 37 (Admin). In this much more recent case, Silber J endorsed Lord Fraser's guidelines, but also dismissed the suggestion that a mother's right to respect for her family life would supersede a competent child's autonomy, and right to have their privacy respected if the child wanted this. This case had involved Mrs Axon seeking to challenge government guidance that had advised that children aged under 16 who were contemplating abortions should have their meetings with doctors kept confidential (see Department of Health (2004) *Best Practice Guidance*, 29 July).

Given that ***Axon*** supports widely circulated and accepted professional guidance and other common law authorities, it is clear that, despite her young age, Marcie can fully expect that Dr Smith should keep their discussions private[6] – with the exception that if he is very concerned as to her safety and well-being, he should disclose that to child protection agencies. Given also that most of the Fraser questions can already be answered 'yes' in her case, Dr Smith will be able to go ahead and provide Marcie with the implant[7] as long as he believes that this is in her best interests.

[6] This is one of the two questions you are asked – so make sure you answer this in your conclusion.

[7] This is the second question you need to answer. Always make sure that your concluding words answer *all* of the questions you face.

Make your answer stand out

- Refer to the Department of Health guidelines (issued 29 July 2004) as to Best Practice Guidance for doctors on providing sexual and contraceptive advice to children aged under 16.
- Could child safety/exploitation issues mean that Dr Smith should breach Marcie's request for privacy? Consider the risk that she may be being sexually exploited – and she *is* under the legal age to give consent for sexual intercourse. If this was the case, and Dr Smith believed that the risks to Marcie outweighed her request for privacy, he may feel obliged to alert Child Safeguarding services – see Department for Education (2013) *Working Together to Safeguard Children*. Statutory guidance, London: DfE.
- Look also at Rachel Taylor's article on the *Axon* case where she argues that Silber J could have recognised the mother's Article 8 right without this changing the outcome of the case – see Taylor, R. (2007) Reversing the retreat from *Gillick*? *CFLQ*, 19: 81.

! Don't be tempted to . . .

- Tell us all you know about the facts of *Gillick* and *Axon*. While this question is clearly focusing on these cases, you need to spend your time analysing how the judgments in each case will impact upon the facts of the problem.
- Spend any time at all on the possibility of Marcie's father giving consent – the facts you are given make clear that he does not have parental responsibility and, in any case, has no contact with Marcie.

www.pearsoned.co.uk/lawexpressqa

Go online to access more revision support including additional essay and problem questions with diagram plans, You be the marker questions, and download all diagrams from the book.

7 Mental health

How this topic may come up in exams

Mental health law can often be taught separately from medical law; it is a complex area of law in its own right. If this does form part of your overall medical law module, the likely focus in exams will be how and why the treatment of mental disorders is addressed differently to physical health problems. When setting essay questions, examiners will often focus on the ethical issues, while any problem questions will expect you to demonstrate your knowledge of the practical application of the law. Showing that you understand the overall scheme of mental health and capacity legislation will stand you in good stead.

Before you begin

It's a good idea to consider the following key themes of mental health before tackling a question on this topic.

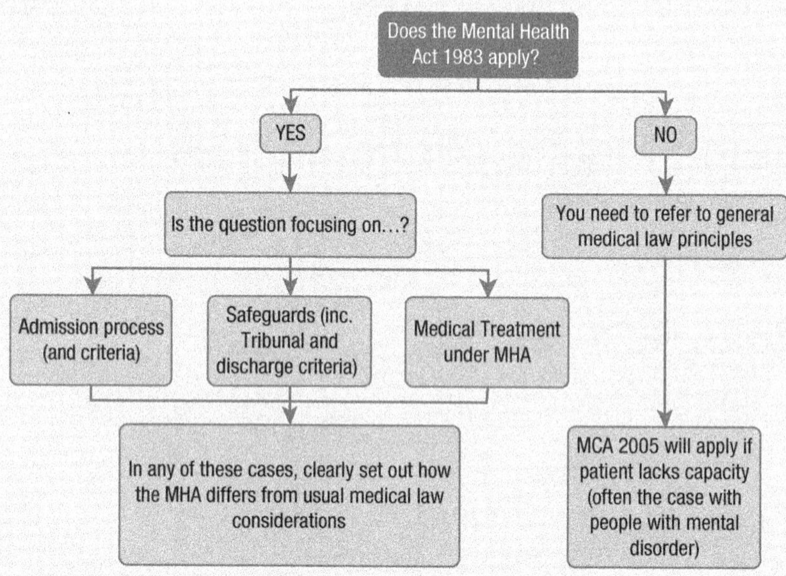

A printable version of this diagram is available from **www.pearsoned.co.uk/lawexpressqa**

Question 1

There have been legislative provisions to provide for the care and treatment of those with a mental disorder since 1324. Why is it still necessary that we should have a Mental Health Act?

Answer plan

- Explain that there are two pieces of legislation currently dealing with this area.
- Explain the limits of common/statute law to impose treatment.
- Consider why compulsory detention and treatment might be necessary.
- Concentrate on the Mental Health Act in its current form.
- Consider briefly the ethical issues – autonomy versus paternalism; public and individual safety in light of impaired judgement; patient's right to treatment.

Diagram plan

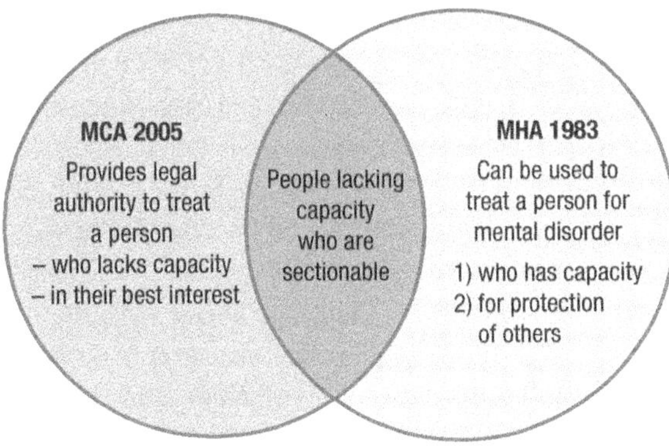

A printable version of this diagram plan is available from **www.pearsoned.co.uk/lawexpressqa**

Answer

There are currently two statutes providing for the care and treatment of those with a mental disorder.[1] The Mental Health Act 1983 (as amended in 2007) (MHA) provides a comprehensive code for the admission to hospital and compulsory treatment of patients with a mental disorder. The Mental Capacity Act 2005 (MCA) is largely a codification of the previous common law as to the legality of treating those without capacity to consent to care and treatment in their best interests. While there is

[1] This is of course the Mental Health Act's focus – but don't forget that the Mental Capacity Act 2005 also has a role in this. The point of this question is what does the MCA *not* cover?

some inevitable crossover between these pieces of legislation,[2] the MHA provides for detention and treatment of those suffering from a mental disorder with capacity who would object to this, and also legalises care and treatment for the protection of others, not just the patient himself.[3]

[2] This demonstrates good understanding of the application of these Acts.

[3] This is a vital point which you should include in any question about the purpose of, or necessity for, mental health law.

The Mental Health Act in its current form largely dates back to 1959, although it was preceded by a number of other statutes and was amended as recently as 2007. Historically therefore, Parliament has clearly recognised the need for those with a mental disorder to be forced to accept treatment for their condition. The Act applies to those with a 'mental disorder' (s. 1 MHA 1983), and provides a legal means to ensure that mentally disordered individuals who present a risk to themselves or others are admitted to hospital ('sectioned') and provided with treatment (widely defined in s. 145 MHA 1983).

In law, those who have a mental disorder are treated differently to those with physical health conditions. If you are physically unwell and in need of treatment, this will not be forced upon you if you are capable of consenting and refuse this – ***Re T (Adult: Refusal of Medical Treatment)*** [1992] 4 All ER 649. Even if your decision to refuse treatment is unwise or illogical, if you are assessed as having the necessary capacity to make the decision to refuse treatment, this cannot be imposed upon you, even if this will result in your death – ***Re C (Adult: Refusal of Treatment)*** [1994] 1 All ER 819. If you are not capable of giving a valid consent to treatment because of an 'impairment or disturbance if the functioning of the mind or brain' (s. 2 MCA) and therefore unable to give consent (see s. 3 MCA) then treatment can only be given to you if it is reasonably believed to be in your best interests. Under the MCA, treatment cannot be given in the best interest of, or for the protection of, anybody else – and a person cannot be 'restrained' for that treatment to be given unless there is a risk of harm to *that* person – sections 4 and 6 MCA. The MCA does not allow for restraint or treatment to be given to an individual, even if they aren't capable of making their own decisions, if the intention is to protect other people.[4]

[4] While you may feel that referring to the MCA in such detail is not the point of this question, you are wrong. It is only by explaining what the MCA doesn't cover that you can begin to address the need for a separate MHA.

However, the Mental Health Act is very different:[5]

[5] The two points following are the major issues that you have to get across in this answer – these are the areas where the MHA stands alone within English law, and by highlighting these clearly, in their own paragraph, but clearly separated, you are showing the examiner that you know what he/she wants you to address. These issues may well come up in a variety of questions about the MHA so you need to be clear that you understand these and can explain them.

1 The MHA allows for an individual to be detained against their wishes in hospital and also for medical treatment for their mental disorder to be imposed upon them regardless of whether they have capacity. Except in a few cases – see sections 57, 58 and 58A[6] which are

[6] By mentioning these sections your examiner will appreciate that you know the details of the Act – most students will not mention these, so this is a good opportunity to gain credit.

made subject to either the patient consenting or the approval of a second-opinion independent doctor – once a patient with mental disorder is subject to the Mental Health Act, then section 63 provides that the patient's consent to medical treatment for their mental disorder[7] is not necessary as long as it is given under the direction of the Approved Clinician in charge of their treatment.[8]

2 The MHA provides that an individual can be sectioned if they are suffering from mental disorder 'of a nature or degree' (see sections 2 and 3 MHA) and medical treatment for that mental disorder[9] is necessary in the interests of the patient's own health and safety, or for the protection of others.

The Mental Health Act therefore clearly has a different focus to the MCA – providing legal authority to detain and treat people who have capacity to refuse the advised therapeutic options, and also allowing for the detention and compulsory treatment because of perceived risks to others, and not simply focusing on the best interests of the patient himself. This can involve extremely invasive and unpleasant interventions into the life of an individual, requiring them to be detained in a hospital with consequent significant reductions of their freedoms, and the possibility of unpleasant and unwanted treatment, which may in itself have equally abhorrent side effects. Why is this necessary?[10] As set out above, there are no similar provisions for the compulsory treatment of those who are physically unwell. I can identify two possible grounds:

1 People who have mental disorders often do not themselves understand that they are mentally unwell, or that treatment might be of benefit to them, and it could be argued that the availability of the MHA allows for these individuals to access treatment that would be otherwise denied to them. This lack of 'insight' can prevent them accessing medical treatment and therefore allowing a chance of recovery from distressing experiences such as the symptoms of schizophrenia. However, such a person would probably also be deemed to be incapable under the MCA tests as, for example, they might be deemed incapable of 'understanding' or 'weighing up' the information as required by section 3 of the MCA.[11] Arguments have been made[12] that this contravention of a capable individual's autonomous right to refuse what is done to his body can be justified on 'social' grounds – that the mentally well individual can therefore function better as part of society.

2 This in turn links to the second ground. It is explicit in the Mental Health Act that detention and the consequence of compulsory

[7] It is important to make sure that you get this phrase right – this is the cornerstone to authorising treatment without consent.

[8] This again is lifted straight from the important wording of section 63 – it is the fact that the treatment is given under the direction of the Approved Clinician which means that consent is not necessary, NOT the fact that the patient is detained under the MHA.

[9] Here is that phrase again – don't be afraid of repeating it, by doing so you are making clear that you understand when the MHA applies.

[10] By asking this question yourself, you are again focusing on the main point under discussion.

[11] This sophisticated argument will catch the eye of the examiner, showing you are able to think beyond the question.

[12] If you are going to refer to such 'arguments' try and refer to the originators of these – see Bartlett and Sandland (2013).

treatment can be justified when the individual poses a danger to 'others'. If a person has a mental disorder which causes them to be a risk to others, it is only the Mental Health Act that provides legal authority for them to be detained, prior to them committing an imprisonable offence. The MHA therefore allows for detention because of a prediction of risk.

[13] In your concluding paragraph, you must take the opportunity to link back to the question you are asked, and to sum up your issues.

The continued existence of the MHA[13] can be seen as necessary because it allows for compulsory care and treatment of those who present a risk to others, whereas other legislative provisions, such as the MCA, do not. This does, however, raise concerns as to the MHA being used in a paternalistic, risk-averse fashion, creating real and unpleasant interventions into an individual's life and autonomy which is not otherwise considered appropriate in society and may potentially breach an individual's human rights.

✓ Make your answer stand out

- When discussing whether medical treatment should be enforced upon mentally disordered people with capacity, consider the academic views that this is a violation of autonomy – see Bartlett, P. and Sandland, R. (2013) *Mental Health Law: Policy and Practice* (4th edn). Oxford: Oxford University Press, and Herring, J. (2012) *Medical Law and Ethics* (4th edn). Oxford: Oxford University Press.
- Consider the difficulty of how to predict that a mentally disordered person is likely to be a risk to others – see Peay, J. (2003) *Decisions and Dilemmas: Working with Mental Health Law*. Oxford: Hart Publishing.
- In your conclusions, consider whether these points could allow for arguments to be made as to a breach of the European Convention on Human Rights – perhaps Articles 8 and 14.

! Don't be tempted to . . .

- Tell us all you know about the Mental Health Act – this question asks you to focus on the reasons for its continued existence, so think carefully about why mental health treatment needs are different to physical health.
- Ignore the MCA just because the question only makes reference to the MHA – you are being asked specifically why there is a need for the MHA, and you can only answer this by referring to the other legal options currently available.
- Veer off into general discussion of the Mental Capacity Act – you are asked about the MHA, and while the MCA is an important point of comparison, that is NOT the focus.

 Question 2

To be detained under the Mental Health Act 1983, a patient needs to be suffering from a 'mental disorder'.

Discuss whether what is a 'mental disorder' is sufficiently well defined in this context.

Diagram plan

Definition of 'mental disorder' – is it too broad?

Does the lack of definition and 'medical prism' cause problems, e.g. ethical issues?

Section 1, Mental Health Act 1983

Exclusionary and any statutory definitions?

Why are these necessary? What is the historical context?

How does this compare with the European Convention and case law, i.e. need for 'medical view'

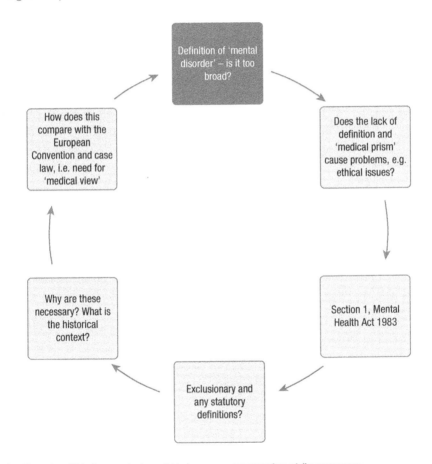

A printable version of this diagram plan is available from **www.pearsoned.co.uk/lawexpressqa**

Answer plan

- Recognise that the need to be 'mentally disordered' is a prerequisite for detention and treatment.
- Point out, however, that to be detained requires more than just 'mental disorder'.
- Explain section 1 MHA and the exclusions/limitations.
- Consider the wider exclusions pre-2007 amendments.
- Review implications of the very broad current definition – who decides what constitutes a mental disorder? Does it accord with Article 5(1) ECHR?

Answer

The use of the Mental Health Act 1983 (MHA) is limited to those who can be said to be 'mentally disordered',[1] and therefore this is the gateway to the Act's legal powers to detain in hospitals, compulsorily treat, and also make patients subject to compulsion in the community. These powers are draconian,[2] and therefore to prevent their abuse, it is crucial that the criteria used should be clearly defined and easily understood by those who are given authority under the MHA.[3]

Section 1(2) of the MHA defines 'mental disorder' as 'any disorder or disability of the mind', which is a very broad definition. However, while a person needs to have a mental disorder for the Act to be used at all, this alone does not enable a person to be 'sectioned' as the mental disorder also has to be of either a nature or a degree to 'warrant' detention (see section 2 MHA) or to make this 'appropriate' (see section 3 MHA),[4] and also there has to be a risk identified either to the patient or members of the public. Both 'nature' and 'degree' were explained in the 2008 version of the MHA Code of Practice,[5] with the former referring to the type, length, prognosis and response to treatment of the mental disorder, and 'degree' referring to the current level of symptoms. Therefore for a section to be lawfully imposed, the patient's mental disorder is required to be either currently serious, or with the clear risk that it will become so if left untreated.

Within the MHA, there is one statutory interpretation of the phrase 'mental disorder', confirming that this should only be used to describe people suffering from a learning disability[6] if that is associated with

[1] This is what the question is getting at – what are the risks of this phrase being defined too loosely?

[2] It is vital to highlight the ethical issues surrounding MHA powers.

[3] Don't be afraid to answer the question in your first paragraph, as long as you go on to properly develop your argument in the rest of the essay.

[4] Your precision here in explaining that there are different grounds for section 2 and section 3 is the sign of a good lawyer.

[5] If you can, summarise paragraph 4.3 of the 2008 Code in this way rather than quoting it word for word – it shows that you understand these rather difficult concepts.

[6] 'Learning disability' is itself defined at section 1(4) but you don't need to set that out here.

the patient's 'abnormally aggressive or seriously irresponsible conduct'. This limits the potential use of the Act for people with learning disabilities, although this limitation only applies to detentions potentially lasting for longer than 28 days (s. 1(2A) MHA). Since the 2007 amendments, there is also now just one exclusion to what can be considered to be a mental disorder – 'dependence on alcohol or drugs' (see s. 1(3)). Prior to those amendments, the Act also specifically excluded 'promiscuity or other immoral conduct [and] sexual deviancy' from being considered to be a mental disorder. This was in itself a reflection of the practice, prior to 1983, of using the MHA to detain people on the grounds of their sexual orientation or societal views of their sexual or other 'immoral' conduct. While the shorter exclusion now in place might suggest that it is again permissible to detain individuals for such behaviour, the MHA Code makes clear in chapter 3 that involvement in unusual or dangerous illegal, antisocial or immoral behaviour should not of itself be enough to give a diagnosis of 'mental disorder'. These changing views[7] as to what should be excluded from the ambit of the Act, however, are illustrative of the need for the law to be explicit in setting out what should, and should not, be considered to be a 'mental disorder'. Without such clear guidelines, there would be a risk of the MHA (as it has in the past) being used to lock away and forcibly treat individuals who may be considered 'different' enough to warrant such repressive measures.[8]

[7] You will see that I come back to this interesting point in the final paragraph as a good way of bringing this essay to a strong conclusion.

[8] You can be brave in your views. At degree level, your examiner will be looking for you to express a view on the adequacy (or otherwise) of the law.

As being 'sectioned' under the Act will involve a deprivation of liberty, the MHA needs to accord with the European case law on how 'unsound mind'[9] is defined – while the case of ***Winterwerp* v *Netherlands*** (1979) 2 EHRR 387 agreed that this could not be given a 'definitive interpretation' because of the changing societal views and medical considerations of what was unsoundness of mind, the European Court of Human Rights (ECtHR) insisted for the need for 'objective medical expertise' to diagnose the presence of 'a true mental disorder'. This putting the decision in the hands of doctors by the ECtHR has clearly been reflected in section 1 of the MHA, but the section 1(2) definition has been criticised as 'worrying' in 'providing clinicians with a very wide discretion in identifying which conditions come within its scope' (Jones, R. (2013) *Mental Health Act Manual* (16th edn). London: Sweet & Maxwell). The Upper Tribunal case of ***DL-H* v *Devon***

[9] Remember that Article 5(1)(e) allows for the lawful deprivation of liberty of someone with 'unsound mind'.

Partnership NHS Trust [2010] UKUT 102 (AAC) pointed out the risks of leaving the decision as to what is a 'mental disorder' in the hands of doctors – they, and their professional guidance (in the forms of the diagnostic manuals ICD-10 and DSM-IV) do not always agree. It is instructive to note that the Upper Tribunal too, in that case, shied away from making a definitive statement on what constituted a 'mental disorder', with UT Judge Jacobs saying 'this was an issue that will have to be considered by the Upper Tribunal in an appropriate case' (see paragraph 24) but also commenting 'There must be an answer that provides protection for patients from vague or differing definitions while ensuring that those who present a danger are not left free to harm themselves or others for failing to meet overprescriptive criteria'.[10]

While the broad, medically led definition of 'mental disorder' therefore clearly accords with the European Convention, this in itself brings ethical issues relevant to society as a whole. Should doctors be best placed to decide when legal powers should be used to detain and compulsorily treat people?[11] The changing views as to what should be excluded from the scope of the Act[12] are illustrative of the legal need to limit an otherwise wide medical discretion when considering what is a 'mental disorder', and this is clearly an area which needs to be kept under review.

[10] These statements are a good illustration of the problem faced by trying to define what is a 'mental disorder'.

[11] If you are going to pose a question like this, be prepared to answer it, as this does in the concluding sentence.

[12] This is a reference back to what was previously discussed in the main body of the essay, and you are doing well if you can tie your argument together like this. A well-considered conclusion will always gain marks.

✓ Make your answer stand out

- Refer to ethical issues. The diagnosis of what is a 'mental disorder' often is dependent on a subjective view rather than a clear medical diagnostic test (such as an X-ray or blood test) – therefore there needs to be thought given as to *who* decides this vital question?
- When explaining that the MHA also requires the mental disorder to be of a 'nature or degree', point out the exception in section 136 – this only needs a police officer to consider that the person has a 'mental disorder'.
- Reflect that in *W* v *L* [1974] QB 711, the Court of Appeal suggested that the words 'mental illness' were 'ordinary words [which] have no particular medical significance'. How does that square with the current definition and the need for a 'medical' interpretation?
- Include the views of commentators such as Emily Jackson, and Bartlett and Sanderson that the removal of the 'sexual deviancy' exclusion was to allow sexual offenders (i.e. paedophiles) to be locked away under the MHA – see Jackson, E. (2013) *Medical Law: Texts, Cases and Materials (3rd edn).* Oxford: Oxford University Press; Bartlett, P. and Sandland, R. (2013) *Mental Health Law: Policy and Practice* (4th edn). Oxford: Oxford University Press.

! Don't be tempted to . . .

- Just explain the ethical concerns – remember this is a medical *law* question!
- Forget about a structure – this model answer has no subheadings, but answers the question in the first paragraph and ties the general discussion in the subsequent paragraphs neatly together in a strong conclusion.
- Ignore the European Convention – it is usually relevant to any discussion of mental health law.
- Focus on one case (i.e. *DL-H* v *Devon*) which you think answers the question. Poorer students will do this, setting out at length the facts of a particular case. Your examiner is asking you here for a more general discussion, and if (like in the suggested answer here) you do mention the case, explain the *ratio*, not the facts.

Question 3

The necessity for 'appropriate treatment' to be available to a patient detained under the Mental Health Act 1983 imposes a high barrier to detention.

Discuss with reference to the relevant law.

Diagram plan

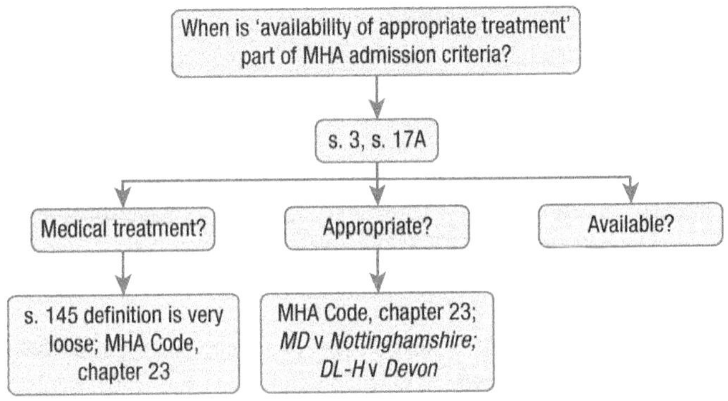

A printable version of this diagram plan is available from **www.pearsoned.co.uk/lawexpressqa**

Answer plan

- Explain what this phrase refers to in the context of the MHA admission criteria.
- Recognise that the test doesn't apply to all detentions.
- Review how the Code of Practice interprets this ground for admission.
- Consider relevant Upper Tribunal case law.
- Reach a conclusion that this does (or does not) often create a barrier to detention under the Act, given its interpretation in the Code and decided cases.

Answer

The amendments to the Mental Health Act 1983 (MHA) which became effective in November 2008[1] introduced a new ground to be considered when applying for the detention of a patient detained for longer than 28 days or subject to a Community Treatment Order – the need for 'appropriate medical treatment [to be] available for him' (section 3(2)(d), MHA[2]). There are other criteria that must also be met, such as the nature/degree of a patient's mental disorder and the need for detention to protect that patient or others,[3] but unless it can be said that 'appropriate medical treatment is available' the Act cannot be used.

This requirement would appear at first glance to impose a high barrier to detaining an individual under the MHA, and would suggest that if there is no medical treatment that can be made available to a patient, then he cannot be sectioned for longer than 28 days. However, interpretations of this phrase by the MHA Code of Practice (which should be followed unless there are cogent reasons not to do so[4]) and the Upper Tribunal have significantly reduced the 'height' of this 'barrier' and it has been argued by Emily Jackson that compulsory detention and treatment can remain lawful under the MHA even if in practice the patient will receive no treatment at all (Jackson, E. (2013) *Medical Law: Texts, Cases and Materials* (3rd edn). Oxford: Oxford University Press).

By breaking the phrase down,[5] one can see why Jackson and other commentators, such as Mason and Laurie (2013) and Herring (2012), have taken the view that this is an easy criterion for a mentally unwell person to pass in order to be detained (see Mason, K. and Laurie, G. (2013) *Mason & McCall Smith's Law and Medical Ethics* (9th edn). Oxford: Oxford University Press; Herring, J. (2012) *Medical Law and Ethics* (9th edn). Oxford: Oxford University Press).

[1] This introduction is a confident and knowledgeable start, letting the examiner know that YOU know where this phrase comes from, and also allows you to slip in the fact you are aware of the date the law changed.

[2] You should always include the exact details of the statutory reference if you know this.

[3] You should make clear that this is not the only issue that needs to be satisfied for a patient to be detained, or you risk the examiner thinking that you have misunderstood the law.

[4] This guidance about the Code of Practice comes from the House of Lords in the case of *R (Munjaz) v Ashworth Hospital* [2005] UKHL 58. Whenever you refer to the MHA Code in an answer, make sure that you let the examiner know that you are aware that this case exists and that it means that the Code is more than 'mere guidance' and should generally be followed.

[5] You can therefore introduce some structure into this essay.

1. 'Medical treatment'

This is loosely defined in section 145(1) of the MHA as including (but not limited to) 'nursing, psychological intervention, specialist mental health habilitation, rehabilitation and care' and can therefore include a very wide range of potential interventions with a mentally disordered patient.

Under section 145(4) the purpose of the medical treatment must be to 'alleviate or prevent a worsening of the disorder or one or more of its symptoms and manifestations', but taking these phrases together, this can clearly be interpreted as meaning that medical treatment can be as little as providing medication to a patient, intending this to reduce his symptoms, without ever being confident that this 'medical treatment' will improve the patient's mental illness. The MHA Code of Practice makes this clear by saying that for some patients, 'management of the undesirable effects of their disorder may be the most that can realistically be hoped for' (see MHA Code of Practice, para. 6.15).[6]

[6] If you can remember the quote or are in an open book exam, please quote this exactly; if not it will be sufficient for you to refer to the Code backing up what you have said in the previous sentence.

2. 'Appropriate'

It is unhelpfully stated in section 64(3) of the MHA that this means 'treatment which is appropriate'. This circular and self-explanatory definition is repeated in the Code of Practice. The Code also makes clear that the treatment available does not have to meet all the medical issues raised by the patient's mental disorder – it can be 'appropriate' even if it just meets some (see para. 23.13). So far, the Upper Tribunal have not encountered a case where it has been successfully argued that the medical treatment on offer to a detained patient is *not* appropriate. In the case of ***MD* v *Nottinghamshire Health Care NHS Trust*** [2010] UKUT 59, it was accepted by the court that just because the 'milieu therapy' offered by the ward environment had the *potential* to benefit the patient, that was enough to make it appropriate for him. In the case of ***DL-H* v *Devon Partnerships NHS Trust*** [2010] UKUT 102, a patient who was refusing to engage in psychological therapy argued that meant this was inappropriate for him. The Code of Practice says that an unwillingness by a patient to cooperate does not make this treatment 'inappropriate', and that it can continue to be appropriate as long as it is on offer (paras. 23.19–20). The Upper Tribunal were cautious of this and warned that it was dangerous to rely on assertions that such a patient would eventually succumb to persuasion by staff, as that could mean locking someone up without treatment, for public safety grounds.

3. 'Available'

The Code does make clear that the appropriate medical treatment does have to be available in actuality, not in theory (para. 23.14). However, the generous interpretations described above means that this threshold is easily met; for example, a nurse being available to limit a patient's distress.

The Code of Practice does say that simply locking someone up in a hospital does not constitute 'medical treatment' (para. 23.18),[7] but given the loose interpretation that has been given to this particular ground for detention, it is hard to agree that the necessity for appropriate treatment to be available does prevent people being sectioned – even if it is highly unlikely that they will receive any benefit in terms of cure.[8]

[7] As you'll have noticed, this essay refers to the Code extensively. Don't worry about this. In setting this question, the examiner knows that the major discussion points about the 'appropriate treatment test' will be found in the Code, and therefore will expect a good answer to make repeated reference to it. Also, don't panic if you can't remember the specific paragraph numbers, it is more important that you remember what the Code says. However, if you are in an open book examination, it would be useful to have these helpful paragraphs marked.

[8] In an essay question like this, when you are specifically asked to discuss an issue, always make sure that your conclusion does exactly that – you must conclude and sum up your argument, one way or another.

Make your answer stand out

- Explain that this test replaced the 'treatability test' under the previous MHA, which came under criticism for excluding potentially dangerous offenders (see, for example, Francis, R. (2006) *Report of the independent inquiry into the care and treatment of Michael Stone*. South East Coast Strategic Health Authority).
- Include an introduction and a conclusion in these essay-style questions. Here you are asked to discuss a particular legal phrase; use the introduction to explain what it is and where it comes from; and use the conclusion to sum up the legal points, and set out your view.
- Refer to relevant Upper Tribunal cases. Weaker students tend to spend time discussing the facts of these; stronger students will be able to explain the *ratio* of the case concisely and use this to support their argument.
- Use a structure such as the one suggested; it will help you organise your thoughts and you'll produce a crisper essay.

! Don't be tempted to . . .

- Ignore the Code of Practice. While this is not primary legislation, it is more than 'mere guidance' in the words of the *Munjaz* case, and is the key to answering this question correctly. In many mental health questions, the Code will be useful as a point of reference, as it remains the main 'guide' to the Mental Health Act itself.
- Just summarise the Code; you may manage a bare pass on a good knowledge of the Code, but if you are aiming for a high-class degree, you will need to demonstrate that you have a wider knowledge of the law, and can make your own argument.
- Get caught up in a political discussion of whether it is right for the MHA to be so loose in this regard – it is far better to make legal points which demonstrate the lack of clarity in the law and save the politics for a different degree!

? Question 4

Sally is aged 23. She has suffered from anorexia nervosa since the age of 14, and at times restricts her diet considerably. She is now significantly underweight and also has depressed mood. Twice, within the last week, she has threatened suicide and says that she has no hope that she will ever be able to live a 'normal' life. Her consultant psychiatrist is concerned that if she remains at home without treatment her mental illnesses will get worse and has recommended the following treatment plan:

- admission to a local eating disorders unit where her dietary intake can be monitored;
- use of nasogastric feeding if Sally refuses to eat the food recommended by the nutritionist;
- regular attendance by Sally at group counselling sessions within the unit to address the underlying causes of Sally's problems;
- family therapy with Sally and her parents, for the same reasons as above. Sally is adamant that she will not participate in this;
- anti-depressant medication to treat Sally's depression.

Following an application made by an Approved Mental Health Professional, Sally has been admitted today to the eating disorders unit under section 3 of the Mental Health Act 1983. Explain and discuss the legal authority that could be used by her Responsible Clinician to ensure that Sally abides by the treatment plan.

Answer plan

- Identify that Sally has been detained under section 3, and as such Part 4 of the Mental Health Act governs the legality of administering all medical treatment for Sally's mental disorder.
- Set out how Part 4 applies to detained patients.
- Identify which parts of the treatment plan are safeguarded treatments where special rules apply.
- Explain whether nasogastric feeding can be classed as medical treatment for mental disorder and thus fall within Part 4.

Diagram plan

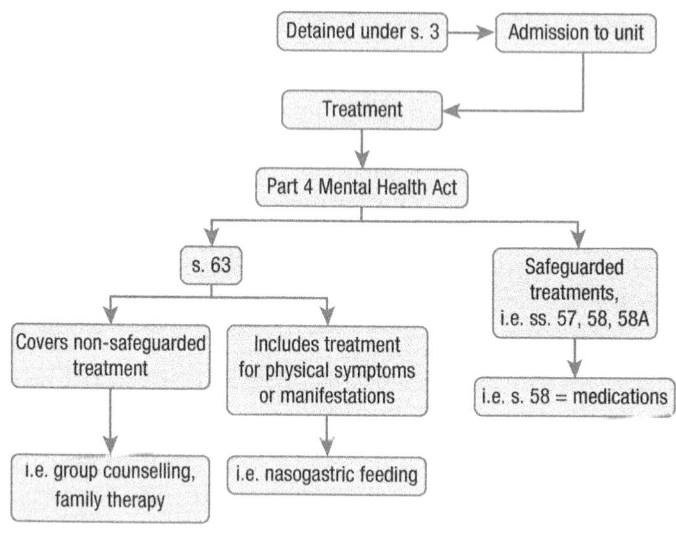

A printable version of this diagram plan is available from **www.pearsoned.co.uk/lawexpressqa**

Answer

Sally has been detained today under section 3 of the Mental Health Act 1983[1] (MHA). The legal grounds for section 3 (set out in section 3(2)) are that Sally is suffering from a mental disorder of a nature or a degree to make it appropriate for her to receive medical treatment in a hospital; that it is necessary for Sally's health or safety or for the protection of others that she should receive this treatment

[1] You need to clarify this right at the start – as it is the fact that Sally has been detained under one of the longer-term sections of the MHA that allows for her treatment.

and it can only be provided if she is detained under section 3. Appropriate treatment also has to be available to her while she is detained in hospital. The element of 'treatment' is therefore a vital reason for her detention, and I will go on to discuss whether the various 'treatments' proposed under the care plan can all be authorised under the MHA.[2]

Her team wish her to undergo a range of treatments:[3]

1. Group counselling and family therapy

When a patient is detained under section 3, Part 4 of the MHA will apply to all the treatments that are to be administered to her for her mental disorder(s). Section 63 of the MHA provides the legal authority[4] for medical treatment for the patient's mental disorder[5] to be given to the detained patient. Both of these proposed 'treatments' fall within the very wide definition of 'medical treatment' set out in section 145(1) MHA. The intention of these 'talking therapies' is to try to positively treat the anorexia and depression and as section 145(4) requires that the 'purpose of the treatment should be to alleviate or prevent a worsening of the disorder or one or more of its symptoms or manifestations', these treatments clearly have that purpose.

Sally has indicated that she does not agree to undergo family therapy. Section 63 states that treatment can be provided lawfully to a detained patient without their consent as long as it is given under the direction of the Approved Clinician in charge of all of the proposed treatment. There is therefore a lawful authority for this, but it may still be impossible practically for the family therapy to proceed without Sally's active participation.

2. Medication

As above, medication can be lawfully administered to a detained patient if it falls within both sections 145 and 63.[6] As it is anti-depressant medication, to be given to Sally to seek to treat her mental disorder, this clearly falls within the treatment provisions in Part 4. Medication is potentially, however, one of the 'safeguarded' treatments given special regard under the MHA as, after three months after it has first been administered, it is covered by section 58 of the Act. After this time, Sally will either need to be certified as capable of

[2] This is a good start – setting out that you understand the question is asking you to link the various treatments with their legal authority, and indicating that they need to be looked at individually.

[3] In order to answer this question clearly, it is sensible to separate out the different medical treatments and deal with these individually. You then need to plan in which order to deal with these. The order suggested here is a sensible one, dealing first with the non-safeguarded treatments which clearly fall within section 145.

[4] This is the main point here.

[5] As with previous answers, when you are discussing section 63, it is vital to get this phrase in – it is the fact that it is 'medical treatment for the patient's mental disorder' which allows section 63 to ignore the patient's need to consent.

[6] As you have already explained this above, you do not need to repeat the whole information here – this is why a structure is so important.

giving consent and consenting to the medication; or if she is capable of consenting but refusing, or incapable of giving consent, a Second Opinion Appointed Doctor will need to assess Sally and the medication, and confirm that it is appropriate for this treatment to continue to be given. However, for the first three months of administration of this medication, section 63 alone will provide the legal authority for this to be administered to her.

3. Nasogastric feeding

Feeding of Sally (potentially against her wishes given her anorexia) is more controversial. Providing food to a detained patient does not at first sight appear to be treatment for her mental disorder. However, in the case of ***B* v *Croydon HA*** [1995] 1 All ER 683,[7] the Court of Appeal held that the legal authority to provide medical treatment for a mental disorder under section 63 includes treatment of the symptoms of the disorder (as well as the disorder itself) and includes a range of acts ancillary to the core treatment. In that case, Thorpe J[8] found on the facts that force-feeding a patient who was refusing to eat due to her personality disorder was 'ancillary' to the core treatment of her mental disorder.

As explained above,[9] a medical intervention can be classed as 'medical treatment for a mental disorder' under section 145(4) of the MHA if its 'purpose' can be said to alleviate or prevent a worsening in one of its *symptoms or manifestations*' (my italics). This change to the MHA was made in the 2007 amendments,[10] and reinforces the common law in this area following ***B* v *Croydon***.

Sally's refusal to eat will be seen as a 'manifestation' of her anorexia, and providing her with food via a nasogastric tube is supporting (or 'ancillary to') the core treatment for her eating disorder (the talking therapies discussed above). This will therefore fall within the definition of 'medical treatment' for her 'mental disorder', and can be legally authorised under Part 4. As nasogastric feeding is not a 'safeguarded' treatment under sections 57, 58 or 58A of the Act,[11] the authority for its administration comes from section 63.

[7] This is the vital case to remember in this context – without including this you will definitely lose marks.

[8] If you can remember the name of the Judge, always add this in. Don't worry if you can't however – the main thing to get right is the name of the case and its *ratio*.

[9] Again, this is the value of a good structure – you can refer to what you have already said without repeating it and losing time.

[10] This is not strictly necessary but will indicate that you know this area.

[11] If you have the space and time, it is worth displaying this little bit of knowledge – that you know what the safeguarded treatments are – to reassure your examiner that you are fully aware of the details of this area of law.

Make your answer stand out

- Focus on the fact that Sally has been detained under section 3 for treatment – can the treatment suggested in the care plan be delivered lawfully under the MHA?
- Consider your structure carefully – what is going to be the most efficient way of explaining this so you don't repeat yourself?
- Make reference to chapter 6 of the MHA Code of Practice, in particular paragraphs 6.18 and 6.19, to indicate to your examiner that you appreciate the argument that Sally's refusal to participate in treatment does not make it any less appropriate.
- In your conclusion, consider whether these arguments could allow for arguments to be made as to a breach of the European Convention on Human Rights – maybe Articles 8 and 14?

! Don't be tempted to . . .

- Just launch into an explanation of Part 4 and ignore the need to address the specific treatments under discussion here.
- Forget about subheadings and structure. Although this looks easy, this is a complicated question! The best way to approach it is to plan out in advance in which order you will address the legal issues.
- Veer off into general discussion of the Mental Capacity Act – you are asked about the MHA, and while the MCA is a useful point of comparison, that is NOT the focus.

? Question 5

Annie is aged 54 and has suffered from schizophrenia for many years. She is prescribed antipsychotic medication for this, tablets which are kept by her husband, John. When John gives the tablets to Annie each morning with her breakfast, she accepts these. Annie has always been reluctant for a nurse to visit her at home but has seen her psychiatrist for an outpatient review every six months. Even though Annie has continued to take her tablets, her mental health has worsened recently, and she has begun to experience auditory hallucinations which are upsetting for her. John is very concerned about her and feels unable to care for her at home; he would like her to be admitted to a psychiatric hospital to 'see if she can be helped'. He is not sure whether Annie will agree to this.

Consider and discuss the legal issues that arise in this case.

Answer plan

- Set out that there are two ways for Annie to be admitted to a psychiatric hospital – compulsorily under the Mental Health Act 1983, or informally.
- Explain the legal procedure for admission under the 1983 Act and the specific criteria.
- Consider for what purpose Annie is going to be admitted and in this context show that you understand the differences between section 2 and section 3.
- Explain how 'informal' admission can take place – the vital issue here is whether Annie will be compliant with the admission and assessment/treatment for mental disorder in hospital.
- Consider the legal safeguards for Annie available under each route, and compare the two options.

Diagram plan

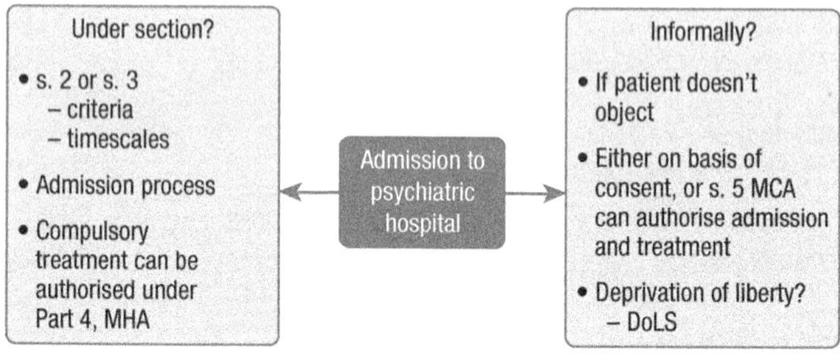

A printable version of this diagram plan is available from **www.pearsoned.co.uk/lawexpressqa**

Answer

Annie is suffering from schizophrenia, a mental illness, and her husband feels that she requires admission to a psychiatric hospital for assessment and/or treatment of her mental disorder.[1] There are two potential ways[2] for this to occur: Annie could be admitted and detained under the Mental Health Act 1983 (MHA), or she could be admitted 'voluntarily' to hospital.

1. Admission under the Mental Health Act 1983[3]

An application could be made for Annie's admission (and subsequent detention, assessment and treatment) for mental disorder under

[1] You will see here that I have not copied the question. Please don't waste time by doing this, but it is a good idea to summarise the question by picking out the relevant points.

[2] You have now set out a structure to focus your essay and avoid getting side-tracked.

[3] Don't be worried that by using subheadings you are wasting words out of your maximum word count. It will often save repetition in the long run.

section 2 or section 3 of the Act. Section 2 allows for detention for assessment (and any treatment) for up to 28 days, and section 3 authorises her detention in hospital for treatment for an initial period of six months which can then be renewed. In either case, Annie will need to be seen to be suffering from a mental disorder of a nature or degree that legally justifies her detention, and there must be a risk to her health or safety, or the protection of others, if she is not so detained. If section 3 is to be used, appropriate medical treatment must also be available.[4]

[4] This is a neat summary of the differing legal criteria for detention under both sections 2 and 3. It is much quicker than writing these out in full and also demonstrates that you have understood the common points between the two.

In either case, the application could be made by John, or an Approved Mental Health Professional (AMHP), relying on reports from two doctors (one of whom must be an authorised mental health specialist) that Annie meets the criteria set out above. If an AMHP makes the application for a detention under section 3, then John[5] would need to be specifically consulted (this doesn't apply for section 2), but given the facts here, it is unlikely that he would object to Annie being sectioned, as he supports her need for admission.[6]

[5] John gets the right to make the application and to object to section 3 because he is Annie's 'Nearest Relative' under the 1983 Act.

[6] Remember this is a problem question and you do need to reflect the facts in your answer. Please don't forget this and instead treat this as an essay-type discussion.

Annie has been suffering from schizophrenia for 'many years' and has an established diagnosis and treatment plan. Assuming Annie meets the criteria, it will be the applicant's choice whether to use section 2 or section 3; the MHA Code of Practice (paras. 4.25–4.27) suggests that section 3 should probably be used in this situation, but commentators such as Richard Jones[7] suggest that assessment under section 2 would be more suitable given the unknown reasons for her recent deterioration (see Jones, R. (2013) *Mental Health Act Manual* (16th edn). London: Sweet & Maxwell).

[7] You might recognise that this is a comment he has made over various previous editions of his *Mental Health Manual*.

Whichever section is used, Annie can be detained in a psychiatric hospital and (at least for the first three months[8]) given medication there even if she doesn't agree to this.

[8] Section 58A states that after three months, Annie will need to consent or a Second Opinion Appointed Doctor will have to approve this.

2. Informal admission

It is important to realise that Annie doesn't have to be sectioned to be admitted to psychiatric hospital – the majority of patients are admitted 'informally'.

As long as Annie does not object[9] to the planned admission to psychiatric hospital or her assessment and medical treatment there, Annie can be admitted without using the 1983 Act. Legal authority can come from Annie's consent to this – but only if she has the mental capacity to provide this. The Mental Capacity Act 2005 states that a person 'should be assumed to have capacity'[10] unless it is established otherwise and just because Annie has schizophrenia, it should not be assumed that she does not have capacity to consent to her admission.

However, if it is established that Annie does not have the ability to make this decision because of an impairment of, or disturbance in the functioning of her mind,[11] then legal authority for her admission can come from section 5 of the Mental Capacity Act 2005, if it is reasonably believed that the admission to hospital and the planned assessment/treatment there are in her best interests. However, if Annie will be deprived of her liberty whilst in the psychiatric hospital, then Article 5 of the ECHR requires that this be done 'lawfully' and with a right to contest this, so a legal authorisation will be necessary under the Deprivation of Liberty Safeguards.[12]

3. Comparison of the options

If Annie is going to object (and John is not sure that she will agree[13]) to the planned admission, then no choice is available – she will have to be sectioned under the Mental Health Act. While this may be felt to be stigmatising, it does provide certain safeguards – her Nearest Relative (John) can object to her detention and request her discharge, Annie herself gets the right to appeal to be discharged, and her treatment and care will be overseen by a Second Opinion Appointed Doctor and the Care Quality Commission.

However, if Annie is admitted informally, her rights may be significantly reduced. If she has capacity, she can choose to refuse treatment and leave, but if she does not, her admission to hospital and medical treatment there can be authorised under the Mental Capacity Act, and she will not have any of the safeguards provided to sectioned patients.

[9] This is *the* vital point that you have to get across when discussing informal admission – it only becomes an option if the patient is not objecting to the admission. If she is, then informal admission cannot be used.

[10] One of the guiding principles of the MCA 2005 – see section 1(2).

[11] This phrase comes directly from section 2 of the MCA – if you can remember this, please use the exact wording.

[12] Of course, if Annie is sectioned instead, then the legal safeguards provided under the Mental Health Act make this compliant with Article 5.

[13] Again, when answering problem questions it is important not to forget that you need to apply the law to the facts you are given.

Make your answer stand out

- Adopt a structure such as the one suggested here. You are asked to consider the situation and discuss – this is pointing you in the direction of identifying the legal options and making a comparison.
- Discuss whether section 2 or section 3 of the Mental Health Act would be most appropriate in the circumstances of this case. Don't forget this is a problem question and you need to apply the law to the facts you have been provided with.
- When discussing informal admission, point out that this is the case for every admission to hospital for a physical health problem; the Mental Health Act is an exception to the usual rules in medical law.
- Consider the implications of Annie being deprived of her liberty in hospital – and refer to Article 5 ECHR.

! Don't be tempted to . . .

- Just launch into an explanation of how people can come into a psychiatric hospital. By thinking about this before you put pen to paper, you can recognise for yourself that there are two routes, and by setting this out at the start it shows the examiner that you know what you are talking about here. This also helps you to create a structure.
- Forget that 'informal admission' doesn't mean that there are no rules. There still needs to be legal authority for an informal admission, whether this comes from a capable patient's consent, or by the appropriate application of the Mental Capacity Act.
- Spend the majority of time discussing the Mental Health Act, as on these facts, Informal admission could equally apply. Remember that Annie has been accepting of treatment at home for many years, but do bear in mind that she might not be so happy to accept the need to go into hospital.

? Question 6

Simon Andrews (d.o.b. 09.05.1971) was detained under section 2 of the Mental Health Act 1983 on 4 January. He was then placed under section 3 of the Act on 29 January. It is now 3 March. Simon would like to have his section discharged, as he does not accept that he is mentally unwell, and does not think that he needs to be kept in a psychiatric hospital. He thinks that it 'must be contrary to human rights law to lock me up when there is nothing wrong with me'. Simon's solicitors have already confirmed to him that his section itself was correctly applied. His Responsible Clinician, Dr Yates, is opposed to Simon's request as he believes that Simon is suffering from a delusional disorder. Although Dr Yates accepts that Simon's symptoms have now improved following treatment with antipsychotic tablets, he is concerned that Simon will leave hospital and stop taking his prescribed medication should the section be discharged. Simon's Nearest Relative is his mother Betty. She and the rest of Simon's family all agree with Dr Yates's viewpoint.

Explain how Simon can seek to have the section discharged, and the relevant law that will be applied to the decision to discharge him.

Answer plan

- Focus on Simon's rights of challenge to a lawful detention – he has the right to apply to the Tribunal and also the Hospital Managers.
- Concentrate on the Tribunal; setting out that this is the body which is compliant with Article 5(4).
- Set out Simon's right to appeal to the Tribunal; where does this derive from? How often can he appeal?
- Consider and discuss the legal grounds for mandatory discharge under section 72(1)(b). Relevant issues for discussion are: is there a mental disorder? If there is a mental disorder, is it of a nature or degree to justify his continued liability to detention? What risks does he present to himself and others? Is appropriate treatment available?
- Also explain that the Hospital Managers can exercise a power of discharge; set out how they will approach an appeal by a patient.

Diagram plan

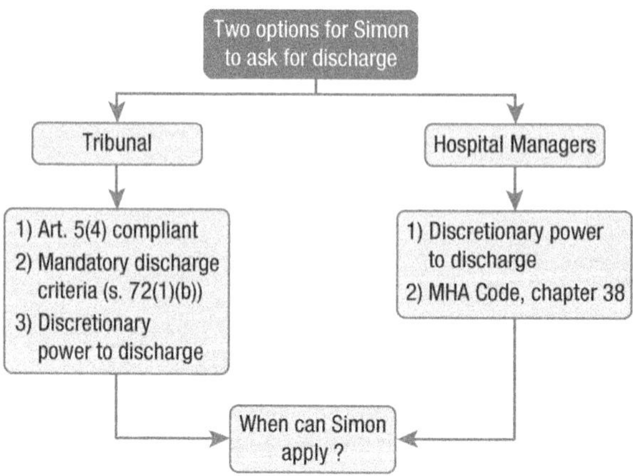

A printable version of this diagram plan is available from **www.pearsoned.co.uk/lawexpressqa**

Answer

Simon is currently detained under section 3 of the Mental Health Act 1983 (MHA) and objects to this; he would like the section to be discharged. There are a variety of ways in which that can happen, but both his Responsible Clinician and his Nearest Relative (who each have a power to effect his discharge under section 23[1]) think that he needs to remain under section currently. Simon himself can challenge his detention under section 3 in two ways, by appealing to the Mental Health Tribunal and the Hospital Managers.[2] Both of these bodies have the power to discharge Simon, even if Dr Yates and Simon's family want the section to remain in place.

Under section 72 of the MHA,[3] the Tribunal have a discretionary power to discharge Simon's detention (they 'may' do so in any circumstances (see section 72(1)) although this is rarely exercised in practice) and they are also mandatorily required to discharge Simon if certain criteria are met. The Tribunal therefore provides the domestic law mechanism ensuring compliance with Article 5(4) of the European Convention on Human Rights – that persons of 'unsound mind' deprived of their liberty by being sectioned under the MHA can 'take proceedings' to a 'court' which can 'speedily' decide on the lawfulness of a section and order release.[4]

Under section 66 of the MHA, Simon has the right to apply to the Tribunal once and at any time during his initial period of detention under section 3 (from 29 January to 28 July). The Tribunal must discharge Simon if the criteria set out in section 72(1)(b) are met:[5]

1. Is Simon suffering from a mental disorder of a nature or degree which makes it appropriate for him to be liable to be detained in a hospital for medical treatment?

Simon's own view is that there is 'nothing wrong with him'; Dr Yates thinks he has a delusional disorder. Simon might not have insight into the fact that he is unwell, but the Tribunal would need to consider whether he is mentally disordered at all by considering the evidence. Even if the Tribunal are satisfied that Simon does have a mental disorder, they must still discharge him if they are not satisfied that it is of a nature or degree to make medical treatment in hospital appropriate. In the case of ***R* v *MHRT for South Thames Region, ex parte***

[1] Although the question is asking you to concentrate on Simon's options to challenge the section, this is a short and easy way to demonstrate to the examiner that you know there are other routes to discharge, and where these come from. Showing off is OK as long as you don't get distracted and ignore the question.

[2] By giving the (very short) answer to this question in your opening paragraph it reassures the examiner at the start that you are headed in the right direction.

[3] Use acronyms if you can as they will save time, but always make sure that you have explained them first.

[4] This summary is a comfortable and well-explained 'mapping' of the language of the European Convention onto the domestic law, with the quoted extracts demonstrating that you know the source material and can apply it. This is much more impressive than simply quoting Article 5(4).

[5] This is the major part of the question, dealing with the specific criteria for mandatory discharge and how these might apply to Simon. If you can remember the specific subsection setting out the criteria, please include this.

Smith [1998] EWHC 832 (Admin), the court held that this test was 'disjunctive' and that the Tribunal were not obliged to discharge a patient whose symptoms (the 'degree' of the illness) had disappeared if the 'nature' was still present.[6] Given the fact that Simon no longer has symptoms they may be satisfied that the *degree* of his mental disorder no longer makes it appropriate for him to receive treatment, but if they accept Dr Yates's view that he might stop medication if released from the MHA's legal powers to make him accept this,[7] then the Tribunal may not be satisfied that the *nature* of his mental disorder requires his discharge.

[6] The difference between 'nature' and 'degree' was discussed in the *ex parte Smith* case and is now repeated in paragraph 4.3 of the MHA Code of Practice.

[7] This is an important point, recognising that while Simon is detained under section 3 he can be forced to take medication even if he does not want this (under section 63) and this may be why the nature of his illness makes it appropriate for him to remain sectioned, even if his symptoms have disappeared. This element of the Act can be criticised for allowing for 'preventative' detention.

2. Is it necessary in the interests of Simon's health or safety or for the protection of others that he should receive such treatment?

Dr Yates is worried that Simon will stop his medication if the section is lifted. Under this subsection, the Tribunal will have to consider if this is likely, and what risks Simon would present to himself or others if he didn't have his medication.

3. Is appropriate medical treatment available for Simon?

The Tribunal have to discharge if not satisfied of this, but given the very wide definition of what is medical treatment found in section 145(1) and (4) of the MHA, and the MHA Code's explanation that as long as there is some element of appropriate treatment for Simon available in hospital (not necessarily *the* most appropriate treatment), this is not likely to lead to Simon's discharge.

Whenever they meet, the Tribunal will consider whether the grounds for discharge are set out at that date – they will not be considering whether the original section was justified.

Aside from an appeal to the Tribunal, Simon also has the right to request that the Hospital Managers discharge his section. They have the power under section 23 to discharge the section, and the MHA Code of Practice[8] sets out that they should consider holding a hearing when the patient requests this. They are not, however, required to discharge – although the Code (at paras. 38.15 and 38.17) suggests that they should do so if a Tribunal would have to do so under section 72(1).

[8] If you have the space, you could make specific reference to chapter 38 of the Code, which is the relevant part. Remember that the House of Lords in the *Munjaz* case [2005] UKHL 58 stated that the Code shall be followed unless there are 'cogent reasons' not to do so.

Make your answer stand out

- When discussing the section 72 discharge criteria of whether Simon has a 'mental disorder', explain that the European Court of Human Rights case of *Winterwerp* v *Netherlands* (1979) 2 EHRR 387 states that objective criteria of 'unsound mind' is required for a lawful deprivation of liberty.
- Consider that the implication of *R* v *MHRT for South Thames Region, ex parte Smith* is that the Tribunal do not have to discharge even if the degree of the mental disorder no longer justifies detention. Explain commentators' concerns as to this – see for example: Bartlett, P. and Sandland, R. (2013) *Mental Health Law: Policy and Practice* (4th edn). Oxford: Oxford University Press, pp. 543–4.
- Remember that the Tribunal also has a discretionary power to discharge a section under section 72(1); however, this is exercised very infrequently.
- Set out the differences between the Tribunal and the Hospital Managers; the Tribunal is a 'court' (see Article 5(4)), its panel of three includes a judge and a psychiatrist, they are required to discharge in certain circumstances, they can discharge on a majority 2:1 decision. In contrast, the Hospital Managers have to vote unanimously for discharge, they can be made up of three 'lay' people, they are never compelled to discharge.

! Don't be tempted to . . .

- Stray into discussion of the powers of the Responsible Clinician and the Nearest Relative to discharge Simon's section – you are specifically told they don't support this.
- For the same reason, don't get involved with any discussion of how a Nearest Relative is allocated to a detained patient and the potential safeguards of this role – this may be an interesting area of law, but entirely irrelevant to this question.
- Forget about the Hospital Managers' power of discharge – this is also available to Simon.
- Discuss claims of habeas corpus or judicial review – while these may be options to challenge an unlawful detention, you are told that the original section was legally obtained.

www.pearsoned.co.uk/lawexpressqa

Go online to access more revision support including additional essay and problem questions with diagram plans, You be the marker questions, and download all diagrams from the book.

8 Reproduction and the law

How this topic make come up in exams

This is a diverse area: medical law mixes with family law, ethics with science. Generally questions fall into two parts: first, essay questions examining the regulation of fertility treatment – here a detailed knowledge of legislation is essential; the second mainstay is surrogacy. Problem or essay questions will invariably focus on the applicability of the status provisions, the enforceability of the surrogacy agreement and the many ethical issues that this area of law generates. In addition we lest not forget the Human Rights Act 1998 – the right to a family life adds a further layer to what is already a complex topic.

Before you begin

It's a good idea to consider the following key themes of reproduction and the law before tackling a question on this topic.

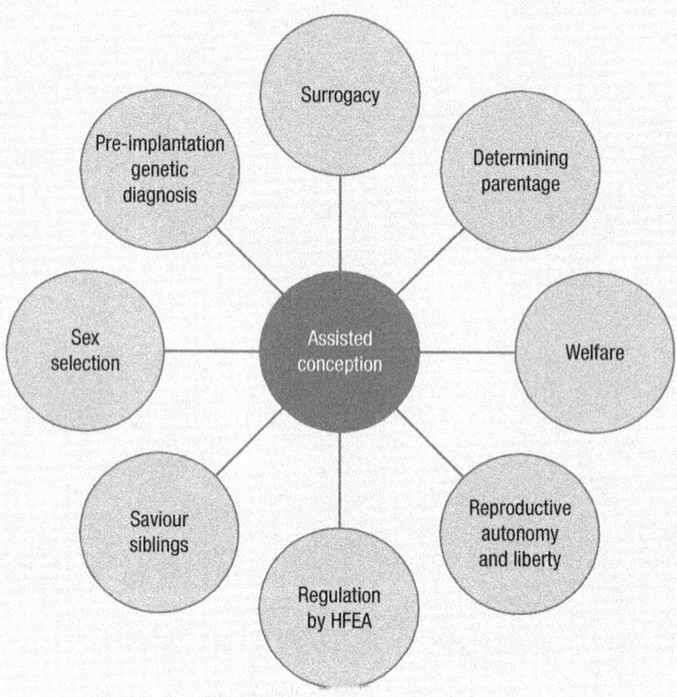

A printable version of this diagram is available from **www.pearsoned.co.uk/lawexpressqa**

Question 1

The welfare provision set out in section 13(5) of the Human Fertilisation and Embryology Act 1990 is an unacceptable barrier to fertility treatment services.

Critically consider the above statement.

Answer plan

- Explain what the welfare provision is.
- Confirm how welfare is assessed and who conducts the assessment.
- Discuss the relevance of reproductive autonomy and reproductive liberty.
- Analyse the impact of the Human Rights Act 1998, in particular:
  - Article 8;
  - Article 12.
- Consider the impact on the prospective child.

Diagram plan

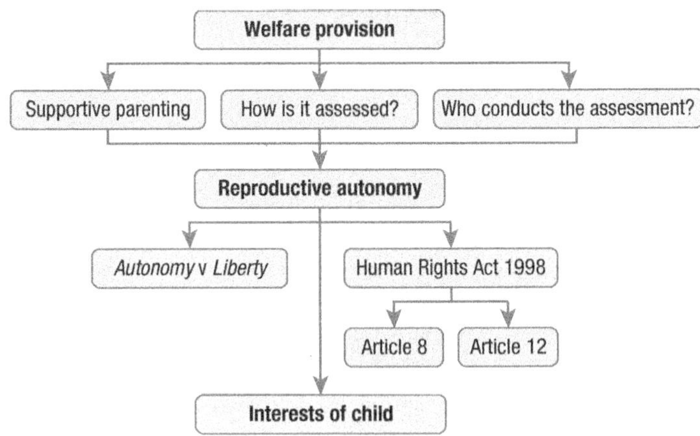

A printable version of this diagram plan is available from **www.pearsoned.co.uk/lawexpressqa**

Answer

This discussion will analyse whether the welfare provision contained in section 13(5) of the Human Fertilisation and Embryology Act 1990 (HFE Act 1990) is in fact a barrier to treatment and, if so, whether it is an acceptable one.[1] It is important to explain the nature and background of the welfare provision.

The welfare provision was amended by the HFE Act 2008. Section 13(5) now provides that a woman will not be able to obtain fertility treatment 'unless account has been taken of the welfare of any child' who would be born 'including the need of that child for supportive parenting'.[2] The reference to 'supportive parenting' is new; the HFE Act 1990 originally made reference to the need to take into account 'the need of that child for a father'. In one respect perhaps the current welfare provision is less of a barrier than the original version. For instance, a lesbian couple can satisfy the 'supportive parenting' condition more easily than the requirement to consider the child's 'need for a father'. The 'supportive parenting' requirement may remain a barrier for single women.

'Welfare' is not defined in the HFE Act 1990. We are familiar with the welfare of the child being a key issue in the family courts; but how is welfare to be approached when a child has not yet been conceived? We need to explore the factors used when determining welfare in relation to access to fertility treatment to determine whether they are a barrier to treatment.[3]

The Human Fertilisation and Embryology Authority (HFEA) must provide guidance regarding the welfare requirement (s. 25 HFE Act 1990). This guidance is set out in the HFEA's Code of Practice (8th edn).[4] The Code states that the treatment centre must conduct an assessment to decide whether 'there is a risk of significant harm or neglect to any child' (para. 8.3). Paragraph 8.10 lists factors to consider including 'previous convictions relating to harming children' and 'violence or serious discord in the family environment'. In reality, most people seeking treatment would not experience difficulty in 'passing' this assessment especially as a presumption exists that prospective parents will be supportive parents (para. 8.11). It is argued the welfare provision is a form of risk assessment rather than a serious consideration of whether someone would be a 'good' parent (if it is even possible to predict this in advance).

Even if we accept that some form of welfare assessment is justifiable, concerns exist about how this is implemented.[5] Clinicians have

[1] This breaks down the reference to 'unacceptable barrier' in the question and indicates the intended structure.

[2] Identify the key elements of the welfare provision. Avoid the temptation to launch straight into your analysis without identifying what the provision actually states.

[3] Show an intention to dissect the terms/ wording used in the question, i.e. do not uncritically accept the provision is a barrier to treatment.

[4] Draw upon a range of material, rather than focusing on the Act alone. The Code of Practice sets out key material too.

[5] Look at the range of issues which arise in relation to the welfare provision, i.e. the issue of who conducts the assessment is also relevant when considering its legitimacy.

[6] The Warnock Report DHSS, (1984) sets out key relevant background information regarding the regulation of assisted conception. It's helpful to draw upon key relevant points made in the report.

the responsibility to conduct the welfare assessment. The Warnock Report (DHSS, 1984) acknowledged that the issue of determining eligibility for treatment was difficult and involved a 'heavy burden of responsibility' on the consultant who would have to make 'social judgements that go beyond the purely medical'.[6] It is questioned whether doctors should conduct this assessment as this is not their field of expertise and could conflict with the duty owed to their patients.

[7] It is important to consider the competing arguments that can be made in this area.

Although the welfare provision may not be a difficult hurdle for prospective parents, it is still a 'test' that has to be 'passed' and is a potential barrier. Is this acceptable? It is argued it is discriminatory as it operates only in relation to those who struggle to conceive. A counterargument to advocate the existence of the welfare provision is based on the key difference between fertile and infertile individuals.[7] In reality the state cannot stop fertile individuals conceiving, but for infertile couples the state is in a position to consider the welfare of the child and withhold access to treatment. The crucial difference is that positive assistance from the state is sought.

[8] Reproductive autonomy and reproductive liberty are key themes so these should be carefully introduced and explained.

[9] This helps to demonstrate strong focus on the angle of the question.

The notion of reproductive autonomy is key. Herring (2012) notes a distinction can be drawn between reproductive liberty and reproductive autonomy[8] (see Herring, J. (2012) *Medical Law and Ethics*. (4th edn). Oxford: Oxford University Press). Reproductive liberty represents the notion that reproductive choices are a private matter. Herring suggests this is 'a negative concept' which prevents state interference, whereas reproductive autonomy extends further, resulting in 'a positive obligation' on the state to treat infertile individuals. Applying the negative concept of reproductive liberty to the welfare principle it can be argued that the state should not use section 13(5) to interfere with the decision reached by prospective parents.[9] Jackson (2002) identifies the need to protect 'decisional privacy' and advocates the abandonment of the welfare principle (see Jackson, E. (2002) Conception and the irrelevance of the welfare principle. *Modern Law Review*, 65:176–203). She argues that even if there is no right to have a child, 'a right to be free from external constraints upon one's decision-making process' should exist and the welfare principle may be 'an interference with infertile people's *negative* liberty'.

[10] This links well from the previous paragraph. Human Rights Act 1998 coverage follows on well from coverage of reproductive autonomy, etc.

Is the Human Rights Act 1998 capable of protecting any rights which do exist?[10] Article 8 'the right to respect for private and family life' and Article 12 'the right to marry and found a family' seem to be relevant. Alghrani and Harris (2006) suggest that although Article 12 does not establish an unqualified right, it does mean some 'impediments' are 'illegitimate' and welfare screening is a 'clear violation of reproductive liberty' (see Alghrani, A. and Harris, J. (2006) Reproductive liberty: should the foundation of families be regulated? *Child and Family Law Quarterly*, 18(2): 191). The impact of Article 8 was considered in ***Dickson* v *UK*** (App. No. 44362/04) (2007) following the refusal to provide a prisoner serving a life sentence access to artificial insemination facilities. Although this case did not deal with section 13(5) it showed that although the state had a positive obligation to protect children this did not mean the prospective parents should necessarily be stopped from attempting to conceive in this instance.[11] A fair balance between the competing interests was needed.

[11] Although not on the point of section 13(5), this case does help to support the argument that Article 8 may be relevant in this area.

When evaluating whether the welfare principle is an unacceptable barrier, the temptation is to focus on the prospective parents' interests, however an interesting issue to assess is how the welfare provision benefits the prospective child?[12] A negative welfare assessment would mean the 'potential child' is never born. As a foetus has no independent rights which are capable of protection (***Paton* v *UK*** (1980) 3 EHRR 408), it is difficult to formulate an argument that the rights of a 'potential foetus' have been violated. The suggestion that a child would have been better off if they had never been born seems inconsistent with the law in areas such as wrongful life (***McKay* v *Essex Area Health Authority*** [1982] QB 1166).[13] Gurnham and Miola (2012) argue it seems settled that the courts will not 'balance the interests in existence with those in non-existence' (see Gurnham, D. and Miola, J. (2012) Reproduction, rights, and the welfare interests of children: the times they aren't a-changin. *KLJ*, 23: 29–35).

[12] Try to develop arguments from different angles.

[13] Where possible make reference to your knowledge in other areas to help support your points.

If the welfare provision is a potential barrier to treatment, this could be an infringement of prospective parents' reproductive liberty. There is little consensus about the nature and extent of parental 'rights' or the role the state should play regarding welfare of a 'potential' child.

Make your answer stand out

- Break down the issues in the question. You need to address the issue of whether the welfare provision is in fact a barrier to treatment (don't uncritically accept it is) as well as considering whether it is 'unacceptable'.
- Develop critical coverage of issues relating to reproductive autonomy and reproductive liberty. There is rich academic debate in this area to help develop your analysis. Consider for instance the conflicting views of: Jackson, E. (2002) Conception and the irrelevance of the welfare principle. *Modern Law Review*, 65: 176–203; and Laing, J.A. and Oderberg, D.S. (2005) Artifical reproduction, the 'welfare principle', and the common good. *Medical Law Review*, 13(3): 328–56.
- Discuss the range of issues posed by the question, for instance avoid the temptation to only consider the prospective parents' 'rights'; note also the impact on the 'prospective' child.

! Don't be tempted to . . .

- Avoid approaching reproductive autonomy and reproductive liberty too broadly. These are pervasive themes which underpin the law in relation to assisted conception. Ensure you apply your coverage to the 'welfare provision' angle of the question and discuss how the welfare assessment may interfere with any rights which do exist.
- Consider only one side of the argument. For instance, even if a strong argument can be advanced that the provision potentially interferes with reproductive liberty, also consider the view advanced that the state should have an interest in the welfare of 'potential' children (as suggested by Laing and Oderberg (2005) for instance).
- Avoid making broad comments about the potential impact of the Human Rights Act 1998. In the absence of case law on the specific issue of the application of section 13(5), make reference to relevant related case law where the welfare of the child was an issue addressed, such as *Dickson* v *UK*.

? Question 2

Annie and Bella wish to have a child. They decide to seek treatment at a licensed clinic.

Annie is worried that the clinic may refuse to treat her as she has several previous convictions for theft when she was a teenager. If they are able to proceed with treatment, their friend Charlie has agreed to donate sperm. Annie and Bella would both like to play a part in creating a child. They would like an embryo to be created using Bella's egg and

Charlie's sperm and for this to then be implanted in Annie's womb. Annie is of the view that Charlie should have a role to play in the future child's upbringing. Bella strongly disagrees and thinks Charlie's identity should remain a secret. Bella worries he could be considered 'the father' if he is involved, whereas she does not want him to have any 'status'.

Consider the legal issues which would arise in relation to the above scenario.

Answer plan

- ➜ Consider how the welfare provision would apply.
- ➜ Identify who would be the child's mother.
- ➜ Identify who would be the second parent (considering the alternative approaches).
- ➜ Discuss whether the sperm donor has any rights.

Diagram plan

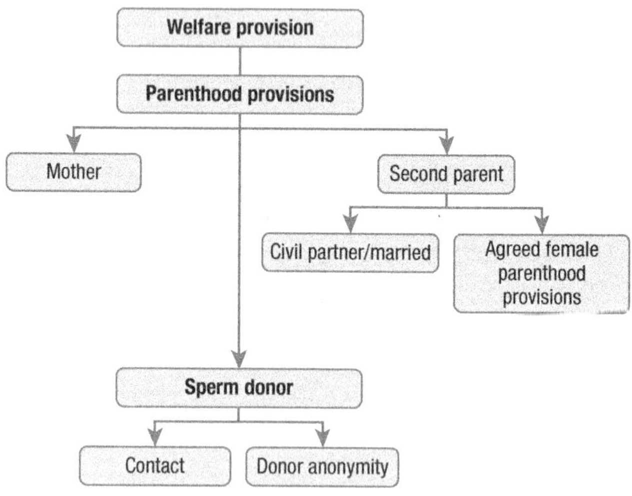

A printable version of this diagram plan is available from **www.pearsoned.co.uk/lawexpressqa**

Answer

Patients must satisfy the 'welfare provision' set out in the Human Fertilisation and Embryology Act 1990 (HFE Act 1990). Section 13(5) now provides that a woman will not be able to obtain fertility treatment 'unless account has been taken of the welfare of any child' who would be born 'including the need for supportive parenting'. The original version of section 13(5) referred to the need to take into account 'the need of that child for a father'.[1] The current reference to 'supportive parenting' will benefit Annie and Bella.

[1] This would demonstrate you understand the history of the welfare provision and how it is now easier for lesbian couples to satisfy the requirements.

Annie worries her previous convictions for theft may result in her treatment request being refused. The HFE Act 1990 does not define welfare, however the Code of Practice produced by the Human Fertilisation and Embryology Authority (HFEA) indicates how the issue of welfare is approached. Annie can be reassured that the Code (at para. 8.11) sets out a presumption that prospective parents will be supportive parents unless there is concern that the child 'may be at risk of significant harm or neglect'.[2] Factors to be taken into account are listed at paragraph 8.10 and include 'previous convictions relating to harming children'. Given Annie's earlier convictions relate to theft when she was a teenager it appears that the welfare requirement will still be met (unless there are other 'risk' factors present of which we are unaware).[3]

[2] When applying the welfare provision try to refer to the guidance set out in the HFEA Code of Practice when discussing how clinics may approach the issue.

[3] It is important to remember to apply the relevant parts of the Code to the particular issues the scenario raises, i.e. concerns about previous convictions.

The parenthood provisions set out in the HFE Act 2008 determine what the position will be regarding legal parentage. The parenthood provisions under the HFE Act 2008 apply where a woman receives treatment using donated gametes.[4] They apply here as an embryo will be created using Bella's egg and sperm donated by Charlie.

[4] Some introduction to the HFE Act 2008 provisions is helpful to show you understand the circumstances where they apply.

It is intended the embryo will be implanted in Annie's womb. Bella will have the genetic tie to the child, whereas Annie will carry and deliver the child. Section 33 provides that a woman who is carrying or has carried a child is to be treated as the mother. So although it is Bella who will have the genetic tie,[5] she will not be considered to be the mother. Nor is Bella automatically entitled to be considered the second legal parent because of the genetic tie as section 47 provides that a woman cannot be deemed to be the child's other legal parent 'merely because of egg donation'.

[5] This explores the effect of section 33 in this scenario.

We need to explore whether Bella could be treated as the second legal parent. We are informed that Annie and Bella are a 'couple' but we need further detail about the status of their relationship.[6] If Annie and Bella are in a civil partnership or married then section 42 applies. This provides that where one party to the civil partnership or marriage

[6] It is important not to make assumptions about the relationship where the scenario is silent on the point. You would need to consider the different possibilities.

receives an embryo or is artificially inseminated, the other party will be treated as parent to the child 'unless it is shown that she did not consent' to the embryo transfer or artificial insemination. Given that Bella will provide the egg it appears that she fully supports the procedure and would automatically be considered the second parent if they are both in a civil partnership or married.[7]

[7] This would show you have carefully considered the 'consent' aspect of section 42.

If they are not in a civil partnership or married, Bella can only be the second parent if the 'agreed female parenthood conditions' are met (s. 43). The conditions are set out under section 44 and apply where the treatment is provided under licence.[8] Given the embryo has been created *ex utero* and implanted this is treatment which would be conducted under licence so the conditions apply. Bella would have to provide a written, signed notice stating that she consents to being treated as parent of the child which results from the treatment. Annie must also provide a notice stating that she agrees to Bella being treated as a parent. Consent must be in place at the time of the embryo transfer. Additionally, Annie and Bella must not be in the prohibited degrees of relationship to each other (s. 58). We will presume they are not.

[8] This is an important point to be aware of. If, for example, the child had been conceived using donor sperm via an 'informal' method, this would not be treatment under licence and the agreed female parenthood provisions would not be applicable.

If a civil partnership or marriage exists or if the agreed female parenthood conditions are met then section 45 states 'no man is to be treated as the father of the child'. Additionally, section 41(1) states that where sperm has been provided with the necessary consent of the donor for the purposes of treatment services the donor is not to be treated as the father. If the consent requirements in Paragraph 5 of Schedule 3 of the 1990 Act are complied with, Charlie could not then be the legal father.[9] Even if Annie and Bella are not married or in a civil partnership and they do not comply with the agreed female parenthood conditions, Charlie would still not be the father.[10]

[9] Remember to explore the potential parental status of all the parties in the scenario.

[10] This would reinforce your understanding of the effect of section 41.

This does not necessarily mean he would have no role to play. If Annie and Bella decide to involve Charlie and at a later date relations become strained, Charlie could commence legal action to seek contact (and possibly residence). In ***Re G; Re Z (Children: Sperm Donors: Leave to Apply for Children Act Orders)*** [2013] EWHC 134 (Fam) the donors (who were known to the mothers) had no legal parental status and required leave of the court to apply for contact.[11] As they had a connection with the children, leave to apply for contact

[11] Always try to make reference to case law to support your point. Examiners like to see this.

was granted. The court considered the applicants' rights under Article 8 ('the right to respect for private and family life') and held that the sufficient connection with the children entitled the applicants to bring a contact application. If Charlie has a relationship with the child it is possible the court would allow him to make a contact application if relations later broke down between the parties.[12]

[12] Try to demonstrate an appreciation of wider, ancillary issues and not restrict your coverage purely to issues regarding legal parentage.

If Annie and Bella decide Charlie will have no role to play, this does not mean that Charlie's identity can remain 'secret'. As the child would have two female parents it will be obvious that another party was involved. There is no legal requirement that a child should be notified in the future they were conceived using donor sperm, but in these circumstances the child would become aware. Under section 31ZA HFE Act 1990 and the HFEA (Disclosure of Donor Information) Regulations 2004 (SI 2004/1511) a child can access non-identifying information from the age of 16, but must be 18 to access identifying information such as the donor's name, date of birth and last-known postal address.

Although the HFE Act 2008 sets out firm provisions for legal parentage, this does not mean necessarily that Charlie would have no role to play in the child's future.[13]

[13] Attempt to bring together the different aspects of your coverage.

Make your answer stand out

- Be able to refer to the various provisions regarding legal parentage and break down the requirements set out in the sections.
- Consider the range of alternative approaches that may be taken in a scenario. For instance, where the scenario refers to the parties as being a 'couple', consider how the situation would differ depending upon whether they were married or in a civil partnership or not.
- In an assisted conception problem question don't focus on legal parentage alone (unless the question instructs you to do so). Identify the range of issues a scenario may raise such as the impact of the welfare requirement and the provisions regarding donor anonymity.
- Demonstrate your understanding of wider issues. Refer to the conflict between the firm HFEA 2008 provisions regarding legal parentage and the more responsive, flexible approach taken in the family law context when determining who should have a role to play in the child's life.

! Don't be tempted to . . .

- Focus only on the parties you think will be legal parents. So, for instance, also explore issues that arise in relation to sperm donors, such as donor anonymity.
- Go astray and begin to critically discuss whether it is a good thing that the HFEA 2008 separates genetic and social parenthood. As this is a problem question, you need to focus on applying the provisions and highlighting the problem areas that arise when doing so.

Question 3

Three decades on since the enacting of the Surrogacy Arrangements Act 1985, UK law is still unable to deal satisfactorily with the complexities raised by a surrogacy agreement. Discuss.

Answer plan

→ Define both full and partial surrogacy.

→ Introduce and critically analyse the Surrogacy Arrangements Act 1985.

→ Focus on the enforceability of agreements, commercialism and status provisions.

→ Introduce the Human Fertilisation and Embryology Acts 1990 and 2008 – what effect have they had?

→ Conclude analysis regarding whether the law is satisfactory.

Diagram plan

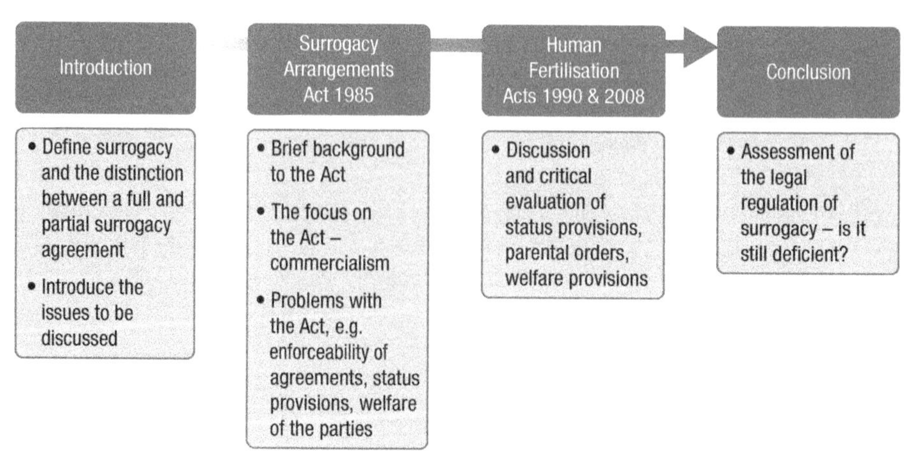

A printable version of this diagram plan is available from **www.pearsoned.co.uk/lawexpressqa**

Answer

Surrogacy is not a new phenomenon, what is, is the science behind it. Surrogacy may consist of a partial surrogacy agreement where the surrogate mother has a genetic link to the child or a full surrogacy agreement where both gametes are provided by the commissioning couple or a donor.[1] To this new science the law has struggled to reply, lagging behind in its attempts to regulate and respond to public opinion. Payments, parental status, the welfare of the child and enforceability of agreements all require legal control, but what form that should take has generated some debate.[2]

[1] At the outset demonstrate that you understand the different forms surrogacy may take.

[2] Give some indication in the introduction of what areas you intend to discuss; it will also keep you on track.

The Surrogacy Arrangements Act 1985 (the SAA) was targeted at the commercial aspect of surrogacy.[3] Coming six months after the ***Baby Cotton*** case (***Re C (A Minor) (Wardship: Surrogacy)*** [1985] FLR 846), the SAA outlawed surrogacy as a commercial business. Advertising, negotiation and any dealing on a commercial basis were unlawful though only commercial organisations could be prosecuted under section 2; the parties to the surrogacy agreement were spared the stigma of a criminal conviction (ss. 2 and 3). The SAA made payments unlawful with the exception of payments in lieu of expenses to the surrogate mother. If the agreement was made by an individual or a non-commercial body and there was no payment, the law left well alone.

[3] As the question is asking you to assess whether the law is better equipped to deal with the complexities of surrogacy since the enactment of the Surrogacy Arrangements Act 1985, the essay should begin with the SAA and chart the development of the law thereafter.

The enactment of the Human Fertilisation and Embryology Act 1990 (the HFE Act 1990) introduced section 1B into the SAA which made no surrogacy agreement enforceable. Consequently the commissioning parents cannot sue the surrogate mother if she fails to hand over the baby, nor can she sue for non-payment or refusing to take the baby after birth. It is acknowledged that the law was merely reflecting what is an everyday reality, a surrogate mother cannot be forced to hand over a child. In the United States, however, (see ***Johnson* v *Calvert*** (1860) 851 P 2D 776) a much more proactive approach has been taken where more emphasis is placed on the parties' *intention* when the agreement was made. In Israel, meanwhile, only a change of circumstances will allow a surrogate mother not to honour the agreement.[4]

[4] It is not always necessary but on occasions referring to the approach taken in other jurisdictions adds an extra dimension to the argument.

Status provisions are addressed by the HFE Acts. Section 33 HFE Act 2008, following on from section 27 HFE Act 1990, states the mother of the child is the woman who gives birth. This may seem unfair when the surrogate has no genetic link to the child but it promotes legal certainty for the child. The definition of father is not as straightforward. If the surrogate is married her husband is the legal father unless he has objected, before the insemination, to the surrogacy agreement (s. 35 HFE Act 2008). Additionally, section 38(2) HFE Act 2008 provides at common law there is a presumption that he is the child's father, only to be rebutted by DNA evidence or proof that he did not consent. The majority of husbands of surrogates will have no desire to be the father of the surrogate child. The position is more complex where the surrogate is unmarried. Previously a surrogate's unmarried partner would be treated as the father if the couple were being 'treated together'[5] (s. 28 (3) HFE Act 1990; ***Re R (A Child)*** [2005] UKHL 33). Section 36 HFE Act 2008 now provides where an unmarried surrogate mother uses donor sperm then her male partner may be the father of the donor-conceived child if he satisfies the fatherhood conditions. This provision assists the partners of surrogates who wish to keep the child, but it does nothing to help the commissioning father if his sperm is used as the agreed fatherhood provisions apply only to men whose sperm was not used in the conception. The HFEA Code of Practice, however, provides for the recognition of one of the commissioning parents as a legal parent from birth at common law (if the surrogate is single).[6]

[5] Here by referring to the old law the essay can analyse whether the new provisions have 'moved things on' in addition to demonstrating the complexity of the parenthood provisions.

[6] The answer refers to the relevant statute but also to the HFEA Code of Practice which details recent changes, see for example para. 6.12 'Legal Parenthood: decision tree'.

The law can respond to changing public perceptions; section 42 of the 2008 HFE Act permits a woman who was in a civil partnership at the time of the insemination to be treated as the other parent unless, as for a married husband, she can demonstrate that she did not consent. Similarly, section 44 of the HFE Act 2008 will apply where the surrogate mother lives with a female partner.

A key problem with surrogacy was the ascription of parentage. Parental orders offer an alternative to adoption. Section 54 HFE Act 2008 widened the parameters of those who may apply to all couples. The section, however, is not straightforward; all parties must consent to the order. In ***Re D*** [2012] EWHC 2631 the Indian surrogate mother could not be traced after the birth of twins; Baker J, however, granted a parental order as he accepted that the commissioning parents had taken reasonable steps to trace her and this outcome was overwhelmingly in the child's best interests. Significantly, single parents are excluded from applying and this unquestionably does not sit happily with Articles 8 and 14 of the European Convention on Human Rights. Finally, the requirement that only payments for reasonable expenses are permitted has been repeatedly flouted, see ***Re C (A Child)***

(Parental Order: Surrogacy Arrangement) [2013] EWHC 2408 (Fam). In ***Re X & Y (Foreign Surrogacy)*** [2009] 1 FLR 733 Hedley J observed that although the law might intend to legislate against commercial surrogacy that was not compatible with the courts' role to consider the welfare of the child. Now that the SAA 1985 permits payments to non-profit organisations we must acknowledge the prohibition on commercial surrogacy is effectively redundant.[7]

[7] Parental orders are unique to surrogacy law; it is important you demonstrate an understanding of the provision and accompanying case law.

The law has addressed some of the difficulties with surrogacy and yet problems remain. The legislation provides no protection for the parties to a surrogacy agreement. Only when faced with difficulties concerning parental orders and multi-jurisdiction issues has the court considered the welfare of the child in a decidedly piecemeal fashion. The SAA is ineffectual; payments to surrogate mothers do happen and the courts will ratify them if the child's best interests are at stake. Margaret Brazier's review in 1998 concluded that prohibiting payments was the way forward, but as Freeman (1999) and the courts have acknowledged the welfare of the child will always take precedence (see Freeman, M. (1999) Does surrogacy have a future after brazier? *Medical Law Review*, 7: 1–20).[8]

[8] It is prudent to acknowledge that there have been previous ineffectual attempts to reform the law.

Status provisions are awkward at best. That the surrogate is deemed to be the child's mother while having no genetic link is unorthodox and fatherhood provisions are out-and-out odd. Of increasing concern are the complications caused by multi-jurisdictional agreements (see ***Re X v Y (Children: Foreign Surrogacy)*** [2008] EWHC 3030 (Fam)), which the courts appear to deal with on an ad hoc basis. The ban on seeking legal advice and the lack of regulation of the agreement provide no solutions to these problems. Surrogacy is here to stay but the SAA has outlived its purpose.[9]

[9] The conclusion refers to what the answer considers are the more important problems with surrogacy and refers again to the question.

Make your answer stand out

- A chronological approach serves best here, charting the development of the law.
- Knowledge of case law is essential. Legislation in this area has been enacted in response to case law and scientific developments. Additionally this is an area which repeatedly brings to light new problems; multi-jurisdictional agreements is one such example.
- Refer to academic opinion if it enhances the argument, e.g. Freeman, M. (1999) Does surrogacy have a future after Brazier? *Medical Law Review*, 7: 1–20.
- Arrive at some sort of conclusion; the question asks whether the law is lagging behind so give a view.

! Don't be tempted to . . .

- Simply list or describe the legislation; you must be selective here and discuss the provisions which illustrate the law's deficiencies.
- Stray into looking at the ethical arguments for and against surrogacy; this question focuses on the law only.

Question 4

Angela and her husband Bob are unable to have a child. Although Angela is able to conceive she cannot carry a child. Bob is infertile. Bob's sister, Carla, offers to carry a child for them. Carla's husband Dan is very unhappy about this and they separate when she says she will go ahead with the proposal. It is intended an embryo will be created using Angela's egg and donor sperm. The embryo will then be implanted into Carla's womb at a licensed clinic. It is planned the baby will live with Angela and Bob following the birth. Carla will be paid £15,000. Angela and Bob want to know what their legal position will be.

Discuss the legal issues in relation to this proposed surrogacy arrangement, particularly the issues which arise regarding legal parentage and the proposed payment.

Diagram plan

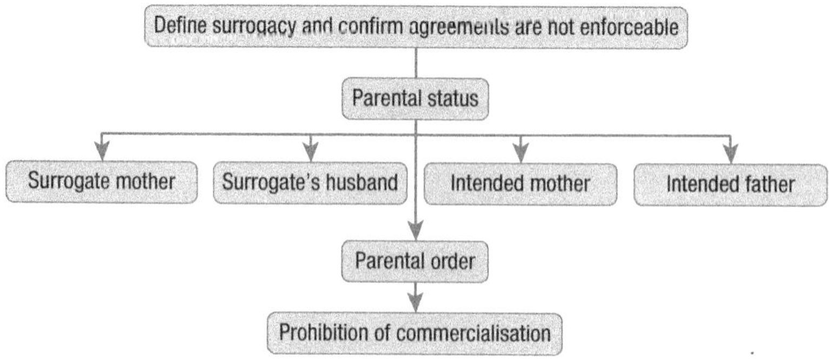

A printable version of this diagram plan is available from **www.pearsoned.co.uk/lawexpressqa**

Answer plan

- ➜ Define what surrogacy is and confirm the surrogacy arrangement is not enforceable.
- ➜ Discuss who would be the legal parents: the surrogate and her husband, or the intended parents?
- ➜ Identify and apply the requirements to obtain a parental order.
- ➜ Comment upon the impact of the prohibition of commercialisation of surrogacy.

Answer

The issues arising from this proposed surrogacy arrangement will be discussed. Surrogacy involves one woman carrying a child where she intends to hand the child over after birth.[1] Carla will carry a child, and then hand the child to the intended parents, Angela and Bob. Surrogacy arrangements are not enforceable (Surrogacy Arrangements Act 1985, section 1B).[2] At this stage there is no reason to suspect that either Carla would refuse to hand the child over or that Angela and Bob would refuse to pay the money.

[1] The examiner would expect you to introduce what is meant by surrogacy.

[2] This is a relevant issue as Angela and Bob seek advice regarding their legal position. Succinct coverage here will suffice. This would require further attention if there is a dispute (e.g. if it appears likely the surrogate mother will refuse to hand the child over).

The issues regarding parentage will be complicated.[3] We must consider the parenthood provisions contained in the Human Fertilisation and Embryology Act 2008 (HFE Act 2008) which apply to determine parentage where a woman is treated using donated gametes. Here an embryo will be created using Angela's egg and donor sperm. The Human Fertilisation and Embryology Authority (HFEA) Code of Practice (8th edn) is also relevant.

[3] As this is a complicated area, it is appropriate to devote a significant amount of your time to the issue of parental status in a surrogacy arrangement.

A woman who is carrying or has carried a child will be treated as the mother of the child (s. 33). Therefore, even though Carla will have no genetic tie to the child, she will be considered the legal mother and will acquire parental responsibility when the child is born. The fact that Angela's egg will be used is irrelevant when determining who is treated as mother, nor is Angela in a stronger position to be considered as the second parent as section 47 reminds us that a woman is not entitled to be the second parent 'merely because of egg donation'.

Who will be considered the second parent? Carla is married to Dan. The common law presumption of paternity in marriage is preserved by section 38(2). Clearly, this presumption could be rebutted with DNA evidence here. Also, section 35 provides that the husband of a woman will be considered the father of the child (where the embryo was not brought about with the sperm of her husband) unless he did not consent to the arrangement.[4] We are told Dan is unhappy about Carla's surrogacy decision. The relevant HFEA form[5] should be completed prior to the embryo transfer to signify that Dan does not consent (although completion of the form itself does not prove lack of consent). It must be shown 'as a question of fact' that Dan does not agree to the arrangement (HFEA Code of Practice, para. 6.6). There should be evidence of a lack of consent (e.g. his opposition to the arrangement) which means Dan will not be the father.

We need to consider whether Angela or Bob could be the second legal parent when the child is born instead. The HFEA amended their Code of Practice in October 2013 to recognise that *one* of the intended parents in a surrogacy arrangement *may* be able to acquire parental status[6] (see Box 6G of the Code). Where donor sperm has been used (as is the case here) the intended father can be the legal father if both the surrogate mother and the intended father provide the necessary consent. However, Bob could not be the legal father here. Carla and Bob are brother and sister and therefore 'within prohibited degrees of relationship in relation to each other' (s. 58). Bob could not be treated as the father of the child as Carla would be her legal mother (notwithstanding the fact neither Bob nor Carla will have a genetic tie to the child as donor sperm and Angela's egg will be used).[7]

It is possible for Angela to be the second legal parent. If Angela and Carla provide the necessary written consent prior to the embryo transfer, Angela will be the second parent when the child was born and would acquire parental responsibility when the birth was registered. The relevant HFEA consent forms[8] would need to be completed by Angela and Carla for this purpose.

However, this would not provide a long-term solution as Carla would still be the legal mother and Bob would have no parental status. A parental order would extinguish Carla's legal status and reassign legal parenthood to Angela and Bob. A court application will be required and the requirements under section 54 must be satisfied for a parental order to be made.[9] The gametes of at least one of the applicants must have been used to create the embryo (s. 54(1)); here Angela's egg will be used. The nature of the applicants'

[4] It is important to remember the surrogate mother's husband may not always be considered the child's father; there is a consent issue to consider.

[5] The relevant form is 'LC Stating spouse or civil partner lack of consent'.

[6] You should stress it would only be possible for *one* of the intended parents to be a legal parent on birth. The surrogate mother will be the legal mother on birth (s. 33). A child can only have two legal parents. The Code of Practice must be carefully considered to identify the circumstances where it will be possible for an intended parent to be a legal parent when the child is born (see Code of Practice, Box 6G).

[7] This would demonstrate good application of the provisions and explains the consequences.

[8] The relevant forms are 'SPP Consent to being the legal parent in surrogacy' and 'SWP Consent (as a surrogate) nominating an intended parent to be the legal parent'.

[9] Try to show a good understanding of the various requirements for a parental order. The examiner will appreciate section 54 is a very detailed section, but try to remember as many of the conditions as you can. Focus on the requirements which may pose a problem (here the payment issue is something to carefully consider).

relationship is also considered under section 54(2); as Angela and Bob are married they automatically satisfy this. Angela and Bob must make an application for a parental order within six months of the birth (s. 54(3)).[10] Both at the time of the application and when the order is made the child must reside with the applicants (s. 54(4)). It is intended the baby will live with Angela and Bob immediately following birth.

[10] Recent case law suggests the court may accept late applications (*Re X (A Child) (Surrogacy: Time Limit)* [2014] EWHC 3135) (Fam). As this scenario focuses on the advice needed before embryo transfer, this is not a key issue to focus on (although the point should be borne in mind in case there is a delay in making a court application following birth).

Under section 54(6) the court must be satisfied that the woman who carried the child and any other person who is parent of the child (but not one of the applicants) have 'freely, and with full understanding . . . agreed unconditionally' to the order. There is nothing to suggest at this stage consent would be withheld.[11] Consent cannot be given in the first six weeks following birth (s. 54(7)). Dan's consent will not be required as he will not be the legal father of the child when it is born. The court must also be satisfied that no money or other benefit (other than reasonable expenses) has been paid 'unless authorised by the court' (s. 54(8)). At this point we should explore the impact of the proposed £15,000 payment.[12] The commercialisation of surrogacy is prohibited under section 2 of the Surrogacy Arrangements Act 1985. No criminal offence is committed by Carla, Angela and Bob for paying or receiving the money. However, the payment could potentially result in the court refusing to make a parental order unless the court then authorises the payment. The court is unlikely to refuse to make a parental order if the child is settled with Angela and Bob as the court must consider the child's welfare.

[11] Although there is no suggestion that Carla would withdraw consent, you still need to cover the consent requirement as it is essential when a parental order is sought.

[12] It is appropriate to link together coverage of the prohibition of commercialisation of surrogacy and the approach the courts take when authorising payments in order to make a parental order.

The questions the court should address when deciding whether to authorise payments were set out in ***Re X and Y (Children: Foreign Surrogacy)*** [2009] 1 FLR 733. Was the sum disproportionate to reasonable expenses? Were the applicants acting in good faith and without moral taint, or were they attempting to defraud the authorities? The sum of £15,000 will be paid. Relatively large sums have been viewed as not disproportionate (for example, ***Re C (A Child) (Parental Order: Surrogacy Arrangement)*** [2013] EWHC 2408) (Fam) where a sum of US$51,200 was paid). There is no suggestion they are not acting in good faith.

If the child lives with Angela and Bob it is likely a parental order would be made in due course. Carla's status as mother would be extinguished and Angela and Bob would acquire parental status.[13]

[13] It is a good idea to summarise what you think the likely outcome could be.

Make your answer stand out

- Show sound understanding of the various possibilities in relation to parental status in a surrogacy arrangement. Although it will often be the case the surrogate mother's husband will be the father, section 35 does contain a consent requirement. If consent is in doubt you then need to consider who else could be the second parent. The HFEA Code of Practice (8th edn) provides a useful flow chart (at para. 6.12) regarding the different possibilities regarding parentage in a surrogacy arrangement which may help with your understanding and revision.
- Demonstrate an awareness of the conflict between the prohibition of commercialisation and the power of the court to retrospectively sanction payments where the court also has to consider the welfare of the child. As this is a problem question focus on how the courts would have to deal with this tension with reference to supporting authority.

! Don't be tempted to . . .

- Lapse into a general critique of the law relating to surrogacy; as this is a problem question careful application is required.
- There is a vast range of case law on the issue of parental orders, so you need to be selective in light of the time constraints you will face in an exam.

Question 5

It is still the position that the current law in England and Wales on reproductive services unnecessarily restricts individuals' reproductive choices.

With reference to pre-implantation genetic diagnosis (PGD) of an embryo critically analyse the above statement.

Answer plan

→ Briefly explain infertility and what is meant by assisted reproduction.

→ Explain what is reproductive autonomy – set out the general arguments for and against.

→ Consider the significance of the Human Rights Act Articles 8 and 12 – discuss case law.

→ Discuss the relevant provisions of the Human Fertilisation and Embryology Acts 1990 and 2008 with reference to reproductive freedom and PGD.

→ Conclude with reference to the question.

Diagram plan

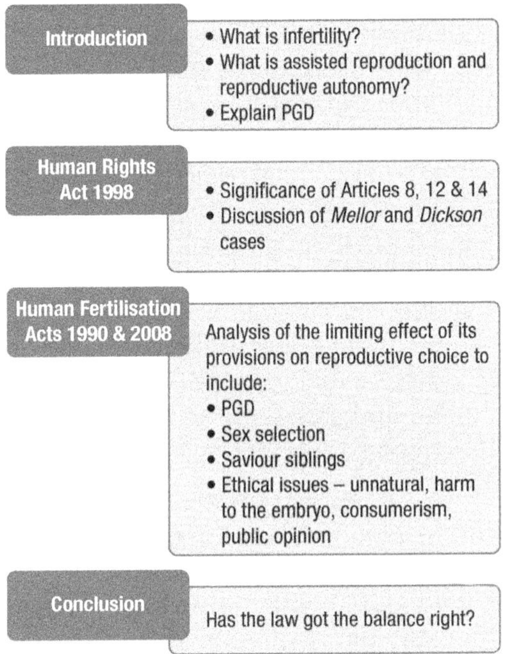

Introduction
• What is infertility?
• What is assisted reproduction and reproductive autonomy?
• Explain PGD
Human Rights Act 1998
• Significance of Articles 8, 12 & 14
• Discussion of Mellor and Dickson cases
Human Fertilisation Acts 1990 & 2008
Analysis of the limiting effect of its provisions on reproductive choice to include:
• PGD
• Sex selection
• Saviour siblings
• Ethical issues – unnatural, harm to the embryo, consumerism, public opinion
Conclusion
Has the law got the balance right?

A printable version of this diagram plan is available from **www.pearsoned.co.uk/lawexpressqa**

Answer

Pre-implantation diagnosis (PGD) allows an embryo to be selected on the basis that it carries a desirable or undesirable characteristic.[1] Usually PGD is used to establish if an embryo has an abnormality but more recently PGD allows for selection of embryos that are of a particular sex or are a good tissue match for an existing sibling. Unfettered reproductive autonomy would mean PGD would allow for embryo selection on any basis. However, PGD may be viewed as devaluing the embryo which is deserving of a limited moral status. This essay will examine if the law has struck the right balance between recognising reproductive rights and restricting these rights in favour of other competing interests.[2]

By accepting infertility as a treatable condition the state has implicitly accepted that infertility is an illness. What, however, is the extent of the state's duty to those seeking treatment? The right to procreate

[1] As always an essay should begin with defining the subject, in this question PGD.

[2] The introduction maps out the structure of the essay. This informs the examiner of what will be discussed and prompts you not to stray away from the issues in the question.

is recognised explicitly in Article 12 of the European Convention on Human Rights, additionally Article 14 provides for the right not to be discriminated against while Article 8 lays down the right to respect for family and private life. Read together, is this an expression of unfettered reproductive autonomy?[3] In ***R v Secretary of State for the Home Department, ex parte Mellor*** [2001] 2 FCR 153 the Court of Appeal held that Article 12 did not give a prisoner an absolute right to reproductive treatment and the state's restrictions were proportionate under Article 12. In contrast in ***Dickson* v *UK*** (Application No. 44362/04) the European Court of Human Rights held that prisoners retained their Human Rights on imprisonment and consequently the state must justify any interference with those rights; not providing treatment services because it would offend public opinion was not sufficient justification. Following ***Dickson*** we can conclude that there are reproductive rights but these rights are not absolute. How then should we interpret this with reference to PGD?[4]

[3] The answer refers to the question again reminding the examiner (and you) of the issues to be addressed. We cannot overemphasise the importance of consistently referring to the question throughout the essay.

[4] Before moving on to look at PGD in detail this paragraph discusses the concept of reproductive autonomy referred to in the question which should be incorporated throughout the essay.

PGD involves removing one or two cells from an embryo in order to test for genetic abnormalities, the affected embryos are disposed of or used for research purposes; the unaffected embryos will be used in fertility treatment. Schedule 2 of the Human Fertilisation and Embryology Act 1990 (the HFE Act 1990) lists the circumstances where PGD is permissible; generally PGD is permitted to prevent a child being born with a serious disability, illness or other medical condition.

Not every condition may be screened for, see the HFEA Code of Practice (HFEA COP). There is no general agreement on what amounts to a serious condition; the family's views on the seriousness of the condition are relevant (HFEA COP 10.4–6). Asch (2003) argues for a liberal approach; all information about each embryo should be given to the parents before selection (see Asch, A. (2003) Disability equality and prenatal testing: contradictory or compatible? *Florida State University Law Review*, 30: 315–342). This approach, however, would entitle parents to choose an embryo with a disability in preference to a 'healthy' embryo which the HFE Act 1990 now expressly prohibits, (s. 13(9)). It is suggested here that legal interference with reproductive autonomy can be justified; parents must be under a moral duty to try and prevent harm to their child. But it seems unlikely any consensus will be reached on what restrictions should be imposed on the availability of PGD.[5]

[5] Reference to academic commentary adds to the discussion and on this occasion it is linked to the statute itself.

PGD is permitted to avoid a sex-related serious physical or mental disability, illness or serious medical condition; but sex selection for social reasons is not, (HFE Act 1990 Sch. 2 Para. 1ZB; HFEA (2003) *Sex Selection: Options for Regulation*. London: HFEA). There are well-versed objections to sex selection: it is discriminatory; the child could suffer psychological problems; and there is a known demographic impact, in China for instance. Yet a woman may try and pre-determine the sex of her child using natural methods and abort her pregnancy if it is the 'wrong sex' if she satisfies a ground within the Abortion Act 1967.[6] Not being able to choose the sex of a child can cause acute distress, as seen in the case of the Mastertons, but does this outweigh the harm sex selection is said to cause? (see Herring, J. (2012) Medical Law and Ethics (4th edn). Oxford University Press, p. 393).[7]

[6] Here a useful comparison is made with the provisions of the Abortion Act 1967.

[7] The Mastertons' case is discussed in more detail in *Medical Law & Ethics* (4th ed) by Jonathon Herring. It illustrates that matters of sex selection on a social basis can give rise to complex social and moral issues.

PGD may be used to choose an embryo on the basis that it is a good tissue match for an existing child with the aim of using the child's tissue to treat a sick sibling, so called 'saviour sibling'.[8] The lawfulness of this procedure was unsuccessfully challenged in ***R (Quintavalle) v HFEA*** [2005] UKHL 28, now see Schedule 2 Paragraph 1ZA(1)(d) of the HFE Act 1990. The practice has restrictions; the procedure can be used to help a sibling only, and only umbilical cord blood stem cells, bone marrow or other tissue from the child may be used. Additionally regard must be given to the various requirements laid down in the HFEA COP paragraphs 10.21–10.28 which include giving consideration to the condition of the affected child, the child who will be born and all other family circumstances. One objection to 'saviour siblings' is the child is used as a means to an end, as PGD does not benefit the embryo and any benefit is intended for the sick sibling. In response it is argued that if the embryo is unharmed then to save the life of a sibling will be of benefit to the child. Another concern is the child will suffer psychological problems knowing that he was conceived solely to cure a sick sibling and, furthermore, what if the intended treatment fails? Are these arguments plausible? Academics such as Sheldon and Wilkinson (2004) contend that the benefits of the child knowing they have saved a life and the enjoyment derived from having the company of a sibling must outweigh any speculative future harm to the saviour sibling (see Sheldon, S. and Wilkinson, S. (2004) Hashmi and Whitaker. An unjustifiable and misguided distinction? *Medical Law Review*, 12(2): 137–163).

[8] After examining sex selection the answer now focuses on another use of PGD demonstrating to the examiner that you have considered all aspects of PGD.

[9] Ensure that you take a balanced approach and address both sides of the argument.

Unless we are of the view that using PGD to choose a 'saviour sibling' is an affront to the embryo's dignity, we may conclude it is morally acceptable.[9]

PGD cannot be used to select an embryo for desirable characteristics such as eye colour or future academic excellence. Were it possible should PGD be utilised in this way? Would it be ethical or morally desirable? Yes, if we accept unfettered reproductive autonomy but if the premise is that PGD should only be used to prevent harm then the answer must be in the negative. PGD is now an accepted practice. Our view on the restrictions on its use depends on our stance towards reproductive freedom. Advocates of total reproductive autonomy argue there should be no limits on right to choose. However, if we accept that the purpose of PGD is to prevent harm, whether that it is to embryo, intended parents or an existing sibling, then perhaps unfettered reproductive autonomy would be a step too far.[10]

[10] In your conclusion it is appropriate to express a view on the purpose of PGD and the current law.

✓ Make your answer stand out

- Much of this answer is taken up with discussing the legislation, therefore ensure you are familiar with the relevant provisions.
- Use academic opinion wisely in this example to support arguments for and against PGD. See for example: Asch A. (2003) Disability equality and prenatal testing: contradictory or compatible? *Florida State University Law Review*, 30: 315–342; and Sheldon, S. and Wilkinson, S. (2004) Hashmi and Whitaker. An unjustifiable and misguided distinction? *Medical Law Review*, 12(2): 137–163.
- Structure here is all important; there are three distinct sections which are each given equal attention.
- There is no right or wrong answer to this question; the aim must always be to present a balanced argument.

! Don't be tempted to . . .

- Only look at one aspect of PGD, this would result in a very limited discussion and would not address all of the legal and ethical issues generated by PGD.
- Stray too much into an ethical debate; you must focus on how the law responds to the complex ethical difficulties generated by PGD.

? Question 6

Assume that you are the legal advisor to Stamcastle Trust. Advise the trust as to the legal and any ethical issues raised by the following situations the trust is currently facing.

(a) Lisa and Leo are parents of a disabled son. Before Lisa embarks on a second pregnancy she wishes to use pre-implantation genetic diagnosis (PGD) to select a healthy embryo as both Lisa and Leo feel they could not cope with a second disabled child. Moreover, Lisa would like to use PGD to choose the sex of her future child as Leo wishes to have a 'healthy' son to carry on the family business.

(b) Eric and Violet have two children, Ada who is perfectly healthy and Lottie who suffers from a serious medical condition that requires daily treatment. Eric and Violet would like to have another child but are anxious to ensure that the tissue of their unborn child would be compatible with that of Lottie; they plan to use their new child's bone marrow and part of her kidney to treat Lottie's condition. Moreover, they wish to know whether it would be possible to treat Lottie's cousin Bella who is similarly afflicted.

Answer plan

- Define and explain what is meant by PGD and 'saviour siblings'.
- Identify and apply the relevant provisions of the Human Fertilisation and Embryology Acts 1990 and 2008 to each scenario.
- Discuss the ethical issues raised by each.
- Conclude – advise the trust.

Diagram plan

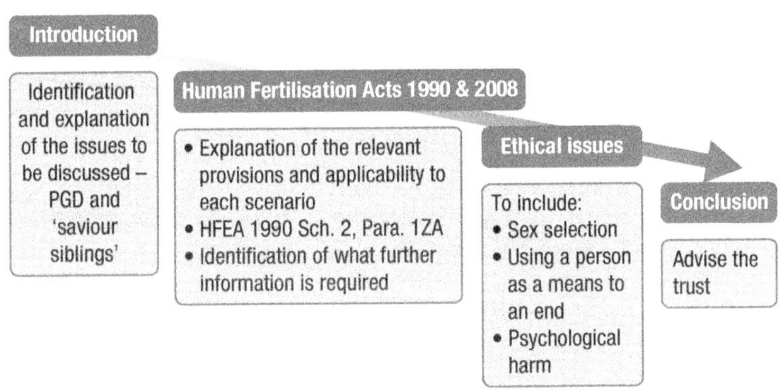

A printable version of this diagram plan is available from **www.pearsoned.co.uk/lawexpressqa**

Answer

Part (a)

[1] Always begin by explaining any legal, ethical or medical terminology.

Lisa and Leo wish to use pre-implantation diagnosis (PGD) which is a screening process where one or two cells are removed from the developing embryo and tested for genetic abnormalities.[1] The process requires a licence from the Human Fertilisation and Embryology Authority (HFEA) and is permitted in limited circumstances, (Human Fertilisation and Embryology Act 1990, Sch. 2). It is not clear from the scenario that Lisa and Leo satisfy the requirements of the Act.

[2] It is essential that you do not make any assumptions about the facts given and instead state what further information is required.

[3] You must consider the HFEA Acts but also discuss the guidance provided in the accompanying Code of Practice for a full discussion of the issues.

[4] It is not necessary and, time will not permit a discussion of all of the criteria in the COP but the answer details some of the factors that may be relevant to this scenario.

We are not informed what Lisa and Leo wish to screen any embryo for. The question states they have a disabled son but does not say that his condition is as a result of a heritable condition or has been caused by some other factor, for example problems at birth.[2] PGD is only permitted for a heritable condition and Lisa and Leo will need to establish this and the condition to be screened. PGD may be allowed in limited circumstances, which include screening to establish if 'the embryo has a gene, chromosome or mitochondrial abnormality that might affect its capacity to result in a live birth' (Sch. 2 Para. 1ZA(1)(a)) and 'to avoid a serious medical condition'(Sch. 2 Para. 1ZA(2)(b)). Lisa and Leo must establish that the condition to be screened meets this criteria, and the trust must also consider the HFEA Code of Practice (8th edn) paragraphs 10.4–10.7 in deciding whether PGD is appropriate.[3] Factors the trust will take account of include the likely degree of suffering associated with the condition and the views of those seeking treatment including their previous reproductive experience.[4]

Assuming that these requirements are satisfied then screening may occur, however the question also states that PGD is to be used to choose the sex of the unborn child. Sex selection is allowed if the genetic illness to be avoided is related to sex either by affecting one sex only or affecting one sex significantly more than the other (Sch. 2 Para. 1ZA(3)). From the question it appears that sex selection is desired only for social reasons (to carry on the family business) and that will not be permitted.

There are several ethical objections to sex selection which include gender imbalance, a concern that the resulting child will suffer from psychological problems believing that they were selected only on account of their sex, and that sex selection is discriminatory. Additionally there are ethical objections to PGD; many view it as discriminatory and arguably valuing the life of a disabled person as worth less than that of a healthy person.[5] However, if Lisa and Leo satisfy the conditions in the Act then they should be permitted to screen their embryos for a heritable condition but not for any social reason.

[5] The question requires a discussion of both the legal and the ethical issues and it is essential you are familiar with both.

Part (b)

As in the Part (a) scenario the prospective parents wish to use PGD. However, on this occasion the tissue typing is to determine whether the intended child would be a suitable tissue match for a sick sibling. Following the decision in ***R (Quintavalle) v Human Fertilisation and Embryology Authority*** [2005] UKHL 28 the HFEA may license tissue typing for this purpose. Under Schedule 2 of the Human Fertilisation and Embryology Act 1990 (the HFEA 1990 (as amended by HFEA 2008)), Paragraph 1ZA(d) allows for testing to be carried out on an embryo produced by Eric and Violet to determine whether the tissue of that embryo would be compatible with that of Lottie if it is established that Lottie 'suffers from a serious medical condition which could be treated by umbilical cord blood stem cells, bone marrow or other tissue'.[6] The question does not reveal what condition Lottie is suffering from, merely that it is a serious condition. Furthermore, the facts do not explain why Eric and Violet have not considered using tissue from their healthy child Ada. We can only assume that she is not a tissue match for Lottie.[7]

[6] In this instance being able to quote from the Act adds clarity to the argument.

[7] Again as for Part (a) the gaps in the information are identified.

Eric and Violet's wish to use part of the organ from the intended child will not be permitted (Para. 1ZA(1)(d)). The resulting child may donate an organ to Lottie but they cannot be selected at the embryo stage for that purpose. Furthermore, the tissue cannot be used to treat Bella, Lottie's cousin, as only an older sibling and no other family member may be treated.

The trust in deciding on the appropriateness of Eric and Violet's application must consider the medical condition of Lottie to include her degree of suffering, the speed of her degeneration and the availability of all treatment options (HFEA Code of Practice para. 10.23). In addition, in cases of saviour siblings the trust must also consider the risks to the embryo of being tested and any likely long-term emotional and psychological implications (Code of Practice para. 10.24). As with the scenario in Part (a), consideration should also be given to the family circumstances (Code of Practice para. 10.25).

[8] After discussing the legal provisions the answer moves on to address the ethical difficulties.

[9] Here the answer concludes with reference to any additional problems the trust may face, again demonstrating to the examiner that you have considered all eventual outcomes to this problem.

There are many ethical objections to 'saviour siblings' which the trust need be aware of.[8] The main objection is that Eric and Violet are effectively conceiving a child whose sole purpose is to cure Lottie; they are using a person as a means to an end. However, it is argued that the intended child will not be harmed by the process and will only benefit from knowing that they have saved the life of their sibling. It is not inconceivable, however, that the child might suffer from psychological problems if he/she believes himself or herself solely created to save the life of a sibling. Problems could occur if the matching ultimately fails and the trust should consider the possibility of any potential legal liability if the eventual child does not provide a cure for their respective sibling.[9]

Make your answer stand out

- Ensure that you deal with all aspects of the question; here you are asked to address the legal and ethical arguments.
- State and apply the relevant legislation to the given facts identifying where further information is required.
- Arrive at a conclusion if possible; you are asked to advise the trust.

! Don't be tempted to . . .

- Lapse into a general discussion of PGD.
- Make too many assumptions without knowing specific facts.

www.pearsoned.co.uk/lawexpressqa

Go online to access more revision support including additional essay and problem questions with diagram plans, You be the marker questions, and download all diagrams from the book.

9 Contraception and the unplanned child

How this topic make come up in exams

This topic may present as a stand-alone question or combined with other areas. There are several tort law issues that can arise: the most frequent is defective contraception and negligence in the sterilisation procedure leading to the birth of an unplanned child. Essay questions focus on a critical evaluation of the judiciary's approach to the assessment of damages, notably the distinction made dependent if the child is born healthy or with a disability. Problem questions involve advising on the scope of the duty of care owed by the doctor and what damages may be awarded for the unwanted pregnancy.

Before you begin

It's a good idea to consider the following key themes of contraception and the unplanned child before tackling a question on this topic.

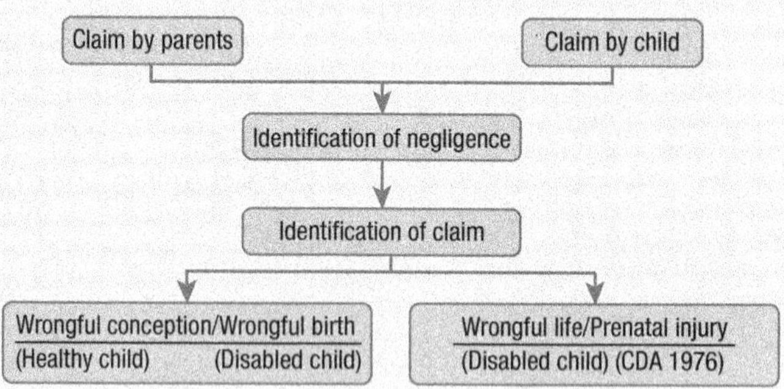

A printable version of this diagram is available from **www.pearsoned.co.uk/lawexpressqa**

Question 1

In a claim for wrongful conception, essentially there is no reason in policy or in law why damages should not be awarded for the birth of a healthy child in a claim for wrongful conception. Discuss.

Answer plan

- Define the claim for wrongful conception.
- Explain the differences in contract and tort and discuss the nature and scope of the duty owed.
- Set out what losses may be compensated for the unplanned birth of a healthy child.
- Critically analyse the reasoning in *McFarlane* for denying recovery.
- Contrast and evaluate the different approach taken in wrongful birth cases and the role of policy.
- Conclude – is recovery denied for policy or legal reasons, or both? Has the law got it right?

Diagram plan

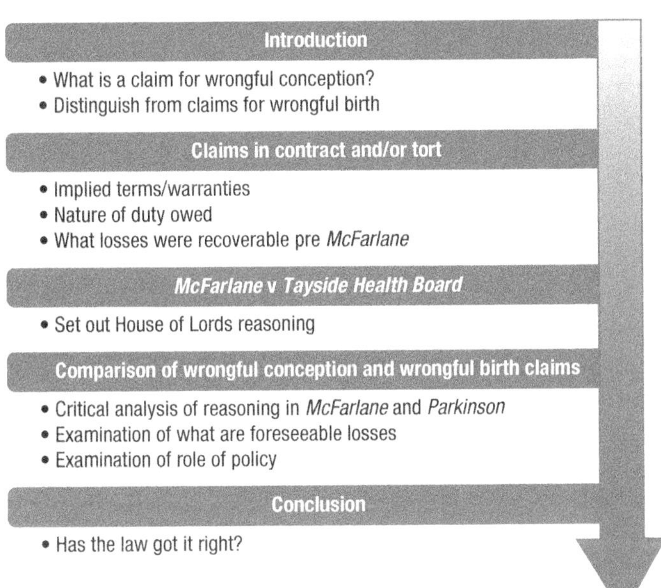

Introduction
• What is a claim for wrongful conception?
• Distinguish from claims for wrongful birth
Claims in contract and/or tort
• Implied terms/warranties
• Nature of duty owed
• What losses were recoverable pre McFarlane
McFarlane v Tayside Health Board
• Set out House of Lords reasoning
Comparison of wrongful conception and wrongful birth claims
• Critical analysis of reasoning in McFarlane and Parkinson
• Examination of what are foreseeable losses
• Examination of role of policy
Conclusion
• Has the law got it right?

A printable version of this diagram plan is available from **www.pearsoned.co.uk/lawexpressqa**

Answer

Until recently the courts awarded damages for a wrongful conception claim (***Emeh* v *Kensington and Chelsea and Westminster AHA*** [1985] QB 1012). The claim is either for the failure of the doctor to advise about the risks of conception following a vasectomy or sterilisation operation or that the procedure was performed negligently resulting in an unwanted pregnancy.[1] The judiciary have struggled to agree on what damages should be awarded for an unplanned healthy child. This essay examines the legitimacy of the judiciary's reasoning from both the legal and policy perspectives and contrasts the approach adopted in wrongful birth claims where the courts compensate for the extra costs associated in raising a disabled child.[2]

[1] Define the claim at the outset.

[2] Use the introduction to map out the structure of your essay.

Claims for wrongful conception may be brought in contract or tort. The courts do not differentiate between the two claims unless the claimant can rely on a specific contractual term guaranteeing sterility.[3] Generally the obligations owed to the private and NHS patient are indistinguishable, to perform the operation in accordance with the ***Bolam*** standard (***Bolam* v *Friern Hospital Management Committee*** [1957] 1 WLR 582). Establishing breach is unproblematic, defining the scope of the duty owed and the level of compensation has proven to be more of a thorny issue as evidenced by the pivotal decision in ***McFarlane* v *Tayside Health Board*** [2000] 2 AC 59.

[3] The answer explains that the claim can be brought in both contract and in tort but the courts do not distinguish between the two claims.

Following his vasectomy the defendant negligently advised Mr McFarlane that he was sterile and the McFarlanes resumed sexual relations without using any contraceptive precautions. Mrs McFarlane became pregnant and gave birth to a healthy daughter.

Generally their Lordships were agreed that damages should be awarded for the pain and discomfort of pregnancy, the exception being Lord Millet who preferred to award a conventional sum for infringement of the McFarlanes' right to limit the size of their family. The claim for damages for the upkeep of a healthy child, an economic loss claim, was not so straightforward; there was universal accord that the claim should be rejected but no consensus of reasoning. Lord Steyn relied on the concept of distributive justice, that is, to compensate for the birth of a healthy child did not satisfy the 'fair, just and reasonable requirement'. Lord Hope said that the benefits of parenting should be offset against the harm, and yet acknowledged that these benefits were incalculable. Lord Slynn relying on ***Caparo Industries plc* v *Dickman*** [1990] 2 AC 605 queried whether it was fair, just and reasonable to impose a duty on doctors to compensate parents for the cost of upkeep; and Lord Clyde opined that it went beyond reasonable restitution to relieve the parents of all their financial obligations. Lord Millet saw the birth of a child as a blessing and not a detriment and disposed of the claim for upkeep. The ruling in ***McFarlane*** has been criticised for its flagrant disregard of tort law principles.[4] Previously in the Court of Appeal Lord Cullen argued: 'Respect for human life should not be allowed to obscure the fact that couples who have decided that they cannot afford to raise another child have been left to find a way to do so.'

[4] *McFarlane* is at the core of this question – demonstrate that you have read the individual judgments and not simply the headnote.

However, although accepting that a duty was owed to the McFarlanes to prevent the conception of children, Lord Slynn maintained that duty did not extend to recompensing the parents for any costs consequent on a breach of that duty. Ellis (1999) argues ***McFarlane*** is a policy decision; the courts in seeking to limit the liability of the health service have shifted the expenses for rearing the unwanted child on to the parents who sought responsibly to limit the size of their family[5] (see Ellis Cameron-Perry, J. (1999) Return of the burden of the blessing. *New Law Journal* 149: 1887).

[5] There is a wealth of academic commentary on the merits or demerits of the *McFarlane* decision – an essay question such as this demands that you are aware of some academic opinion.

If McFarlane represents an unsatisfactory departure from tort law principles, is it a sound policy decision?[6] The dominant argument against awarding damages for the birth of a healthy child is that a child is a blessing, yet this overlooks that parenthood has been forced upon the parents. Moreover, how is McFarlane to be reconciled with ***Parkinson* v *St James and Seacroft University Hospital NHS Trust*** [2002] QB 266, a case similar in facts save that the unplanned child was born with a disability for which the courts awarded compensation? Hoyano (2002) asks why should a surgeon assume responsibility for the costs of an unhealthy child which is less statistically possible and yet not the costs of a healthy child?[7] (see Hoyano L.C.H. (2002) Misconceptions about wrongful conception. *Modern Law Review,* 65: 883–906). In both cases the purpose of the sterilisation was to avoid the birth of any child, the duty of care owed to both sets of parents being identical. Mason and Laurie (2013) writes accepting that ***Parkinson*** acknowledged that the child's disability was not attributable to the defendant's negligence this implicitly means that either the decision in ***Parkinson*** or ***McFarlane*** must be wrong

[6] Pay attention to the structure of your answer – there are two aspects to the question: legal and policy matters.

[7] The answer continues by referring to academic commentary but ensuring it is interwoven with the arguments in relation to the question.

(see Mason, K. and Laurie G. (2013) *Mason & McCall Smith's Law and Medical Ethics* (9th edn). Oxford: Oxford University Press). The view of Nicky Priaulx (2005) is that the courts erred in focusing on the healthy/disabled distinction (see Priaulx N.M. (2005) Damages for the unwanted child: time for a rethink? *Medico-Legal Journal*, 73(4)). She draws on the example given by Lord Waller in the Court of Appeal in ***Rees* v *Darlington Memorial Hospital NHS Trust*** [2002] 2 All ER 177: 'Assume the mother with four children who had no support from husband, mother or siblings, and then compare her with the person who is disabled but who has a husband, siblings and a mother all willing to help. I think ordinary people would feel uncomfortable about the thought that it was simply disability which made the difference.'[8]

[8] Quoting directly from a case again indicates that you have read widely and are familiar with the more contentious issues.

In ***Rees***, a conventional sum of £15,000 for loss of autonomy was awarded for the unplanned birth of a healthy child to a disabled parent. Emily Jackson asserts that the House of Lords were creating simply a new scheme of compensation to acknowledge a legal wrong but minimising the pay-out, though at least here there is no unpalatable distinction made between healthy and disabled children (see Jackson, E. (2013) *Medical Law: Texts, Cases and Materials* (3rd edn). Oxford: Oxford University Press). That aside, it is difficult to discern anything meaningful from ***Rees*** as there is little commonality in the judgments.

In conclusion the majority reasoning of the Australian High Court in ***Cattanch* v *Melchior*** [2003] HCA 38, a case similar on the facts to ***McFarlane***, is attractive.[9] Damages were awarded for the birth of a healthy child; Kirby J commenting that neither the famous commuter on the Underground nor reliance on Scripture could authorise a court to depart from the usual tort law principles governing the recovery of damages. There remains no plausible explanation why the rules of tort have been disregarded in wrongful conception claims. If damages are awarded for the birth of a disabled child then unless the courts acknowledge on policy grounds that a disabled child is less of a blessing it is difficult to see why such a distinction is adopted.[10] As Priaulx (2005) observes, the current policy adopted by the courts sends out a clear signal that a disabled child is less than a blessing, and that parental choices in reproduction are only relevant if the child is born disabled.

[9] Case law from other jurisdictions can often shed a different perspective on the question.

[10] Note the answer concludes by referring to the two issues posed by the question.

Make your answer stand out

- Again adopt a structured approach and note there are two distinct strands to the question – the law and policy; make sure your answer deals with both.
- Demonstrate that you have read the relevant case law by quoting and analysing the key judgments.
- Read as much of the surrounding literature as possible. This answer referred to a number of articles, notably: Hoyano, L.C.H. (2002) Misconceptions about wrongful conception. *Modern Law Review*, 65: 883–906; Priaulx, N.M. (2005) Damages for the unwanted child: time for a rethink? *Medico-Legal Journal*, 73(4); and Ellis Cameron-Perry, J. (1999) Return of the burden of the blessing. *New Law Journal*, 149: 1887. Use academic opinion to support your arguments in relation to the question.

! Don't be tempted to . . .

- Give a narrative of all aspects of a wrongful conception claim – the question requires you only to address the merits of a claim for an award of damages.
- Focus only on the legal and/or policy issues – the question asks you to address both.
- List academic opinion without integrating and referring to the question.

? Question 2

Advise the following parties of their legal liability, if any:

(a) ABC Ltd who are being sued by Ruth who alleges that she became pregnant as a result of her boyfriend's condom splitting. Ruth alleges that the condom was defective. *(10 marks)*

(b) Ludd NHS Trust who provided fertility treatment to Craig and Cara, the parents of Brian who has been born with an inherited genetic disease. Craig and Cara allege that the trust failed to properly screen their embryos before implantation. *(20 marks)*

(c) Rudley Health Authority who are defending a claim brought by Mr and Mrs Stoat acting on behalf of their severely disabled son Barney. The claim alleges that the doctors treating Mrs Stoat failed to inform her that there was a high likelihood that she had contracted the rubella virus. *(20 marks)*

(d) Mr Lord, a surgeon who performed surgery on Lydia for the removal of cysts on her fallopian tubes. Lydia alleges that Mr Lord guaranteed that the operation would render her sterile, and failed to discuss the possibility that there could be a natural reversal of this. Eighteen months after the operation Lydia became pregnant, but was unaware of her condition until she was four months pregnant. Lydia's GP suggested that she may abort the pregnancy, however Lydia disapproved of abortion in any circumstances. Lydia subsequently gave birth to May who has severe learning difficulties. Lydia believes that Mr Lord should be responsible for May's upkeep as she only resumed sexual relations on the strength of his assurances following her operation. *(50 marks)*

Answer plan

- Explain what area of law is being discussed – (a) defective contraception; (b) Congenital Disabilities Act 1976; (c) wrongful life and (d) wrongful birth.
- Consider the current state of case law ((a), (c), (d)) and the extent to which the courts recognise the rights of the parties to claim compensation.
- Identify and apply the relevant provisions of the Congenital Disabilities Act 1976 (scenario (b)).

Diagram plan

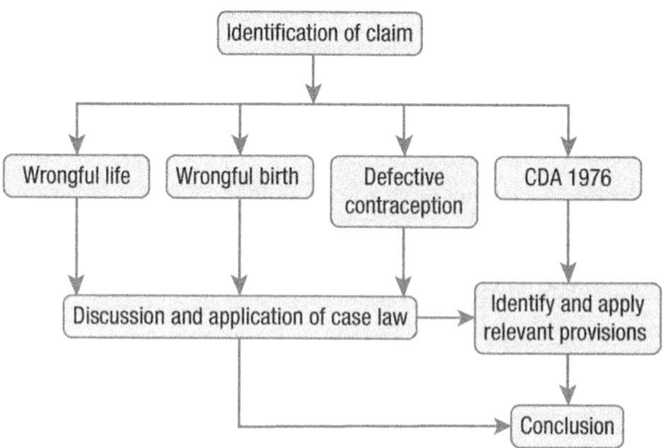

A printable version of this diagram plan is available from **www.pearsoned.co.uk/lawexpressqa**

Answer

Part (a)

[1] The answer succinctly sets out the position and then concisely states the three strands of the argument in support.

Ruth will not be able to recover any compensation from ABC.[1] In ***Richardson* v *LRC Products*** [2000] Lloyd's Rep Med 280, a case with identical facts to the question, a claim against a manufacturer failed for three reasons. First, a split condom was held not to be defective, the court ruling that no contraceptive is 100 per cent effective. Now that condoms are widely available and inexpensive there is a clear practicality to this reasoning. Second, despite knowing that the condom was defective the claimant failed to take the morning after pill. We are not told what Ruth did following the failure in contraception but it seems she took no further steps as she is now pregnant.[2] Finally, following ***McFarlane* v *Tayside Health Board*** [2000] 2 AC 59 damages are not available for raising a healthy child.

[2] It will not always be the position that assumptions can be made, but on the facts given this is an appropriate conclusion to reach.

Part (b)

[3] Begin by simply defining the nature of the claim and the relevant legislation.

[4] Try and remember as accurately as possible the wording of the relevant provision.

[5] Remember to consider all angles of the question. Here the answer speculates as to whether Brian or Cara knew of the risk of disability.

This is a claim for pre-natal injuries and falls under the Congenital Disabilities (Civil Liabilities) Act 1976.[3] Under section 1A (1) a child may have a right of action for disabilities resulting from fertility treatment. Section 1A (1) provides there may be liability where a child is carried by a woman as the result of placing in her an embryo or of sperm and eggs or her artificial insemination is born disabled, and the disability results from an act or omission in the course of the selection, or the keeping or use outside the body, of the embryo carried by her or of the gametes used to bring about the creation of the embryo.[4] Brian claims that Ludd negligently failed to screen the embryos before implantation. However, any claim will fail under section 1A (3) if at the time of insemination either or both Brian and Cara knew the risk of their child being born disabled (i.e. Brian and Cara knew that the screening process was not satisfactory).[5] Moreover, Ludd will generally have a defence if it has complied with the common law test for clinical negligence (***Bolam* v *Friern Hospital Management Committee*** [1957] 1 WLR 582) replicated at section 1(5) of the Act. Only if it was proven that Ludd had further additional knowledge of the risks will Ludd be held to owe a greater duty.

Part (c)

Barney's claim is for wrongful life; a claim for negligently allowing Barney to be born alive in an injured condition.[6] The negligence is Rudley Health Authority's failure to warn his mother that she had contracted the rubella virus and thus depriving her of the opportunity of terminating the pregnancy. This was the gist of the claim in ***McKay* v *Essex AHA*** [1982] QB 1166. Barney's claim is unlikely to succeed on two grounds: first, ***McKay*** stated that such a claim was contrary to public policy as being inconsistent with the concept of the sanctity of human life. Stephenson LJ argued that it would mean not only regarding the life of a handicapped child as less value than that of a 'normal' child but of no worth at all. Second, the court held that they could not evaluate the denial of non-existence for the purposes of awarding damages, declaring that no comparison was possible between the value of non-existence and existence. Consequently the child's claim was struck out although the parents claim for the costs of upbringing was allowed. This approach was confirmed in ***Whitehead* v *Searle*** [2009] 1 WLR 549 and in the Australian case of ***Harriton* v *Stephens*** (2006) 226 CLR 52.[7] The dissenting judgment of Kirby J in ***Harriton*** echoes the views of many academics that the objections to a wrongful life claim are not sustainable. Kirby J argued that a life of severe and unremitting suffering was worse than non-existence and that this loss should be recoverable as by awarding damages would allow the child to lead a more dignified existence. However, the seemingly intractable problem of knowing when a disability is so serious that non-existence is to be regarded as preferable means that Barney's claim will be unsuccessful.[8]

[6] Again, as for Part (b) define and explain the claim.

[7] While a sound knowledge of *McKay* is essential you should refer to more recent case law to reinforce that the position adopted in *McKay* remains unchanged.

[8] Although not essential in a problem question the answer has referred to academic criticism but has made clear in the conclusion that this will not affect the eventual outcome; Barney's claim is not sustainable.

Part (d)

This scenario examines whether damages may be awarded for the birth of an unplanned child suffering from a disability; a wrongful birth claim. Like the claimants in ***McFarlane* v *Tayside Health Board*** [2000] 2 AC 59 Lydia has relied on the negligent advice of her doctor and ceased to take any contraceptive precautions resulting in the birth of an unplanned child. Following the ruling in ***McFarlane*** Lydia may claim general damages for the pain and suffering of pregnancy and childbirth.[9] More controversial, however, is whether Lydia may claim compensation for the costs of May's upbringing. In ***McFarlane*** the claim for damages for bringing up an unwanted child was unanimously rejected by the House

[9] At the outset state what Lydia may claim before moving on to the more contentious issues.

of Lords, however the reasons for doing so were varied. All of their Lordships, however, rejected any argument that the failure by a pregnant woman to have an abortion following discovery that she was pregnant broke the chain of causation between the negligence and the birth or could be described as an unreasonable failure to mitigate her loss. Lord Millet declared that save 'in the most exceptional' circumstances could a refusal to terminate be deemed unreasonable. This view endorses that of the Court of Appeal in ***Emeh* v *Kensington and Chelsea and Westminster AHA*** [1985] QB 1012 and therefore Lydia's continuance with the pregnancy would not be deemed unreasonable.[10]

[10] Deal with all aspects of the question – here the answer comments on the implications of Lydia electing to continue with the pregnancy.

With regard to Lydia's claim for the costs of May's upbringing, ***McFarlane*** held that claims of this type were claims for economic loss and principles such as distributive justice prevented the law of tort from awarding damages consequential on the birth of a healthy child. Furthermore, it was not fair, just or reasonable to impose liability on the defendant doctor. However, in this scenario, the child, May, has been born disabled. In ***Parkinson* v *St James and Seacroft University Hospital NHS Trust*** [2002] QB 266 a mother of an unplanned disabled child was able to recover for the costs of providing for her child's special needs and disability but not for the basic costs of his maintenance. Therefore Lydia would similarly be able to recover for those additional costs related to May's disability such costs not limited to May's 18th birthday.[11] It has been argued that the courts in differentiating between a healthy and a disabled child are implicitly valuing the life of a healthy child as more worthy than that of a disabled infant. LJ Hale in ***Parkinson*** counteracted this argument by observing that 'this analysis treats a disabled child as having exactly the same worth as a non-disabled child. It affords him the same status and dignity. It simply acknowledges that he costs more.'[12]

[11] If you can add relevant additional information then do so; here the answer points out damages are not limited until the age of 18.

[12] This concluding quote aptly summarises the present position regarding wrongful birth claims.

✓ Make your answer stand out

- Clearly state what your advice is with regard to each party.
- Consider and discuss the relevant case law in as much detail as possible. In scenario (b) case law from other jurisdictions was usefully employed to restate the position re wrongful life claims.
- Quotes directly from a case may be used in a problem question – in scenario (d) the words of LJ Hale succinctly sum up the court's reasoning for awarding damages in a wrongful birth case.

! Don't be tempted to . . .

- Stray away from advising the parties – this is a problem question not an essay.
- Look at all material that is not directly relevant to each scenario, e.g. Part (b) is focused on wrongful life claims only.

www.pearsoned.co.uk/lawexpressqa

Go online to access more revision support including additional essay and problem questions with diagram plans, You be the marker questions, and download all diagrams from the book.

10 Abortion

How this topic may come up in exams

Abortion divides both public and political opinion. On the pro-life side abortion is simply regarded as murder of the unborn. The pro-choice camp argue a woman has a fundamental human right to make her own reproductive choices. The law struggles to find a compromise between protecting a woman's autonomy and still affording some rights to the unborn. Essay questions will examine how the law attempts to maintain the right balance and whether abortion is too readily available. Problem questions will focus on the applicability and interpretation of the Abortion Act 1967.

Before you begin

It's a good idea to consider the following key themes of abortion before tackling a question on this topic.

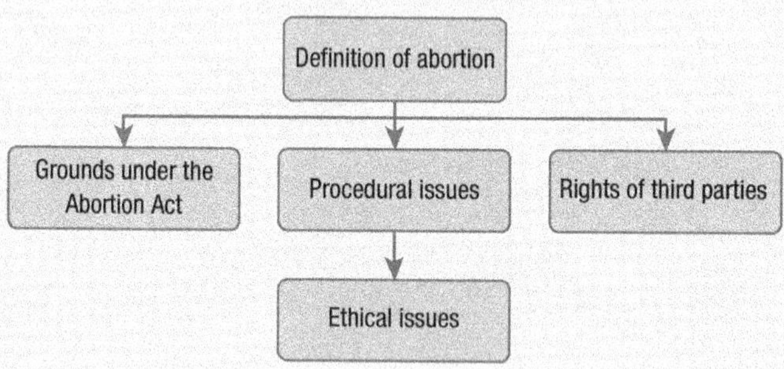

A printable version of this diagram is available from **www.pearsoned.co.uk/lawexpressqa**

Question 1

Molly and Jack are in a relationship. On one occasion they have sexual intercourse without protection and Molly takes the morning after pill, without Jack knowing, the following day. The morning after pill is unsuccessful and she subsequently discovers she is eight weeks pregnant. Molly worries how she will cope as she has just been made redundant from work and her savings are running low. She has been on medication for stress for some months now and she is also a part-time carer for her elderly mother whose health condition is slowly deteriorating. Molly knows Jack would want to have a child so she does not tell him she is pregnant. She attends appointments with two doctors and an abortion is then carried out at her local NHS hospital. Jack discovers what has happened when he reads Molly's diary some months later. He is angry and wants to know whether a criminal offence has been committed.

He cannot understand how the morning after pill can be lawful, how the doctors could find grounds for an abortion and why he was not consulted. Discuss the legal issues relating to the concerns Jack has and whether there is any potential criminal liability here.

Diagram plan

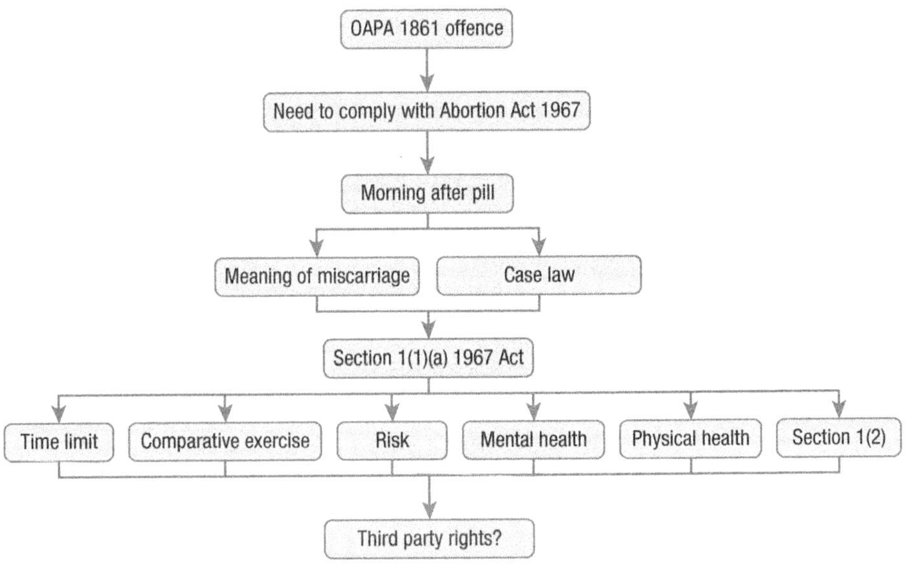

A printable version of this diagram plan is available from **www.pearsoned.co.uk/lawexpressqa**

Answer plan

- Refer to the potential offence under the Offences Against the Person Act 1861.
- Introduce the need to comply with the Abortion Act 1967.
- Discuss issues regarding the morning after pill.
- Analyse the content of section 1(1)(a) of the Abortion Act 1967 Act and apply the requirements to this scenario:
  - 24-week time limit;
  - comparative exercise;
  - use of the term 'risk';
  - meaning of 'mental health';
  - 'physical health';
  - relevance of section 1(2).
- Confirm whether third parties have any rights to prevent an abortion.

Answer

Under section 58 of the Offences Against the Person Act 1861 (the 1861 Act) it is an offence to procure a miscarriage. A defence will be available where two doctors are of the opinion formed in good faith that one of the grounds in section 1(1) Abortion Act 1967 (the 1967 Act) is met. The following issues will be considered: whether there can be any criminal liability in relation to use of the morning after pill and whether the subsequent abortion was lawful focusing on Molly's reasons for seeking an abortion and whether Jack had any rights to prevent this.[1]

[1] It can be helpful to try and breakdown the issues involved in the scenario at the outset. This also gives a clear indication of the intended structure.

Molly has taken the morning after pill (MAP), although this has been unsuccessful. Under section 58 of the 1861 Act an offence will be committed where there is intent to procure a miscarriage (even if the miscarriage does not subsequently happen). So does the MAP cause a woman to miscarry? The legislation does not define miscarriage. It is clear that for a miscarriage to occur, the woman must be pregnant first. We need to determine *when* a pregnancy occurs. The MAP operates to stop a fertilised egg implanting in the womb. So if pregnancy were deemed to occur when the egg was fertilised this would mean that preventing the fertilised egg from implanting would be 'procuring a miscarriage'. Alternatively, if pregnancy occurs only when the fertilised egg implants in the womb, the MAP would not operate to procure a miscarriage, as it stops the pregnancy occurring in the first place.

R (Smeaton)* v *Secretary of State for Health [2002] Crim LR 664 considered this point. The issue was whether offences under the 1861 Act would be committed where pharmacists supplied the MAP. The meaning of the word 'miscarriage' was considered. It was held that the word 'miscarriage' should be used in its ordinary sense, namely the termination of an established pregnancy. Therefore if the egg has not yet implanted, there is no pregnancy which means there can be no miscarriage. In our scenario Molly (or the person supplying the MAP) has no potential criminal liability as it cannot be said that she intended to 'procure her own miscarriage'; rather she wanted to prevent pregnancy occurring in the first place.

Molly discovered she was still pregnant and had a termination. The most common ground for abortions is set out under section 1(1)(a). This ground has a 24-week time limit.[2] As Molly was in the early stages of pregnancy this ground would have been relied on. It provides a justification where two doctors form an opinion in good faith that 'continuance of the pregnancy would involve *risk*, greater than if the pregnancy were terminated, of *injury to the physical or mental health* of the pregnant woman or any existing children of her family' (author's emphasis).[3] This ground demands the doctors undertake a comparative exercise. The doctors would have to compare what the situation would be if the pregnancy continued with what the situation would be if the pregnancy were terminated. The doctors must form the opinion that the termination involves lower risk.

The ground refers to *risk* of injury to the physical or mental health of the pregnant woman. Use of the term 'risk' is significant.[4] Section 1(1)(a) provides no indication what level of risk would satisfy the ground. Herring (2012) asks whether it would have to be shown injury was 'likely or just a possibility' (see Herring, J. (2012) *Medical Law and Ethics* (4th edn). Oxford: Oxford University Press). Department of Health (2014) guidance (*Guidance in Relation to Requirements of the Abortion Act 1967*. London, DoH.) is relevant.[5] Paragraph 13 provides: 'The identification of where the threshold of risk to the physical or mental health of the woman lies is a matter for the clinical opinion for each of the doctors.' If this is the case, this would give doctors a great deal of discretion. Paragraph 14 recommends that the doctors should justify how their opinion was formed following consideration of the relevant information (and that this should be recorded in the patient's record). The scenario does not tell us what happened during Molly's

[2] She is clearly in the very early stages of pregnancy, so will be well within the 24-week limit. You could explore issues relating to when the time limit is deemed to start running.

[3] It may be difficult to remember the precise wording of this provision. Try to set out key parts of it and refer to key terms, namely the need to show 'risk' of 'injury to the physical or mental health' of the woman if pregnancy were to continue.

[4] It is important to consider the wording of the provision very carefully.

[5] The examiner will be impressed if you refer to a range of source material.

consultations with the doctors, but we have no reason to suspect the decisions reached were not in 'good faith', as section 1(1) demands.

It may be relatively easy for the doctors to form an opinion that there was a risk to Molly's mental health. It seems mental health may be broadly interpreted.[6] The World Health Organization defines health as 'a state of physical and mental well-being, not merely an absence of disease or infirmity'. If this approach is taken there was no need for the doctors to conclude that Molly would suffer a recognised mental disorder for this ground to be met, rather it would be enough that they formed the opinion that her mental well-being would be affected. She did not want to continue with the pregnancy and was worried how she could cope, so it seems there would have been a greater risk to her mental well-being if the pregnancy continued. Under section 1(2) account can be taken of a woman's 'actual or reasonably foreseeable environment'.[7] Her financial worries and demanding role as carer (as well as her likely future problems) were factors that could be considered under section 1(2). It appears section 1(1)(a) was satisfied.

[6] This would show you have carefully considered the scope of the ground in light of the reference to 'mental health'.

[7] When looking at the application of section 1(1)(a) it is important to remember section 1(2) is also relevant.

Termination of pregnancy can also be justified where there is a risk to the woman's physical health. Looking at statistical arguments in the early stages of pregnancy the risks to a woman's health by continuing with pregnancy are higher than the risks of termination. It appears the risk to physical health could operate as a justification for termination of early stage pregnancies.[8]

[8] The 'physical health' point can be raised as a side issue, however when answering this question it is more apt to focus on the 'mental health' aspect of the ground given Molly's reasons for seeking an abortion.

Jack believes he should have been consulted. An abortion is lawful when the requirements of the 1967 Act are met. The Act contains no provision for consideration of the wishes of the woman's partner. In ***Paton v Trustees of the British Pregnancy Advisory Service*** [1979] QB 276 a man tried to seek an injunction to prevent his wife's abortion. It was held that a foetus has 'no right of action until birth', so the father could not act on behalf of the foetus. It was also held that the 1967 Act gives no right to a father to be consulted. The case progressed to the European Commission of Human Rights (***Paton v United Kingdom*** [1980] 3 EHRR 408) where his claim was also rejected. Following consideration of the Article 8 arguments advanced it was clear that a woman's right to respect for her private life would allow an abortion.[9]

[9] The Article 8 arguments in this area are also of relevance. This would show you have considered whether the alternative arguments Jack could advance are likely to succeed. This shows you have considered issues beyond the 1967 Act itself.

In conclusion, there appears to be no criminal liability here in relation to use of the morning after pill or in allowing a termination to take place (as section 1(1)(a) could be easily satisfied and Jack had no right to prevent it).

Make your answer stand out

- In relation to the morning after pill coverage the *R (on the application of Smeaton)* v *Secretary of State for Health* decision could be considered in more depth. For instance, consider Munby J's comments regarding the implications should the morning after pill be deemed to procure a miscarriage, such as the effect this would have for the use of other forms of contraception which prevent the fertilised egg from implanting in the womb.
- Consider section 1(1)(a) of the 1967 Act in some detail, and engage in detailed analysis of the wording used.
- Comment further on the 24-week limit. When does the 24-week limit run from? There are different possibilities, e.g. does it run from the date of the woman's last menstrual period, the date of conception or the date of implantation? On this issue read Jackson, E. (2013) *Medical Law: Text, Cases and Materials* (3rd edn). Oxford: Oxford University Press, p. 682. This would be a particularly key point to raise if you need to establish the availability of the section 1(1)(a) ground where the scenario involves a pregnancy close to the time limit (here the pregnancy is at an earlier stage).

! Don't be tempted to . . .

- Stray into giving personal opinions about whether Jack's anger is justified. The question asks you to discuss the 'legal issues' and whether there is any possible 'criminal liability'.
- Apply all of the grounds for abortion under the 1967 Act. Molly is in the early stages of pregnancy, so section 1(1)(a) is clearly the appropriate focus and this will show you understand the significance of the timing of the pregnancy. You would only rely on sections 1(1)(b)(c) or (d) where the 24-week time limit has passed as these grounds contain more onerous requirements. You could, however, refer to them by way of comparison (for instance to compare the 'grave permanent injury' requirement in section 1(1)(b) with the 'risk of injury to physical or mental health' requirement in section 1(1)(a)).

Question 2

Given the ethical and moral difficulties in permitting termination of pregnancy on the grounds of disability it is regrettable that section 1(1)(d) Abortion Act 1967 fails to set any real parameters and safeguards. Discuss.

Answer plan

- ➜ Refer to the need for a defence under the Abortion Act 1967.
- ➜ Introduce section 1(1)(d).
- ➜ Highlight there is no time limit in section 1(1)(d).
- ➜ Discuss the status of a foetus (and a disabled foetus).
- ➜ Evaluate the 'foetal interests' argument.
- ➜ Consider the 'parental interests' argument.
- ➜ Analyse the content of section 1(1)(d), particularly:
  - – issues regarding 'substantial risk';
  - – issues regarding 'seriously handicapped'.

Diagram plan

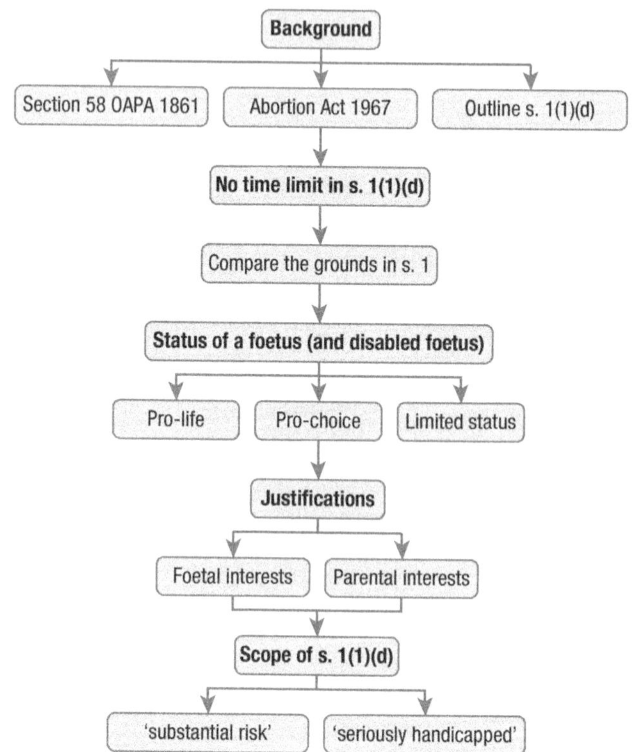

A printable version of this diagram plan is available from **www.pearsoned.co.uk/lawexpressqa**

Answer

If a pregnancy is terminated, the provisions of the Abortion Act 1967 must be satisfied otherwise an offence is committed. Under section 58 of the Offences Against the Person Act 1861 it is a criminal offence to procure a miscarriage. Defences are set out under section 1 Abortion Act 1967. Our focus will be on the ground in section 1(1)(d) which allows termination on the basis of foetal abnormality. We must consider whether termination of pregnancy on the basis of disability can be morally and ethically justified.[1] If moral and ethical difficulties exist the content of the provision must be carefully evaluated.[2] A defence under section 1(1)(d) arises where a pregnancy is terminated if two registered medical practitioners are of the opinion formed in good faith 'that there is a substantial risk that if the child were born it would suffer from such physical or mental abnormalities as to be seriously handicapped.'[3]

It is significant that there is no time limit for carrying out a termination under this ground. This can be compared with section 1(1)(a) where a 24-week limit is applicable. Admittedly, there are no time limits under section 1(1)(b) and (c), but these grounds only apply to avoid a risk to the woman's life or to prevent grave permanent injury.[4] Under section 1(1)(d) there is no requirement that the woman be at risk. Generally, therefore, a non-disabled foetus cannot be aborted after 24 weeks whereas a disabled foetus can be aborted at any time.

We should consider the moral and ethical status of the healthy and the disabled foetus. A strong pro-life approach suggests that abortion is intrinsically wrong and the foetus attains independent moral status following conception. Taking this approach the disabled and the healthy foetus ought to receive the same protection.[5] This can be contrasted with a pro-choice approach which would prioritise the autonomy interests of the woman over whatever interests the foetus is deemed to have (again, this view should not distinguish between the healthy and the disabled foetus). Between these two approaches Pattinson (2014) identifies that a foetus may have 'limited status' and he refers to the 'proportional status position' whereby the moral status of the foetus will develop over time (see Pattinson, S.D. (2014) *Medical Law and Ethics* (4th edn). London: Sweet and Maxwell). This limited status has been recognised in case law (e.g. ***A-G's Reference***

[1] The question sets out a proposition that such terminations are unethical, we need to explore how/if this conclusion is justified.

[2] This confirms the second limb of the question (i.e. we need to evaluate the provision to see if it sets apt parameters and safeguards).

[3] The provision should be introduced at an early point. It may be difficult to remember this precisely. If you are paraphrasing this, try to identify some key words precisely, for example the terms 'substantial risk' and 'seriously handicapped' are important.

[4] Although the question relates to section 1(1)(d), the other grounds can be referred to in comparison. Coverage should be restricted to what is necessary to engage in this comparison – do not stray too far.

[5] This applies the general ethical/moral arguments regarding abortion to the disabled foetus.

(No. 3 of 1994) [1998] AC 245) and the 24-week time limit in section 1(1)(a) also seems to reflect this. Section 1(1)(d) cannot be said to follow this approach, as it would allow a termination at any stage of pregnancy if an abnormality is identified and it does not appear to apply differently as the foetus develops. How can the different treatment of the disabled and the healthy foetus be justified?

One argument considered by Sheldon and Wilkinson (2001) to justify section 1(1)(d) is the 'foetal interests' argument which suggests that abortion can be permitted as it 'benefits the disabled foetus by saving it from a life of suffering' (see Sheldon, S. and Wilkinson, S. (2001) Termination of pregnancy for reason of foetal disability: are there grounds for a special exception in law? *Medical Law Review*, 9: 85–109). However, they concede that very few abortions carried out under this ground can legitimately be categorised as involving sufficiently severe conditions which would result in the child having little or no quality of life. Additionally, the argument that it would be better for a child not to be born at all has been rejected in claims for wrongful life (***McKay* v *Essex Area Health Authority*** [1982] 2 All ER 771).[6] McGuinness (2013) concurs that a 'foetal interests reading would greatly narrow s.1(1)(d)'s practical scope' (see McGuiness, S. (2013) Law, reproduction and disability: fatally 'handicapped'? *Medical Law Review*, 21: 213–242). She argues however that withdrawal of life-sustaining treatment in the best interests of a neonate would be 'a more fruitful analogy' than wrongful life.[7] If a condition is so severe it would justify treatment withdrawal following birth on a best interests basis, then this should also permit termination before birth. This argument has some merit but would still only apply to very serious conditions.[8]

An alternative argument is that this ground is based on 'parental interests' as the welfare of the mother could be affected if, for instance, there would be an increased level of care needed. Arguably, the woman's interests are already catered for under section 1(1)(a) which applies if there is a risk her mental health will be affected if she proceeds with the pregnancy. Morgan (1990) suggests that if parental interests were the basis of section 1(1)(d) this would 'unnecessarily repeat' the basis of section 1(1)(a) (see Morgan, D. (1990) Abortion: the unexamined ground. *Criminal Law Review*, 687–94).

There are doubts regarding the ethical and moral basis of such terminations. Therefore, if terminations based on disability are to

[6] Show your knowledge of other areas of law to support your line of argument here.

[7] The examiner will be impressed if you identify the different lines of argument advanced by academics on whether the foetal interests argument can be supported.

[8] Following consideration of the issues raised regarding foetal interests it would be open to you to reach a different conclusion.

be allowed, the parameters regarding what is permissible should be clearly and narrowly drawn.[9]

[9] Different approaches are possible here. If you had drawn a different conclusion regarding the moral/ethical permissibility of such terminations, you may also take a different approach regarding the existence and scope of section 1(1)(d). This also creates a link to the second limb of the question.

Section 1(1)(d) provides the doctors should form the opinion that there is a 'substantial risk' that the child would be 'seriously handicapped'. The term 'substantial risk' is not defined.[10] It has been argued by Wicks *et al.* (2004) that the lack of guidance regarding the terms used means that this does not fetter discretion of the doctors in reaching their conclusion, but on the other hand this 'fails to provide the guidance sought by doctors' (see Wicks, E., Wyldes, M. and Kilby, M. (2004) Late termination of pregnancy for fetal abnormality: medical and legal perspectives. *Medical Law Review*, 12(3): 285–305). Although it would be for the court to decide whether there was a substantial risk (as this is a legal issue), it is likely that the court would place great emphasis on medical evidence regarding risk. It remains uncertain what level of risk will satisfy this requirement, would a higher than 50 per cent chance be required or could a lower than 50 per cent chance be sufficient if the condition was particularly serious? Herring (2012) notes it could be argued that 'it would be strange if the meaning of "substantial" altered depending on the nature of the disability' (see Herring, J. (2012) *Medical Law and Ethics* (4th edn). Oxford: Oxford University Press).

[10] To evaluate the provision, you need to look very closely at wording used and the impact of this.

The term 'seriously handicapped' is also not defined. Although this is a legal issue, medical evidence will again be significant. It will be difficult to predict what physical/mental conditions will fall within this ground, although admittedly it would be impossible to provide a definitive list of conditions that would permit an abortion.[11] In ***Jepson v Chief Constable of West Mercia Police Constabulary*** [2003] EWHC 3318 an application was made to judicially review a decision not to prosecute where a late abortion was carried out where the foetus was discovered to have a cleft palate. The application was granted and following reinvestigation of the case it was concluded there was good faith on the part of the doctors so the case did not progress further. There is concern that what may be considered relatively minor conditions can fall within the scope of the provision.

[11] This point would address the angle of the question, i.e. the lack of clarity may be *regrettable*, but this acknowledges it may be difficult to identify suitable alternative approaches.

It is clear that the disabled foetus is treated differently from the healthy foetus and it is difficult to justify this disparity.[12] There is little guidance in section 1(1)(d) which leaves doctors with much discretion, whereas clear parameters (where possible) and a restrictive approach are needed.

[12] This conclusion reflects the points made during the course of the essay. Again, for this style of question it is open to students to argue and conclude differently.

Make your answer stand out

- There is scope to develop commentary regarding the moral/ethical and legal status of both the disabled and non-disabled foetus. Explore the academic commentary further and comment on case law such as *Vo* v *France* (2005) 40 EHRR 12.
- Read the articles by Sheldon, S. and Wilkinson, S. (2001) Termination of pregnancy for reason of foetal disability: are there grounds for a special exception in law? *Medical Law Review*, 9: 85–109 and McGuiness, S. (2013) Law, reproduction and disability: fatally 'handicapped'? *Medical Law Review*, 21: 213–242. Develop coverage of the arguments made regarding foetal interests and parental interests, e.g. you could consider the 'parental interests' argument further from a reproductive autonomy perspective.
- Explore the difficulties generated by the terms 'substantial risk' and 'seriously handicapped' further. What is the position where a foetus may only develop a serious illness later in life? Should the term 'seriously handicapped' be removed? Consider how you think the provision could be changed.
- Refer to other source material, e.g. Royal College of Obstetricians and Gynaecologists (2010) *Termination of Pregnancy for Fetal Abnormality in England, Scotland and Wales* – this helps show how the medical profession approach the issue of 'serious handicap'.

! Don't be tempted to . . .

- Stray into coverage of the Abortion Act 1967 as a whole, as the question is very clearly about the ground contained in section 1(1)(d) (although other grounds can be referred to by way of comparison).
- Look solely at the legal issues regarding the content of section 1(1)(d) as the question refers to ethical and moral difficulties too.
- Avoid only looking at one side of the argument; you need to look at the range of arguments that can be advanced.
- Feel you have to agree with the statement in the question. Alternative lines of arguments are also possible.

? Question 3

Juliet, aged 38, is six months pregnant with her first child. She is currently unemployed and living alone in a one-bedroom flat. Her partner Rob left her on discovering that she was pregnant and her parents have refused to speak with her as they disapproved of Rob. Juliet has therefore decided that an abortion would be in her and her unborn child's best interests.

Juliet consults her general practitioner, Dr Dunn, who on hearing the facts agrees to a termination after seeing and counselling her for about ten minutes. He then sends Juliet to one of his colleagues in the practice, Dr Noone, who, after reading her notes, concurs with Dr Dunn's view.

At the hospital to which Juliet was referred, Dr Grim, who was to be in charge of the abortion, was delayed by another case and instructed Nurse Forth to initiate the medical induction method of abortion. Josh, a hospital porter and ardent member of the Pro-Life Group, refused to wheel Juliet into the side-ward where the treatment was to be carried out. Nurse Forth arranged for someone else to do this and then commenced the treatment. The foetus was soon expelled from the womb dead.

Josh subsequently informs his local Pro-Life Group who consult you as to whether there has been a contravention of the abortion legislation.

Advise the Pro-Life Group.

Answer plan

- ➜ Define abortion with reference to the Offences Against the Person Act 1861.
- ➜ Set out and discuss the relevant grounds in the Abortion Act 1967.
- ➜ Critically evaluate whether Drs Dunn and Noone acted in 'good faith'.
- ➜ Consider the scope of section 4 and Josh's actions.
- ➜ Discuss the actions of Nurse Forth in initiating the abortion.

Diagram plan

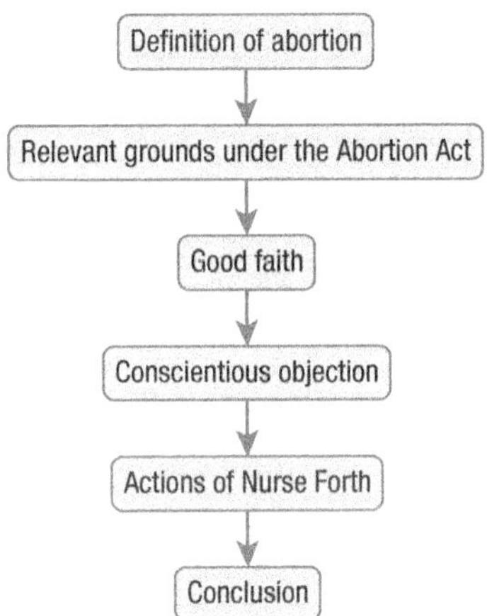

A printable version of this diagram plan is available from **www.pearsoned.co.uk/lawexpressqa**

Answer

An abortion is the termination of a pregnancy due to the loss or destruction of the embryo or foetus before birth.[1] Section 58 of the Offences Against the Person Act 1861 makes it a criminal offence for a woman or a third party to procure or attempt to procure a miscarriage. For Juliet's abortion to be legal she must satisfy the requirements of the Abortion Act 1967 which provides a defence to any potential criminal liability.[2] There is no right to an abortion; rather two medical practitioners must have formed the opinion in good faith that one of the four statutory grounds was present.[3]

As Juliet was six months pregnant, Drs Dunn and Noone cannot rely on section 1(1)(a) of the Act which is the only ground to impose a time limit of 24 weeks.[4] Therefore Drs Dunn and Noone must look to the three remaining grounds in the Abortion Act. Section 1(1)(b) permits an abortion to be performed if 'the termination is necessary to prevent grave permanent injury to the physical or mental health of the pregnant woman'.[5] In considering this section Juliet's 'actual or reasonably foreseeable environment' may be taken into account; (s. 1(2)). From the information given, Juliet may struggle to satisfy this ground. Her socio-economic circumstances are difficult but there is no evidence that she was at risk of any permanent grave physical or mental injury or that the abortion was 'necessary' to reduce that risk.[6]

Section 1(1)(c) states an abortion may be carried out where 'the continuance of the pregnancy would involve risk to the life of the pregnant woman, greater than if the pregnancy is terminated.' A doctor need only show that continuing with the pregnancy may result in the death of the woman and an abortion would reduce the risks to the woman's life. Again, there is no indication that Juliet's life was at risk so it is unlikely that Drs Dunn and Noone would be able to rely on this ground.[7]

Finally, section 1(1)(d) permits a termination where 'there is a substantial risk that if the child were born it would suffer from physical or mental abnormalities as to be seriously handicapped'. This is the only ground to consider the foetus and not the physical or mental health of the woman. Again there is no evidence in the question that Juliet's foetus was suffering from any disability – if this ground

[1] Begin any problem question by defining any medical terminology. Although abortion is a term in common usage it is good practice to give a definition which also provides a good starting point for the discussion.

[2] Although the focus of your discussion is the Abortion Act you should refer to other legislation if appropriate. Here the answer explains that abortion will be a criminal offence under OAPA 1861 unless the Abortion Act 1967 is complied with.

[3] Indicate what will be the key issues for discussion in the introduction.

[4] Do not waste time discussing matters which are not relevant, however demonstrate to the examiner that you are aware of all the grounds in the Act.

[5] You should try and remember the exact wording of the grounds, however as a minimum try and set out the significant parts, e.g. 'grave permanent injury'.

[6] Remember that you must apply the law to the facts in the scenario. The answer refers to Juliet's difficult circumstances but concludes that they are not sufficient to satisfy section 1(1)(b).

[7] Ensure that you explain why Juliet's circumstances do not fall within a particular ground, again demonstrating to the examiner that you fully understand the grounds for an abortion.

were to apply then there needs to have been a substantial risk to the foetus and the handicap must have been serious. The scope of both these terms, however, is often disputed; there is no agreement on how great the risk must be and whether it is Juliet's and not the doctor's perception that matters as to what constitutes a serious handicap.

Drs Dunn and Noone agreed to Juliet's request for a termination. There is some doubt, however, as to whether they have formed their opinion 'in good faith' under section 1 of the Act. Dr Dunn only saw Juliet for ten minutes and Dr Noone did not see her at all, but reached his decision after reading his colleague's notes. In ***R* v *Smith*** [1974] 1 All ER 376 a doctor was found not to have acted in good faith as he had made no internal examination of the patient, nor did he take any medical history and there was evidence that he had received a cash payment for agreeing to the abortion.[8] ***Smith***, however, is apparently unique in being one of the very few reported prosecutions, and providing Drs Dunn and Noone followed professional practice and acted in accordance with the ***Bolam*** test (***Bolam* v *Friern Hospital Management*** [1957] 2 All ER 118), they are unlikely to be liable. We can only speculate, however, as to whether a ten-minute consultation meets current professional standards.

[8] Include the facts of a case to distinguish it from the present scenario.

Juliet's abortion takes place in a hospital – section 1(3) of the Act stipulates that abortions may only be carried out in an NHS setting or other approved place. In refusing to wheel Juliet into the side-ward Josh may attempt to rely on section 4 of the Act which provides that anyone with a conscientious objection to abortion is not under a legal duty to participate in any treatment authorised by the Act. In ***Janaway* v *Salford AHA*** [1989] AC 537 a secretary, who was a Roman Catholic, refused to type a letter referring a patient to a consultant for a possible abortion. The Court of Appeal held that the use of the words 'in any treatment under the Act' indicated that section 4 only applied to 'actually taking part in the treatment'. This interpretation has recently been endorsed by the Supreme Court in ***Doogan* v *Greater Glasgow and Clyde Health Board*** [2014] UKSC 68. In ***Doogan*** Lady Justice Hale said that 'participate' meant taking part in a 'hands-on capacity'. Consequently, Josh's actions would not be interpreted as taking part in the treatment and he could not rely on section 4.

The abortion was initiated and performed by Nurse Forth. In ***Royal College of Nursing* v *DHSS*** [1981] AC 800 the court examined the meaning of 'when a pregnancy was terminated by a registered medical practitioner' in section 1(1). The majority of their Lordships ruled that the Abortion Act did not require the doctor to perform all the procedure, merely that the procedure must be '. . . carried out in accordance with his direction and of which a registered medical practitioner remains in charge throughout' (Lord Diplock).[9] Therefore, although Nurse Forth may perform the abortion, we would need to determine if Dr Grim remained on call throughout the procedure, or instructed another doctor to supervise the nurse's actions.[10] If, however, neither Dr Grim nor any other doctor supervised the procedure then the termination may not be lawful.

[9] It is not essential to quote directly from the case but on this occasion it aptly summarises the point.

[10] Remember, on occasions you may not be able to reach a definitive conclusion. We cannot know from the limited facts in the question whether Dr Grim did in fact supervise the procedure and you should point this out to the examiner.

To conclude it is unlikely that any claim for contravention of the Abortion Act against Juliet or any of the medical personnel involved will succeed.[11] On the information in the question, although it is doubtful that Juliet met the requirements of grounds (b) and (c), Drs Grim and Noone have only to demonstrate that they acted in 'good faith' even if it transpires they were mistaken in their belief. As discussed above, actions against doctors for not acting in 'good faith' are almost non-existent. The best chance of a successful action may lie against Dr Grim for not supervising the procedure.

[11] You must conclude whether there has been a contravention of the abortion legislation otherwise you are not answering the question. It does not matter if you cannot come to a definitive conclusion providing you explain why.

Make your answer stand out

- Adopt a structured chronological approach to the question. Here the answer deals with the events in the same order they appear in the question, i.e. the grounds, the conscientious objection and the procedure. By adopting this structure you will ensure that you cover all aspects of the question.
- Accurately state and apply the provisions of the Act and analyse the more contentious wording. As the question focuses on whether there has been a contravention of the Abortion Act you must know the provisions in detail.
- Be prepared to discuss the differences in interpretation of the wording in the Act. The four grounds for an abortion have all given rise to academic debate as to their meaning and application.
- Use the relevant case law effectively, for example can the question be distinguished on the facts. In this question *R* v *Smith* was discussed to illustrate the excessively high threshold that must be satisfied to demonstrate 'bad faith'.

! Don't be tempted to . . .

- Look at material that clearly is not relevant, for example ground (a) – Juliet is now 24 weeks pregnant so it will not apply.
- Stray into discussing ethical issues, e.g. the rights of the embryo or foetus. The question asks you to focus on any potential criminal liability of Juliet and the medical personnel.
- Enter into a general discussion of abortion law; you must advise the parties whether there has been a contravention of the Abortion Act.

Question 4

The failure of Parliament to seize the opportunity and amend the Abortion Act alongside the Human Fertilisation and Embryology Act was regrettable. Discuss.

Diagram plan

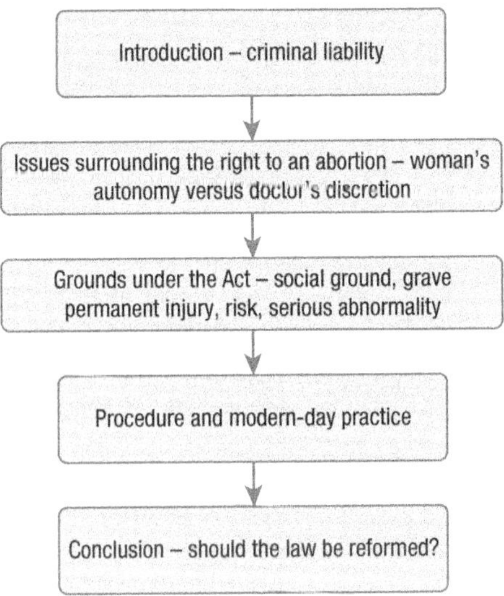

A printable version of this diagram plan is available from **www.pearsoned.co.uk/lawexpressqa**

Answer plan

- ➜ Introduce the purpose behind the Abortion Act.
- ➜ Set out section 1(1) – discuss the 'good faith' requirement.
- ➜ Critically analyse the grounds under the Act.
- ➜ Discuss other provisions in the Act.
- ➜ Conclude making sure you refer to the question set.

Answer

Section 58 of the Offences Against the Person Act 1861 (OAPA 1861) makes it a criminal offence to perform any act to induce an abortion. Until the Abortion Act 1967 doctors had to rely on the common law defence in ***R* v *Bourne*** [1939] 1 KB 687. The Abortion Act brought in a statutory defence and our focus will be on whether the provisions of the Act remain sustainable in the twenty-first century. Has the law kept pace with medical advancement? Does the Act meet society's expectations?[1]

[1] Use your introduction to set out what are the key issues and what will be the focus of the essay in the subsequent paragraphs.

A woman does not have a right to an abortion, rather under section 1(1) two registered medical practitioners must form the opinion in good faith that her circumstances fall within one of the four grounds in the Abortion Act (grounds (a)–(d)). ***R* v *Smith*** [1974] 1 All ER 376 is the only successful prosecution against a doctor for not acting in 'good faith' and it is now questionable whether the 'good faith' requirement adds anything of substance. Sheldon (2012)[2] argues that the decision to have an abortion should rest with the woman alone (see Sheldon, S. (2012) The Abortion Act's paternalism belongs to the 1960s. *Guardian*, 22 March), but ***ABC* v *Ireland*** [2010] ECHR 2032[3] confirmed the law remains unwilling to give a woman this right. Below it is argued that if a woman is in the early stages of pregnancy then she has a right to an abortion even if the Act refuses to formally acknowledge it.

[2] Refer to specific academics if you are able; it will indicate that you have read widely.

[3] Try to include recent case law in your argument. Here the *ABC* decision illustrates that as yet the law is unwilling to embrace the view of academics such as Sheldon who argue for a woman's unfettered autonomy.

The grounds for abortion are contentious. The majority of abortions rely on section 1(1)(a), commonly referred to as the 'social ground' and the only ground to impose a time limit of 24 weeks. Parliament has consistently refused to lower the 24-week limit which critics argue is too high and ignores the advances in neo-natal medicine. However, as the remaining sections of the Act provide for abortion until full term, this is something of a moot point.

Under ground (a) a pregnancy may be terminated 'if the continuance of the pregnancy would involve risk, greater than if the pregnancy were terminated, of injury to the physical or mental health of the pregnant woman or any existing children of her family'. The wording is far from clear. What is 'mental health'? What degree of risk will suffice?[4] By definition a woman carrying an unwanted pregnancy will be distressed which will affect her mental well-being. Critics of ground (a) argue it is nothing more than abortion on demand, as in the early stages of pregnancy there is always less of a risk posed to the health of the woman by termination than by continuing with the pregnancy. Section 1(2) adds that in determining the risk of injury to the health of the woman or her existing children 'account may be taken of the pregnant woman's actual or reasonably foreseeable environment'.[5] The application of section 1(2) means that risks to the woman's health beyond the pregnancy itself are also considered, for example would a pregnancy impede career advancement? It has been suggested by Swift and Robson (2012) that the vagueness of this section would allow an abortion if a woman were carrying a child not of her desired sex (see Swift, K. and Robson, M. (2012) Why doctors need not fear prosecution for gender-related abortions. *Journal of Criminal Law*, 76(4): 348–57).[6] Should Parliament have amended this section, for example by listing those reasons which would satisfy this ground?[7] Inevitably this type of amendment would mean that a woman would simply select from the 'acceptable' reasons. By leaving the Act undisturbed, the doctor's discretion remains unfettered and the woman must still prove her case.

[4] The ambiguities in the wording of ground (a) are discussed to illustrate the problems caused in interpretation of the Act – a powerful reason for reform which the question requires you to address.

[5] It is easy to forget that section 1(2) is considered alongside grounds (a) and (b). Here the answer speculates what factors would fall within the ambit of this section.

[6] Again, the question refers to academic commentary to illustrate once again the lack of clarity in the wording of the Act.

[7] It is perfectly acceptable to put forward a suggestion of how the law should be amended and then to give reasons why this would not be feasible. In so doing you are demonstrating that you have critically considered an alternative approach to current legislation.

The remaining three grounds in the Act are not without difficulty. Section 1(1)(b) provides an abortion may be performed where 'the termination is necessary to prevent grave permanent injury to the physical or mental health of the pregnant woman'. The inclusion of the word 'necessary' has been interpreted to mean no other measure will suffice.

Section 1(1)(c) is similar to the social ground save that the risk considered is to the pregnant woman alone. What amounts to a 'grave' injury? What degree of risk is necessary? The wording of the Act raises more questions than it answers.[8]

[8] Although arguably not as contentious as grounds (a) and (d) the answer should refer to all four grounds in the Act as these are at the heart of the movement for reform.

The final ground under the Act (section 1(1)(d)) permits a pregnancy to be terminated if there is a 'substantial risk that if the child were born it would suffer from physical or mental abnormalities as to be seriously handicapped'. This section is controversial; by its inclusion it is implicit that disabled foetuses are denied any protection whatsoever. The risk considered is only to the foetus, neither the woman nor her family need be at risk. Key words are not defined; what is a 'substantial risk', or a 'serious abnormality'? Would a risk of developing a condition in later life, for example Huntington's disease, suffice? Furthermore, is it the doctor's or mother's perception of risk that matters? In ***Jepson* v *Chief Constable of West Mercia Police Constabulary*** [2003] EWHC 3318 it was argued, ultimately unsuccessfully, that an abortion on the grounds that the foetus had a cleft palate was not within the ambit of ground (d). It is suggested that the current wording of this section means that any abnormality would satisfy this ground, presumably not what Parliament intended.[9]

[9] Any discussion of possible reform to the Act should refer to ground (d), which is arguably the most ambiguous and controversial ground for its singling out of disabled foetuses.

We have focused on the ambiguous wording of the grounds; however other sections of the Act are problematic.[10] Section 1(3) states any treatment must take place in a licensed place. In ***BPAS* v *Secretary of State for Health*** [2011] EWHC 235 (Admin) 'treatment' was interpreted to mean the diagnosis and prescription and taking of the medication. The woman may return home thereafter. Greasley (2011) points out that, although a correct decision on strict statutory interpretation, it is unsympathetic to the woman who may be faced with the onset of an abortion while making her way home (see Greasley, K. (2011) Medical abortion and the 'golden rule' of statutory interpretation, *BPAS* v *the Secretary of State for Health* [2011] EWHC 235. *Medical Law Review*, 19: 314–25). Moreover, given that the majority of abortions are now medicinal abortions and often nurse-led, Parliament could have taken the opportunity to amend section 1(1) in line with the decision in ***Royal College of Nursing* v *DHSS*** [1981] AC 800. In ***RCN*** the court held section 1(1) did not require the doctor to perform all the procedure, merely that the procedure must be carried out under his direction and supervision. The law has again not kept pace with modern-day medical procedures.

[10] It is not possible to discuss all the provisions of the Act in the time allowed; be selective and focus on those you consider are worthy of discussion.

To conclude, the Abortion Act has many deficiencies.[11] For those who advocate a woman's right to choose, Parliament missed an opportunity to remove the stigma of criminal liability. Currently a woman's entitlement to an abortion depends on the doctor she happens to see. The ambiguity in the wording in the Act means that in practice the power to grant or deny an abortion lies with the doctor. However, for the present it seems that until there is political will, the Act is likely to remain undisturbed.

[11] Use the conclusion to refer to the question again, and if appropriate give an opinion on whether future reform is likely.

Make your answer stand out

- Adopt a structured approach to the question; here the answer examines the grounds in the Abortion Act and then moves on to discuss the procedural requirements.
- Demonstrate a precise knowledge of the provisions of the Act. The question requires you to analyse the deficiencies with the Abortion Act and it is essential that you are familiar with its provisions and the disagreements in interpretation.
- Use up to date and topical academic opinion: for example, Greasley, K. (2011) Medical abortion and the 'golden rule' of statutory interpretation, *BPAS* v *the Secretary of State for Health* [2011] EWHC 235. *Medical Law Review*, 19: 314–25; Sheldon, S. (2012) The Abortion Act's paternalism belongs to the 1960s. *Guardian*, 22 March; and Swift, K. and Robson, M. (2012) Why doctors need not fear prosecution for gender-related abortions. *Journal of Criminal Law*, 76(4): 348–57.
- Weave the question in to your answer. The answer consistently identifies provisions which are problematic and additionally gives an opinion on how the law should be reformed.

! Don't be tempted to . . .

- Get into a debate about the rights and wrongs of abortion – avoid a rant.
- Become side-tracked and discuss ethical issues; the question asks you to analyse the law.
- Try and discuss all the provisions of the Act; you will end up with a superficial answer.

www.pearsoned.co.uk/lawexpressqa

Go online to access more revision support including additional essay and problem questions with diagram plans, You be the marker questions, and download all diagrams from the book.

11 End of life issues

How this topic may come up in exams

This is always a topical legal area giving rise to considerable legal and ethical debate. It frequently comes up in either essay or problem form and lends itself to an examination of ethical issues. It comprises a number of elements that may be examined, through assisted suicide and the right to die to the refusal of life-sustaining treatment and decisions to withhold or withdraw such treatment. Answering treatment-based questions requires a sound knowledge and understanding of consent and capacity issues. Assisted suicide questions may be narrowly focused, only covering assisted suicide. It is important to be clear about the scope of any question, as confusion can arise over terminology.

Before you begin

It's a good idea to consider the following key themes of end of life issues before tackling a question on this topic.

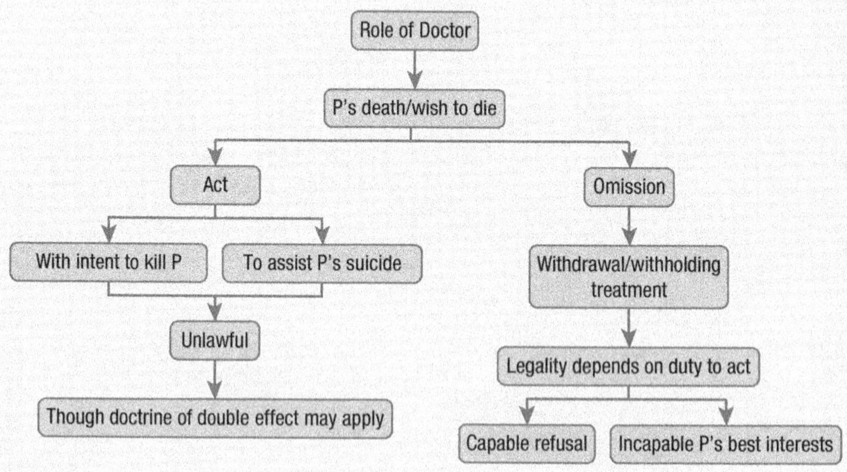

A printable version of this diagram is available from **www.pearsoned.co.uk/lawexpressqa**

Question 1

James, aged 54, has an advanced deteriorating neurological condition with a limited life expectancy. His condition will deteriorate to the point where he will need to be ventilated and tube fed, requiring constant nursing care. With such care he may survive in this condition for some time. James has described this as a 'living death' and 'never wants to end up like that'.

Although he is currently able to breathe for himself he has almost no movement, is totally reliant on carers for assistance with all bodily functions and is now struggling to swallow. He has been admitted to hospital with a respiratory infection which is affecting his breathing. His consultant, Dr Black, has informed James, and his wife Jill, that he needs intravenous antibiotics and because of his weakened state and compromised breathing he may need to be placed on a ventilator.

James says he has had enough, his life has become intolerable and things will only get worse as his illness develops. He wants 'nature to take its course' and to be allowed to die now in as dignified and pain free manner as possible. Dr Black explains that without the treatment James is likely to die very quickly. James still refuses the treatment and his condition rapidly deteriorates until he loses consciousness. Jill pleads with him to reconsider and begs Dr Black to 'do something to save him', accusing him of 'just helping to kill James'.

Advise Dr Black as to the legal position in treating/not treating James.

Diagram plan

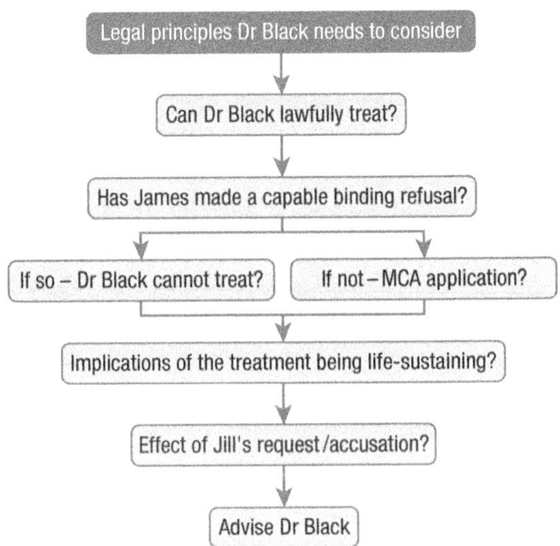

A printable version of this diagram plan is available from **www.pearsoned.co.uk/lawexpressqa**

Answer plan

- Identify the legal principles that Dr Black must consider in making the decision whether James can or should be treated.
- Consider whether James has made a valid refusal of treatment.
- Consider the implications of James's loss of capacity.
- Consider the implications of Jill's request and allegations.
- Advise Dr Black accordingly.

Answer

In order to advise Dr Black, we will need to consider the legal principles that apply to James's treatment. In particular we will need to identify whether James has made a valid and binding refusal of treatment. We will need to consider the implications of James' loss of capacity and his likely imminent death and to what extent, if at all, Jill's request and accusations affect the legal position.[1]

[1] Remember you are being asked to advise on the legal position.

1. Legal principles

Although this scenario involves consideration of James's wishes to die, in fact, since the legal issue in question is whether Dr Black can and/or should treat James, then the basic principles of consent to treatment apply.

The treatment in question (medication and ventilation), is required to prevent James from dying. However, James, if capable to do so, is entitled to refuse any treatment and it is settled case law (see ***Re T (Adult: Refusal of Medical Treatment)*** [1993] Fam 95) that he cannot be treated without his consent even though he may die as a consequence. This is not suicide,[2] but simply his right to autonomy. In ***Re T*** [1993] Fam 95, the Court of Appeal confirmed the capable adult's right to choose which 'exists notwithstanding that the reasons for making the choice are rational, irrational, unknown or even non-existent'.

[2] Take care not to get bogged down in the definition of suicide/assisted suicide here.

If James is making, or has made, a valid refusal of treatment[3] then Dr Black cannot treat James, even though he will die as a consequence. Dr Black will not be 'assisting James to die' but will be abiding by James's wishes, as Dr Black is legally bound to do.

[3] This would need to be considered under the Mental Capacity Act 2005 if James has now lost capacity.

2. Valid refusal

If, however, James has not made a binding refusal of treatment, then the question as to whether he may and/or should now be treated will depend upon whether he now lacks capacity to make his own decision and his best interests (under the Mental Capacity Act 2005, (the MCA)).

Although James has clearly stated that he does not want the treatment proposed, we need to consider whether this amounts to a valid and binding refusal of treatment. It seems likely on the facts of the case that James has lost capacity (and will not regain it in time to make the decision) in which case the MCA would now apply.

[4] This is clearly the case so there is no need to be too detailed with the capacity presumption and assessment.

We are told that James is now unconscious, in which case he will clearly lack capacity in accordance with the definition and tests of capacity set out in sections 2 and 3 of the MCA.[4] The MCA will now need to be considered to assess whether James can and/or should be treated. It may be possible that James will regain capacity, at which point he will be able to make the decision to refuse treatment again for himself.

[5] You may wish to identify that section 5 is actually a defence to any claim that would otherwise arise for treating without consent.

[6] Note the distinction between the two tests here.

Assuming James continues to lack capacity, then the MCA will provide Dr Black with an authority[5] to treat James in his best interests (s. 5 and s. 4). This authority is subject to limitations, including where James has made a valid and applicable advance decision (AD) refusing the treatment (s. 26). James may not be treated if Dr Black is 'satisfied' (s. 26) that James has made such an AD and Dr Black will be legally protected where James dies as a result of not being treated so long as Dr Black had a reasonable belief that James had made a valid, applicable AD (s. 26(2)).[6]

[7] You may wish to detail the definition and assessment of capacity if time/word count allows. There is, however, nothing to suggest that James had any impairment or disturbance of functioning.

To be binding the AD must be 'valid' and 'applicable'. It will be valid if James (who is clearly over 18) had capacity when he made it. Capacity is presumed under section 1 and assessed in accordance with sections 2 and 3 of the MCA. There is nothing to suggest that James lacked capacity[7] when he made the refusal of treatment.

He will also have to have been clear what treatment he was refusing, so as to ensure that the AD applies otherwise his AD may be held 'inapplicable' (s. 25(3)). Again, in the context of the scenario it seems clear what treatment James was refusing and that he appreciated the circumstances and consequences of this.

Where the refusal is of life-sustaining treatment, however, as in James's case, then the AD must be in writing, signed, verified and witnessed (s. 25(5) and (6)).

There is nothing to suggest that James has done this. If he has then there would appear to be a binding AD and the treatment could not be given.[8]

[8] Remember, the court can not intervene to override a valid applicable AD, although the court may be asked to adjudicate on its validity.

3. MCA otherwise

However, if James has not complied with the procedural aspects then the AD will not be binding. It will, however, be seen as an advance statement of James's wishes. The decision whether James can/should be treated will then depend on whether the treatment is in James's best interests as assessed in accordance with the checklist set out in section 4. James's wishes will be highly influential in making the decision, but the test is an objective one, ultimately. Dr Black must also take Jill's views into account[9] in assessing James's best interests. If treatment is not in best interests then it would not be lawful to provide it (see ***Aintree University Hospitals NHS Foundation Trust* v *James*** [2013] UKSC 67).

[9] Remember it is Jill's views as to James's best interests that are relevant here.

4. Summary of advice

Dr Black should be advised to consider whether James, who currently lacks capacity, is likely to regain capacity to make the decision for himself. If so, and if it is practicable to wait for James to be able to make his own decision (again), then this should happen. However, it seems unlikely that this is a practicable option on the facts.[10]

[10] Although you need to take care not to make inappropriate assumptions, the facts of this scenario are fairly clear.

Otherwise Dr Black will need to consider if James's earlier refusal of treatment amounts to a legally binding AD. Although on the facts of the scenario it appears likely that James had capacity, was clear what treatment he was refusing and in what circumstances and thus would appear to be a valid, applicable AD, it may be that the procedural requirements have not been satisfied.

If this is the case, Dr Black will need to carefully assess James's best interests in accordance with section 4. It is likely that considerable

[11] If time allows, you may wish to expand on this case and identify that it is to be compared with the decision in the *Re L* case ([2012] EWHC 2741 (COP). However, you may wish to raise the point that it is not necessarily decisive – and refer to the facts of the *Re E* case.

[12] There may be an Article 8 issue if Dr Black failed to consult appropriately with Jill. See *R (Tracey)* v *Cambridge University Hospitals NHS Foundation Trust & Ors* [2014] EWCA Civ 822).

weight (see ***Re E*** [2012] EWHC 1639) (COP)[11] would be placed on James's clearly expressed contemporaneous wishes, even though Jill is opposed to not treating him. If Dr Black assesses that the treatment is not in best interests then it would not be lawful to provide it. In cases of genuine doubt or disagreement (Jill)[12] then an application could be made to the Court of Protection[13] (s. 15) to determine the issue of James's best interests and James could be treated to preserve his life in the interim (s. 6(7)).

[13] There have been many recent cases where the court has considered best interests in the circumstances of withdrawal of life-sustaining treatment in an incapable P, you could demonstrate a good level of up-to-date knowledge by selecting appropriate aspects to incorporate into your answer.

✓ Make your answer stand out

- Make sure you are familiar with and refer to up-to-date case law – there have been many relevant and important cases over the last few months (such as *Aintree University Hospitals NHS Foundation Trust* v *James*, the first Supreme Court consideration of the MCA). See also *R (Tracey)* v *Cambridge University Hospitals NHS Foundation Trusts & Ors* (margin note 12) in relation to family involvement and Article 8 arguments.
- Keep clearly focused on the facts of James's case and the issue of treatment.
- Be realistic on the facts and tailor your answer accordingly, provide a good level of detail on the key issues – whether the AD is valid and consequences where it is not.
- Make sure you identify with sufficient precision and detail the key aspects of the MCA and their application to the facts and understand the ethos and principles of the Act.

! Don't be tempted to . . .

- Be side-tracked into detailing suicide and assisted suicide provisions. Jill's comments are a red herring, to some degree.
- Get bogged down in unrealistic factual outcomes. James is unlikely to regain capacity in time to make the decision.
- Spend too long going into detail about his capacity where we are told he is unconscious.
- Simply recite the key provisions of the MCA without applying it to the scenario.

? Question 2

David, aged 53, has had a stroke, leaving him almost completely paralysed, with some very limited head movement. He is totally reliant on others for his care, although his condition is not life-threatening and he may well live for many years in this condition. David describes his life as 'intolerable, a living hell of indignity and suffering'. He simply wants to die now and to have some control over the manner and timing of his death.

David's clinician, Dr Grey, sympathises with David's plight and has built up a strong relationship with David. Since David has no close family, this is particularly important to him.

David has now asked Dr Grey to 'help him die'. He wants Dr Grey to either administer a lethal injection of painkillers (or other medication that would kill him quickly and painlessly), or, if Dr Grey feels unable to do this, wants Dr Grey's help to arrange a trip to the Dignitas clinic in Switzerland, where it would be lawful for them to assist David to die.

He has also requested that he not be given any treatment that may become necessary should he get an infection (which he is susceptible to), other than to keep him comfortable and as a last resort will stop eating and drinking and wants Dr Grey to agree that he will not medically intervene to forcibly feed or hydrate him.

Advise Dr Grey as to the legal position.

Answer plan

- Provide an overview of the relevant legal provisions.
- Identify and apply the legal provisions relating to David's request that Dr Grey administer medication to kill him.
- Identify and apply the legal provisions relating to David's request that Dr Grey assist him to attend Dignitas to be assisted to die.
- Consider the legal position in Dr Grey withholding treatment from David as requested.
- Analyse to what extent Dr Grey may comply with David's wishes.
- Conclude your advice to Dr Grey.

Diagram plan

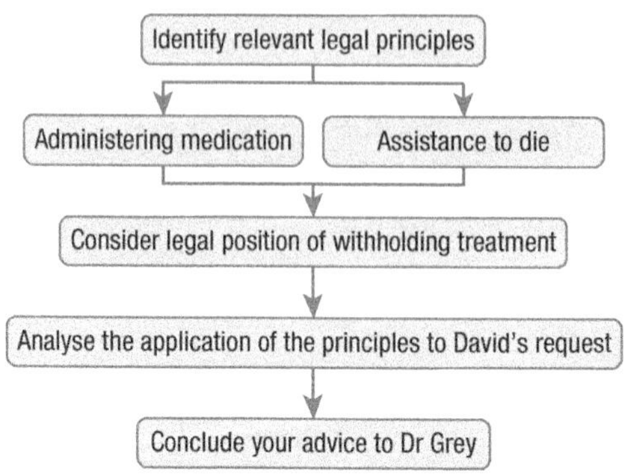

A printable version of this diagram plan is available from **www.pearsoned.co.uk/lawexpressqa**

Answer

David has requested that Dr Grey assist him to end his life.[1] This is by (1) administering medication to kill him; (2) by assisting him to plan a trip to/visit the Dignitas clinic where his death may be brought about in accordance with the law there; and (3) by withholding any treatment that may become necessary. The requests raise different legal considerations and so will be separately examined.

[1] Take care not to get bogged down with non-legal terminology such as euthanasia, active and passive euthanasia. The terminology may be used in different ways by different commentators and in a problem question is rarely useful or necessary to your answer to spend time discussing this.

1. Administration of medication

In administering medication as requested to kill David, Dr Grey would appear to be committing murder. The legal position is clear, an act with the intent to kill David (and which did cause his death and to which there was no legal defence) would be unlawful regardless of the fact that Dr Grey is David's doctor and acting at his request and that it may be argued that this would be a 'mercy killing' and regardless of how imminent death may be in any event. See the cases of ***R* v *Cox*** ((1992) 12 BMLR) and ***R* v *Moor*** (1999, Crim LR 2000).[2]

[2] Although unreported, most texts refer to the case and the judge's direction to the jury so it is acceptable to include this in your answer.

Although there may be evidential difficulties in proving beyond reasonable doubt that the doctor's intervention actually caused the patient's death, as in ***R* v *Cox***, this is less likely to be an issue in David's case, where his life is not imminently at risk and he has a reasonable life expectancy.[3] There does also seem to be a reluctance to criminalise doctors in this way (see the reported judge's direction to the jury in ***R* v *Moor*** (quoted in Dyer, C. (1999) British GP cleared of murder charge. *BMJ*, 318: 1306). Jackson (2013) notes that 'no doctor who has complied with a patient's request to end her life has ever been convicted of the full offence of murder' (Jackson, E. (2013) *Medical Law, Text, Cases and Materials* (3rd edn). Oxford: Oxford University Press, p. 876). However, clearly there would be a substantial risk to Dr Grey.

[3] Don't forget to apply the law to the facts.

In certain circumstances of 'mercy killings' it may be argued that there is a defence to the charge of murder. For family members, for example, there may be an argument they suffered from an 'abnormality of mental functioning' while carrying out the act, reducing the offence by means of diminished responsibility (s. 2 Homicide Act 1957).[4] This would not appear to be an available defence to Dr Grey.

[4] Although some knowledge of the relevant criminal law offences and defences will be necessary to answer such a question, the focus, however, should still be on the 'medical law' aspects and you need to resist too much focus on the criminal law elements.

[5] Note there has been much recent case law in this area and it is important to stay up to date.

Recently, in the case of ***Nicklinson***,[5] (***R (Nicklinson and Others) v Ministry of Justice and Others*** [2014] UKSC 38) following lines of argument advanced in ***Re A ((Children) conjoined twins)*** [2001] Fam 147, it has been contended that the common law defence of necessity should be an available defence in situations such as that faced by Dr Grey. However, it is unlikely such a defence would be available.

Finally, although the so-called 'doctrine of double effect' (see ***R v Cox***) may enable Dr Grey to lawfully administer medication in order to treat David including to relieve pain, that may have a consequence of hastening death, this would not be applicable in the scenario envisaged here.

2. Assistance to attend Dignitas

The second request David makes is that Dr Grey assists him to make the necessary arrangements to travel to Dignitas where he may be assisted to die. This scenario can be distinguished legally from that considered above, where Dr Grey would be actually administering the lethal injection. In this scenario, Dr Grey would be providing David with practical assistance to travel to Switzerland.

We need to consider here, whether Dr Grey may be committing an offence of assisting suicide under the Suicide Act 1961 (as amended). Although suicide itself is not an offence the act of assisting suicide is. This means that Dr Grey would be committing the offence if he can be said to be doing an act 'capable of encouraging or assisting the suicide or attempted suicide of another' and his act was intended to do so. It appears likely that Dr Grey may well fall within this definition. This provision has been the subject of considerable judicial scrutiny (see for example ***Nicklinson; Pretty (R Pretty) v Director of Public Prosecutions***, [2001] UKHL 61 and ***Pretty v UK*** (2002) 35 EHHR 1) and ***Purdy*** (***R (Purdy) v Director of Public Prosecutions*** [2009] UKHL 45). Prosecution can not proceed without the leave of the Director of Public Prosecutions (DPP) and guidance has been issued to assist in identifying relevant factors the DPP will take into account in making the decision to prosecute. One of the factors tending in favour of prosecution is where the person is acting in a medical professional capacity.[6]

[6] See the DPP Policy for Prosecutors. Although you would not be expected to be familiar with all the detail of this guidance (which of course may change), you should be familiar with the relevant elements within the context of the medical profession.

Clearly then, Dr Grey would be at risk of committing a criminal offence and prosecution for this. In addition Dr Grey will need to consider the implications for him professionally and any sanctions the General Medical Council (GMC) may take.[7]

[7] You may find it useful to refer to the GMC website and its guidance for doctors on a range of legal and ethical issues.

3. Withholding treatment

Finally, we need to consider David's request that Dr Grey withhold treatment from him. Even though this request is still motivated by David's wish to die, legally there is a distinction made between acts and omissions (see ***Airedale NHS Trust* v *Bland*** ([1993] AC 789)). Although an act carried out with the intention of killing would probably be murder, as we have seen, the legality of the doctor's actions characterised as an omission, will depend on whether he is under any duty to carry out such acts (i.e. treatment). A failure to provide appropriate treatment which is legally authorised may well be a serious criminal offence,[8] however a doctor cannot provide treatment, even life-sustaining treatment without legal authority and not against the capable wishes of an adult (see ***Re T (Adult: Refusal of Medical Treatment)*** [1993] Fam 95). In such circumstances where David has capacity[9] (see the Mental Capacity Act 2005 (MCA)) he may refuse any treatment and Dr Grey could not lawfully provide it. This would include any feeding or hydrating of David which required medical treatment (procedures) to provide it (see ***Bland***). Consequently, David can validly refuse treatment which Dr Grey would not be lawfully obliged (or allowed) to carry out.

[8] You may wish to expand upon this and note that this may be manslaughter or murder depending upon the circumstances.

[9] Don't forget he could also make an advance decision under the MCA to refuse it in the future too (ss. 24–26 MCA). This could be included in your answer.

4. Summary of advice

Dr Grey could not accede to David's request that Dr Grey administer medication to kill David as this is likely to be murder, even if the chances of Dr Grey being successfully prosecuted seem low. Dr Grey would also probably be committing the offence of assisting suicide if he agrees to assist David with his Dignitas plans. However, Dr Grey would be bound by David's refusal of treatment, so long as David had capacity to refuse or had made a valid advance decision to that effect.

Make your answer stand out

- Demonstrate that you are up to date with case law and relevant guidance, including the GMC position.
- Identify the implications for Dr Grey from a professional perspective.
- Keep your answer clearly focused on David's specific requests.
- Demonstrate a clear understanding of the legal distinctions between acts, omissions and assisted suicide.

! Don't be tempted to . . .

- Simply recite case facts, even though there may be many recent key judgments on similar cases to David's.
- Get too bogged down in criminal law at the expense of analysis of the implications from a medical perspective.
- State your own views or opinions on what the legal position should be where this isn't what the question is asking for.
- Forget to answer fully all parts of the question.

? Question 3

Sasha is six months old. She was born with a severe congenital condition. She can barely move, is unable to breathe unaided, cannot swallow and has seizures. She requires ventilation and artificial feeding to keep her alive. She has never left hospital and is likely to only live for a few weeks, up to six months at the most. Her doctor, Dr Pink, and the rest of the clinical team feel it is time to withdraw further treatment, which will result in her death within a matter of minutes. They feel that to continue treating Sasha is inappropriate and that all they are doing is prolonging Sasha's suffering needlessly. They also do not want to provide Sasha with any invasive treatment, such as resuscitating her, should this become necessary at any stage (which is likely), or to treat any infections that she might contract aggressively. Reena and Jonathan, Sasha's parents, are devoted to Sasha and have barely left the hospital since her birth. They insist that her condition is improving and that she experiences pleasure at the sound of their voices and when she is bathed. They are hoping for a 'miracle' and in any event their firm religious beliefs don't allow for 'euthanasia' as they call any suggestion of treatment being withdrawn or withheld.

Advise Dr Pink and the clinical team as to the legal position in withdrawing or withholding treatment from Sasha.

Answer plan

- ➜ Identify the legal issues raised by the withdrawal/withholding of treatment.
- ➜ Consider the application of these principles to Sasha.
- ➜ Consider the role of Jonathan and Reena and their insistence on treatment.
- ➜ Identify the role of the court and the principles the court would rely on to make a decision.
- ➜ Analyse the application of these principles to Sasha.
- ➜ Conclude your advice to Dr Pink and the team.

Diagram plan

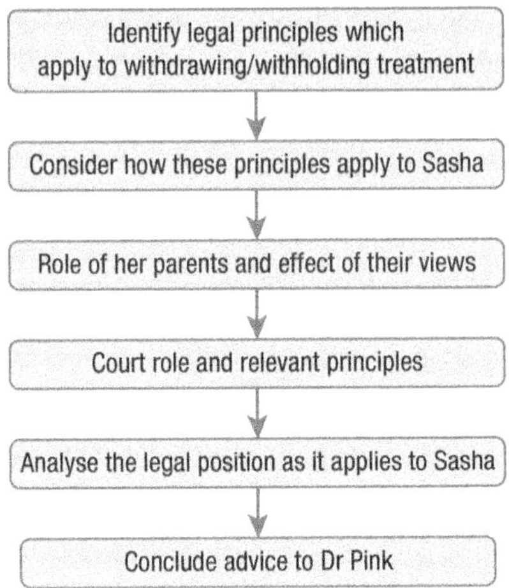

A printable version of this diagram plan is available from **www.pearsoned.co.uk/lawexpressqa**

Answer

In order to advise Dr Pink and team we need to identify the relevant legal principles that apply to the question of withdrawing or withholding treatment where Sasha will die as a consequence. We need to consider in what circumstances this may be lawful, the effect of her parents' refusal to consent to the proposals and whether an application to court needs to be made and the likely outcome of such an application.

1. Legal principles

Although Dr Pink and the team will owe a duty of care to Sasha to provide appropriate treatment, this does not mean that all available treatment must always be given. If the treatment is no longer in Sasha's best interests then Dr Pink need not continue to treat her, indeed to do so would be unlawful (see ***Aintree University Hospitals NHS Foundation Trust* v *James*** [2013] UKSC 67), even though Sasha's death will inevitably follow.

Legally a distinction is drawn between an act and an omission (see ***Airedale NHS Trust* v *Bland*** ([1993] AC 789)). An act with the intention of causing death is likely to be murder, regardless of how well intentioned the motive is (see ***R* v *Cox*** ((1992) 12 BMLR)). However, both the withholding and withdrawing of treatment is legally seen as an omission. Although withholding treatment is clearly an omission, in ***Bland*** the court held that the withdrawal of treatment was also an omission. This means that there will be no criminal act committed, even if Sasha dies as a result, provided Dr Pink is not under a duty to act. Whether there will be such a duty on Dr Pink[1] will depend upon an assessment of Sasha's best interests.

[1] You may wish to refer the the fact that an individual clinician will not be required to act contrary to his own professional judgement.

2. Role of parents

Sasha's parents want the treatment to continue. Legally a person with parental responsibility (PR) may consent to treatment on behalf of a child (see the Children Act 1989). On the assumption Sasha and Jonathan have PR for Sasha[2] they could consent to the treatment. However, the right to do so has to be exercised in Sasha's best interests, not theirs, and there are limits to the rights of a parent in this context (see ***Re S (A Minor) (Medical Treatment)*** [1993] 1FLR 376). Further, they have no right to demand treatment (see ***Burke*** (***R (Burke)* v *GMC*** [2005] EWCA Civ 1003)). Although they presumably want what they see as best for Sasha, Dr Pink can not be required to treat based on their request.[3] In many cases where the decision has been taken not to continue to treat, the treatment will simply be discontinued without application to the court. However, in a situation where Sasha's parents do not agree with such a decision, then it would be advisable, if not legally necessary, for Dr Pink to involve the High Court under its inherent jurisdiction and ask for a court determination of the question. In the case of ***Glass* v *UK*** (App. No. 61827/00) a failure to take such

[2] Clearly Sasha is not able to consent and there is no point considering *Gillick* competence here.

[3] You may wish to identify that such PR consent can't be relied on where treatment is not in Sasha's interests.

steps where there was a dispute between the clinicians and the family as to treatment and where there was sufficient time to do so, was held to be a breach of the child's Article 8 rights.[4]

[4] Note the Court of Appeal in *Burke* that the decision here was based on a misunderstanding of the English legal position. If time allows you could develop this point.

3. Court role

Where there is a dispute between healthcare professionals and parents, or an issue arises that causes disagreement as to the appropriate course to take, then an application may be made to the court to determine the issue. The court retains its inherent jurisdiction in relation to minors. An application could also be made[5] via the Children Act 1989 by means of a section 8 (specific issues) application. When exercising its jurisdiction the court will treat the child's welfare as 'paramount' (Children Act 1989 s. 1).

[5] There is generally no need to detail the different types of application further.

In ***Burke***, the Court of Appeal noted that[6] 'the true position is that the court does not authorise treatment that would otherwise be unlawful. The court makes a declaration as to whether or not proposed treatment, or the withdrawal of treatment, will be lawful.' This would mean a failure to apply to the court would not render any treatment decision unlawful. This has to be considered, however, in the light of the European Court's decision in ***Glass*** and the substantial risk a failure to make such an application may be seen to be a breach of Article 8.

[6] The extent to which you may be able to include quotations from the judgments/ commentators may well depend upon whether the exam is open or closed book.

4. Best interests

The focus for the court is on the child's best interests, the child's welfare being paramount. In cases where the child is dying and the continued treatment is simply prolonging the child's suffering or where it is futile, the issue may be an easier one to assess.[7] More difficult, however, is the situation where the child is not dying and may not be aware or suffering. Here it is maybe more difficult to say that the treatment is no longer in the child's best interests and to carry out any balancing exercise at all to determine what is in the child's best interests.[8]

[7] You may wish to refer to the Royal College of Paediatrics and Child Health Guidelines as to when treatment may be withheld or withdrawn.

[8] You could mention *Re J* [1990] 3 All ER 930 and address the approach of the court in *Bland* here.

The courts have previously approached this by application of an 'intolerability' test, that is whether the life of P is so intolerable it is no longer in their best interests for the treatment to be given (see ***Re J (A Minor)*** [1990] 3 All ER 930). More recently, however, the Court of Appeal held in ***Burke*** that it was not appropriate to reduce the issue to one single question. Following the more recent case of ***Re Wyatt (A Child) (Medical Treatment: Parents' Consent)*** ([2004] EWHC 2247 (Fam)) it is clear that the test is simply one of best interests to be assessed using the 'balance sheet approach' (see ***An NHS Trust* v *MB*** [2006] EWHC 507 (Fam)), where the advantages known and anticipated are balanced[9] against the disadvantages of the treatment.

[9] The balance sheet approach is clearly illustrated in the *Re MB* case and worth reading.

5. Summary of advice

In Sasha's case, bearing in mind the position of Sasha's parents Dr Pink should consider an application to the court for a declaration as to whether the continued treatment of Sasha is in her best interests.[10] The court will carry out a balancing exercise and will frequently rely heavily on the medical evidence and views of the healthcare professionals (see ***Wyatt***). In Sasha's case she has a very limited life expectancy, there is evidence she may be suffering pain and that invasive treatment would be distressing. This would be balanced (see ***Re MB***) against the parents' evidence she experiences some pleasure and any argument that Sasha's awareness may be limited. On balance the court may well conclude further treatment – and certainly any invasive treatment – is no longer in her best interests.[11]

[10] Note this is the question, not whether it is in her best interests to die – see *Aintree*.

[11] You could also discuss *Re K* [2006] EWHC 1007, (Fam) where a distinction appears to have been drawn with *Re MB* based on the more limited cognitive development of *K*, and also Jackson's comments (Jackson (2013: 948)).

✓ Make your answer stand out

- Demonstrate that you have a clear appreciation of the role of parents and the court.
- Refer to recent cases and be able to identify relevant principles and their application to Sasha.
- Demonstrate a detailed knowledge and understanding of key cases in this legal area, including *Airedale NHS Trust* v *Bland*, *Aintree University Hospitals NHS Foundation Trust* v *James* and *R (on application of Burke)* v *GMS*.

! Don't be tempted to . . .

- Simply recite detailed case facts.
- Limit your references only to cases involving children.
- Simply provide your own views on whether treatment should be withdrawn in such cases. You must apply the law.

Question 4

Amanda, aged 26, suffered a serious head injury in a car crash and has never regained consciousness. She is now in what the doctors describe as a permanent vegetative state (PVS), reliant on being fed and hydrated through a tube (artificial nutrition and hydration – referred to as ANH). From time to time she gets infections and these have to be treated. She is likely to carry on living for many more years in this condition. The doctors are satisfied that she will not recover nor will her condition improve and that her diagnosis is properly diagnosed as one of PVS. The doctors now want to withdraw the tube, which will mean that Amanda will starve to death over a period of days.

Amanda's parents Ian and Fran are horrified that their daughter is in such a condition, however they refuse to accept that she should be starved to death, saying 'you wouldn't do that to a dog'. They also believe that 'only God should take a life'.

Amanda's husband Dan says he 'just wants it to be all over' and that Amanda would never have wanted to be kept alive in this condition and that she had very clear views on this having studied medical law.

Advise the clinical team.

Diagram plan

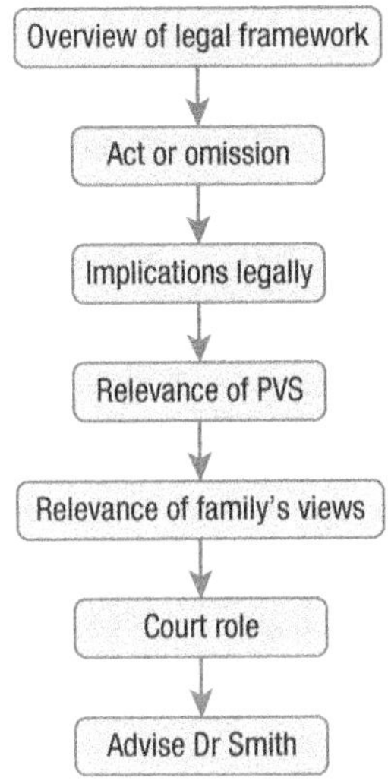

A printable version of this diagram plan is available from **www.pearsoned.co.uk/lawexpressqa**

Answer plan

- Provide an overview of the legal principles that apply to withdrawal of Amanda's feeding tube.
- Consider whether withdrawal will constitute an act or omission and implications of this.
- Address the implications of Amanda being in PVS.
- Consider the role of Amanda's family.
- Consider whether such withdrawal would be lawful and any prerequisite steps the clinical team should take.

Answer

Amanda has been diagnosed as being in a permanent vegetative state (PVS) and the clinical team now wish to withdraw and possibly withhold treatment from her. This is supported by her husband but opposed by her parents. In order to advise the team we need to consider the applicable legal principles, whether the team can lawfully withdraw treatment where Amanda's death will inevitably follow and whether withdrawal of food and hydration (ANH) amounts to treatment which can be withdrawn. We also need to consider what steps the clinicians need to take to ensure any decision is lawful.

1. Legal framework

The key issue in this case is whether treatment may be withdrawn even though Amanda will die as a consequence. The legal position is clearly set out in the case of ***Airedale NHS Trust* v *Bland*** ([1993] AC 789), which also involved the withdrawal of ANH from a patient in PVS.

2. Act or omission

In that important case[1] the House of Lords had to grapple with the question whether treatment could ever lawfully be withheld or whether, where the patient would inevitably die as a consequence, such an act would be a criminal offence.[2]

[1] You need to be familiar with this case and demonstrate that in your answer.

[2] There is no need to spend too long discussing the criminal law aspects.

It was affirmed that a deliberate act to kill a patient, regardless of motive, would probably be murder and unlawful – this could be distinguished from an omission. Where a clinician omitted to treat, so that the patient dies from the pre-existing medical condition, this would be

[3] With a problem question where you are asked to advise on the legality of treatment there will be limited scope for consideration of the ethical issues.

[4] Because of the importance and direct relevance of the *Bland* decision you will need to provide some detail of that decision.

lawful so long as the doctor was not under any duty to treat. Although the sanctity of life is important it is not absolute.[3]

In order for the conclusion to be reached that ANH could be withdrawn in ***Bland***[4] this meant that the Court had to be satisfied that the withdrawal of ANH was an omission, that ANH was treatment and that there was no legal duty on his doctors to continue to provide it.

The importance of the act/omission distinction was highlighted by Lord Goff, who referred to the deliberate act by a doctor to bring about the death of a patient as 'crossing the Rubicon', between proper patient care on the one hand and euthanasia on the other. The distinction is made, however, between the doctor withholding or withdrawing treatment and thus omitting to treat any further, and the 'interloper' who enters the hospital room and switches the ventilator off. The latter would be an act, interfering with the proper provision of treatment. Where the doctor simply omits to continue treatment, the patient dies as a result of their medical condition rather than through the doctor's act. Although the distinction may be uncomfortable the case clearly establishes that withdrawing treatment is to be treated legally the same as withholding treatment in the first place and, as an omission, its legality depends on whether there was a duty to treat.

3. Is ANH treatment?

One other key issue addressed in ***Bland*** was whether ANH could be seen as treatment at all. Is it in fact simply feeding the patient and giving them fluids, a basic form of care that can never be withheld? This is a particular issue in relation to the PVS patient.

[5] Note an advance decision under the MCA can not refuse basic care only treatment. You may wish to reflect this in your answer.

Ultimately the court held that ANH was seen by the medical profession as treatment, it required medical expertise to site the tube and maintain it safely. Consequently the provision of ANH, unlike offering a patient food or water by natural means,[5] was properly viewed as medical treatment and could thus be lawfully withdrawn so long as there was no duty to continue to provide it.

4. Best interests

The ***Bland*** case predates the Mental Capacity Act 2005 (MCA) which now applies to provide the legal authority (s. 5) for the care and treatment of adults who lack capacity (ss. 2 and 3) in their best interests (s. 4).

Any consideration of Amanda's best interests must now fall under the MCA and would be subject to any decision made by someone with a lasting power of attorney (LPA) or any advance decision Amanda may have made to refuse the treatment in advance (ss. 24–26). However, although the courts will apply the best interests assessment and balance sheet approach to such treatment withdrawal decisions, where the patient has some level of consciousness[6] (see ***Re M (Adult Patient)*** [2011] EWHC 2443 (Fam)) there is a clear difficulty in attempting to assess the best interests of someone who has no awareness at all.

[6] Such as a minimally conscious state (MCS). You will need to have a basic understanding of the medical terminology to answer questions about withdrawal of treatment.

Where a patient may have awareness and may suffer pain or distress then it is easier to identify factors that need to be balanced against the advantages of treatment. Where the PVS patient has no awareness at all it may be difficult to find factors to balance against the interests of simply keeping the person alive. The court in ***Bland*** did identify that it was no longer in Tony Bland's best interests to continue to be treated, even though he had no awareness. From cases such as ***Re CW*** [2010] EWHC 3448 (COP) it now seems accepted by the courts where they are asked to make a declaration in a PVS case that if the patient is in such a state and that this is clearly established then treatment is futile and no longer in best interests. Once such a decision is made then treatment can and should stop. If no longer in best interests there can be no legal authority for continuing to provide it[7] (see ***Aintree University Hospitals NHS Foundation Trust* v *James*** [2013] UKSC 67). Withdrawal of treatment in such circumstances would not breach Amanda's human rights.[8]

[7] Remember, for an adult there is no one else who can provide legal authority by consenting to the treatment. Make sure your answer reflects your understanding of this key aspect.

[8] Such as Articles 2 and 3 – see *NHS Trust A* v *MNHS Trust B* v *H* [2001] Fam 348, although this decision has been criticised. This may be something you want to incorporate in your answer if time allows.

5. Prerequisite steps

In order to lawfully withdraw ANH from Amanda the team will need to make an application to the court for a declaration. The requirement that such matters be brought before the court was established in ***Bland*** and has been recognised by the Court of Protection, even though the MCA requires no special procedures for the decision. The court will need to be satisfied that a proper diagnosis of PVS has been made and certain procedural steps followed.[9]

[9] Safeguards were set out in *Bland* and you could summarise these and consider to what extent subsequent case law has deviated from the initial safeguards.

6. Summary of advice

In order to lawfully withdraw the ANH from Amanda, the team should make an application to the court once they are satisfied that the diagnosis is clear and that any procedural requirements have been satisfied. It seems likely the court will make the declaration once satisfied that Amanda is in PVS. The usual assessment of best interests, including assessment of her views and those of family as to her best interests would not appear to be of relevance in the way they would if Amanda had a level of awareness.[10]

[10] See section 4 MCA. Remember no one can demand treatment – see *Burke*. Make sure your understanding of this is clear in your answer.

✓ Make your answer stand out

- Demonstrate a detailed understanding of the arguments and issues raised in the *Airedale NHS Trust* v *Bland* case.
- Demonstrate a clear understanding of the particular issues that arise in relation to PVS patients, in particular in assessment of best interests.
- Explain the impact of the MCA clearly.
- Introduce key case references and quotations to support your arguments.

! Don't be tempted to . . .

- Simply provide a case summary of *Bland*.
- Get too involved in the views of family and best interests under section 4 MCA.
- Fail to recognise and distinguish the particular issues that arise where Amanda is a PVS patient.

Question 5

The time has now clearly come for Parliament to legislate as to when a person may be assisted to die by a physician. Discuss.

Answer plan

→ Provide an overview of the current legal framework.

→ Consider the Suicide Act and relevant criminal law provisions.

→ Consider case law and the act/omission distinction and withholding/withdrawing treatment.

→ Consider case law developments and the call by the courts for Parliament to intervene.

→ Analyse in the context of the question and role of the doctor.

→ Conclude your answer.

Diagram plan

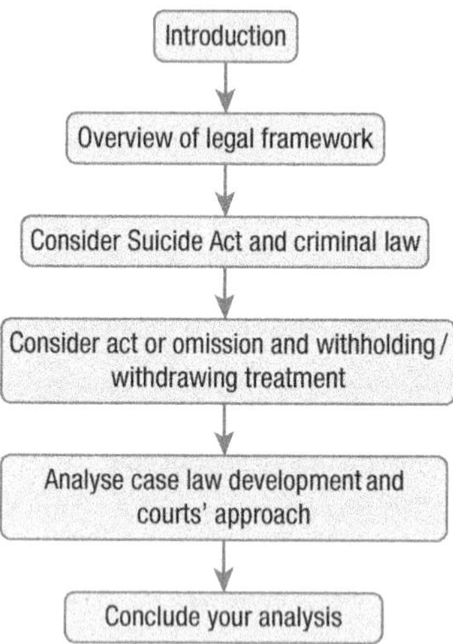

A printable version of this diagram plan is available from **www.pearsoned.co.uk/lawexpressqa**

Answer

To address the issue raised by this question we need to consider the current legal framework and case law developments, the 'call' by the courts for Parliament to intervene and why, in the particular context of the physician, this may now be said to be necessary.

Currently there is no statutory authority allowing someone to be assisted to die by a physician (or anyone), unlike some jurisdictions (such as Switzerland[1]). Any doctor carrying out an act to kill or assist a patient to die is likely to be committing an offence.

[1] For example , you may wish to refer to the Dignitas clinics there.

Where a doctor withholds or withdraws life-sustaining treatment, legally this is an omission rather than an act (see ***Airedale NHS Trust* v *Bland*** ([1993] AC 789). A doctor will only be liable where he is in breach of a duty to act.

In recent cases the courts have had to grapple with whether there may be a defence at common law where the patient is helped to die in order to save him from suffering (see ***R (Nicklinson and Others)* v *Ministry of Justice and Others*** [2014] UKSC 38) or save the life of another (see ***Re A (Children) (Conjoined Twins)*** [2001] Fam 147). This has led to pleas that parliamentary intervention is necessary (see for example ***Bland*** and ***Nicklinson***). Despite numerous private Bills being introduced over the years,[2] Parliament has avoided legislating.

[2] For example by Lord Falconer – you need to keep up to date with developments in this fast-developing area and make sure this is reflected in your answer.

1. Acts causing a patient's death

In carrying out an act with the intention of killing the patient (P), a doctor is likely to be committing a criminal offence, such as murder regardless of the fact that the doctor may be acting at P's request, regardless of motive and of how imminent P's death may be. See ***R* v *Cox*** ((1992) 12 BMLR 38).

The courts appear reluctant, however, to criminalise doctors (see ***R* v *Moor*** (1999) CrimLR 2000), Dyer, C. (1999) British GP cleared of murder charge. *BMJ*, 318: 1306). Jackson (2013) notes that 'no doctor who has complied with a patient's request to end her life has ever been convicted of the full offence of murder' (Jackson, E. (2013) *Medical Law, Text, Cases and Materials* (3rd edn). Oxford: Oxford University Press, p. 876). This may well indicate that the law is not in keeping up with society's attitudes and that Parliament should now intervene.[3]

[3] This was clearly reflected in the judgments given in the *Nicklinson* case which you may wish to expand on in your answer.

Recently, in ***Nicklinson***[4] (following lines of argument advanced in ***Re A***) it was argued that a defence of necessity should be available where a doctor is being asked to assist the death of a capable but physically incapable patient. It is unlikely such a defence would be available without clear legislation being introduced. The Supreme Court refers to the need for parliamentary action.

[4] Note there has been much recent case law in this area and it is important to stay up to date.

The so-called 'doctrine of double effect' (see ***R* v *Cox***) may enable a doctor to lawfully administer medication in order to treat P's pain which would also have the consequence of hastening death. However, this may depend upon the approach of the individual doctor and how defensive he/she is to the possibility of a charge of a criminal offence. To have to rely on the individual doctor's willingness to prescribe such medication, would seem to be an unsatisfactory position.

2. Assisted suicide

Although suicide itself is not an offence the act of assisting suicide is (Suicide Act 1961 as amended). A doctor would be committing the offence if he does an act 'capable of encouraging or assisting the suicide or attempted suicide of another 'and the act was intended to do so'. This has been the subject of considerable judicial scrutiny (see for example ***Nicklinson; Pretty*** (***R (Pretty)* v *Director of Public Prosecutions***, [2001] UKHL 45 and ***Pretty* v *UK*** (2002) 35 EHHR 1) and ***Purdy*** (***R (Purdy)* v *Director of Public Prosecutions*** [2009]UKHL 45). Prosecution requires leave from the Director of Public Prosecutions (DPP) and guidance has been issued to assist in identifying relevant factors the DPP will take into account in making the decision to prosecute. One of the factors tending in favour of prosecution is where the person is acting in a medical professional capacity.[5]

[5] See the DPP Policy for Prosecutors. Although you would not be expected to be familiar with all the detail of this guidance (which of course may change), you should be familiar with the relevant elements within the context of the medical profession.

3. Withdrawal/withholding treatment

A binding refusal of treatment (whether contemporaneous or in advance[6]) will legally prevent the doctor from treating P, even where the decision is wholly motivated by P's wish to die. This is due to the distinction drawn between acts and omissions (see ***Bland***). Such a decision in respect of an incapable P would depend on P's best interests.[7] Where a doctor withdraws or withholds treatment this is an omission and would only be unlawful where the failure to act amounted to a breach of a duty to do so (see ***Bland***). This leads to the unpleasant reality of P being left, in some cases to slowly starve to death, when treatment is withdrawn, when a lethal injection would surely be more humane (see ***Bland***).

[6] Such as under the MCA sections 24–26. The refusal will need to be valid, with P capable of making it and an advance refusal will need to comply with the procedures set out in the MCA. You may wish to incorporate this into your answer.

[7] You could expand on this and refer to the MCA for an adult or 16–17-year-old, or Children Act 1989 for an under 16. Ensure the basic point that if the treatment is no longer in P's best interests then there is no duty to provide it (indeed it would be unlawful probably to do so – see *Bland*) is clear in your answer.

4. Case law developments

The need for parliamentary intervention has been highlighted in cases going back to ***Bland*** itself, where concerns were raised at the need to categorise withdrawal of treatment as an omission to avoid legal consequences of it being an act. The need for intervention was clearly highlighted in the ***Re A*** case, where the courts struggled with how to render lawful an operation to separate the conjoined twins which would inevitably kill one, but save the other. In ***Pretty*** and ***Purdy*** attempts have been made to challenge the legality of the current law on human rights grounds (Articles 2 and 8). However, it is clear that considerable leeway is granted to the State to make its own laws within the margin of appreciation. Without legislation court challenges seem likely to fail. Most recently this is illustrated through the case of ***Nicklinson***, where, although arguments failed, the need for Parliamentary intervention was highlighted.

5. Summary of analysis

As seen, the law does not allow a physician to assist P to die. P's only option would seem to be a refusal of treatment, with the unpleasant consequences and potentially slow death that may result. It is clear that the courts consider it inappropriate for them to make decisions which fundamentally impact on the legal position, which should be dealt with by Parliament. There are a number of ethical concerns about any legalising of 'euthanasia' in whatever form, from the religious and moral views that the sanctity of life is absolute, to concerns expressed about the 'slippery slope'. Ultimately, however, as per Lady Hale in ***Nicklinson***, it can't be beyond the legislature to provide clear safeguards to protect against such concerns whilst still allowing those who wish to die to do so in a peaceful and dignified manner with appropriate medical assistance.

✓ Make your answer stand out

- Demonstrate that you are familiar with the extensive case law and in this area.
- Ensure your answer remains focused – there is a lot of ground to cover and time/word limit will affect the level of detail.
- Demonstrate an understanding of the ethical issues.
- Show you are up to date – this is a fast-moving area.

! Don't be tempted to . . .

- Just provide your own personal opinion without reference to the legal/ethical arguments.
- Miss out relevant elements of the overall framework.
- Forget to answer the question.

Question 6

By recognising an adult's right to refuse life-sustaining treatment, the Mental Capacity Act 2005 (MCA) has started the law down the slippery slope to euthanasia. Discuss.

Answer plan

- Introduce and identify the scope of the question.
- Identify the relevant provisions of the MCA.
- Detail and analyse the impact of advance decisions.
- Consider the extent to which advance decisions may be said to be a move towards euthanasia.
- Conclude your answer.

Diagram plan

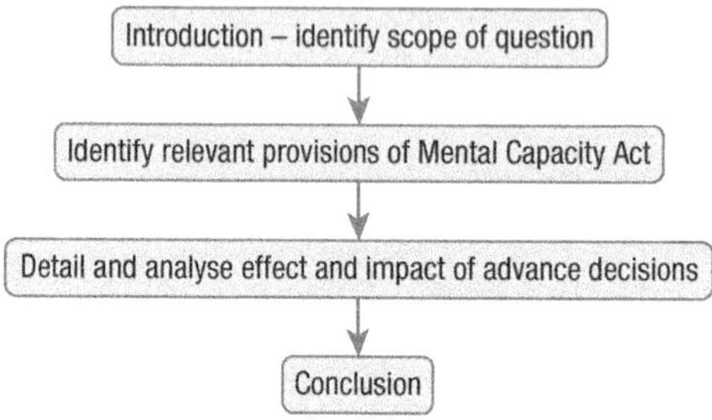

A printable version of this diagram plan is available from **www.pearsoned.co.uk/lawexpressqa**

Answer

The Mental Capacity Act 2005 (MCA) sets out a statutory regime which provides authority for the care and treatment of those who lack capacity.[1] The MCA also provides for a capable adult to make advance decisions to refuse treatment at a time when they have lost capacity. Following concerns raised that these provisions could amount to a legalising of euthanasia, section 62 was added to clarify the effect the MCA has on assisted suicide. We will discuss the relevant provisions of the MCA, consider their impact and the extent to which concerns that the provisions could be said to be a step towards euthanasia are valid.

[1] Of course the MCA also provides for decisions to be made about property and affairs of those who lack capacity – but you don't need to discuss this as the focus here is clearly on treatment provisions.

1. The MCA overview

The MCA provides a statutory framework for the care and treatment of adults[2] who lack capacity, effectively replacing the common law doctrine of necessity, developed in cases such as ***Re F*** (***F* v *West Berkshire*** [1990] 2 AC 1) by the courts to fill a gap in the law.[3] The MCA provides key principles (s. 1), a definition of capacity (s. 2) and an assessment process (s. 3) as to whether P has the requisite capacity to make a particular decision at the relevant time. Where P lacks capacity the MCA may 'authorise' treatment (s. 5) in P's best interests (s. 4), which take into account P's wishes and feelings, past, present and future. This does not prevent P being treated against his/her wishes, however, if such treatment were to be objectively assessed as being in P's best interests.[4] In order to ensure that treatment would not be given in such circumstances P may make an advance decision (AD) refusing treatment which is legally binding.

2. Advance decisions

The relevant provisions are set out in sections 24–26 of the MCA.[5] These provide for an adult, who has the requisite capacity to make such a decision, to make an advance decision (AD) refusing treatment which takes effect if P loses capacity to subsequently make such decisions for himself. An AD will, however, only be binding if it is 'valid' and 'applicable' (s. 25).

To be valid the AD has to be made by a capable adult P and not withdrawn either directly or indirectly by P doing a subsequent inconsistent act.[6] To be applicable the AD must relate to the particular treatment in question, apply in the circumstances within which the treatment is proposed and not be affected by any medical developments to an extent which would not have been envisaged by P, thus making it effectively a different decision to that made by P when he created his AD. An AD can be withdrawn at any time and is of no legal effect if P still has capacity to make the decision for himself (s. 24).

There are special procedural requirements that apply where the treatment refused becomes 'life-sustaining' (s. 25). Then the AD will only be legally binding if it is in writing, signed witnessed and verified. If not, then it will simply be a powerful statement of P's wishes[7] but will

[2] Some of the provisions apply to 16–17-year-olds but that is also outside the scope of this question and you don't need to waste time or word count talking about this.

[3] To fully understand the lengthy process involved in the creation of the MCA you can look at the four consultation papers published by the Law Commission. For a recent consideration of the MCA see the 2014 House of Lords Select Committee Report at http://www.publications.parliament.uk/pa/ld201314/ldselect/ldmentalcap/139/13902.htm. This background information can be used to add depth to your answer.

[4] Remember, although best interests is focused on the individual P it is still an objective assessment and not a 'substituted decision' approach. Make sure this is clearly reflected in your answer.

[5] These are key provisions of the MCA and you will need to be sufficiently precise and detailed in references to them.

[6] For examples and a basic explanation of the effect of this provision see the Code of Practice.

[7] This may be referred to as an advance statement. It is important not to confuse the legal effect of this with an AD.

not be legally binding and a decision may be taken to treat P contrary to the refusal in his 'best interests'.

The AD will prevent a doctor providing P with the relevant treatment only where the doctor 'is satisfied' that a valid applicable AD exists (s. 26). Given the real possibility that the doctor may not know about the AD (particularly in an emergency), the potential that P may not have been capable while making the AD, that P may have changed his mind or that P was not sufficiently clear to which treatment the decision was meant to apply, in fact the creation of a binding AD may be practically difficult. This is demonstrated in the court's approach in the case of ***Re E (Medical Treatment: Anorexia)***[8] ([2012] EWHC 1639 COP).

[8] You could cite this case and *W* v *Healthcare NHS Trust* v *H* [2004] EWCA Civ 1324 as examples of the court's approach.

3. Effect and impact

In fact, despite the considerable concern expressed at the provisions of the MCA which allow for refusal of treatment, actually the MCA only recognises what was already established at common law,[9] namely that a capable P could make a binding refusal of treatment now and in the future (see ***Re C (Adult: Refusal of Treatment)*** [1994] 1 WLR 290). Not to do so would arguably render any requirement for consent to treatment of a P who is inevitably going to lose capacity as their illness progresses, meaningless. A doctor could just wait for P to lose capacity and intervene at that point. This would erode P's right to autonomy which underpins medical law in this context.[10]

[9] It is important you are clear what the relevance is of any of the pre-MCA common law cases you refer to.

[10] You could use *Re C*, *Re MB* ([1997] 2 FLR 426) as an example of this.

In fact it would seem that the MCA has actually made it more difficult for a P to make a binding refusal of treatment, because of the requirement for the doctor to be satisfied the refusal is valid and applicable and the procedural requirements that apply if the refusal is life-sustaining treatment, which was not part of the common law.

The concerns expressed at the inclusion of ADs led to the addition of the somewhat strange section 62, which declares that nothing in the MCA is to be taken as in any way altering the law on murder, manslaughter or assisted suicide. This is clearly aimed at assuaging any concerns that ADs may be used/interpreted as a means of legalising euthanasia.

[11] Take care with the different approaches in this regard and ensure your answer is clear.

Of course the term euthanasia may be used differently by different commentators.[11] It may be argued that allowing patients to refuse any form of life-sustaining treatment is a form of euthanasia, however this is not the legal position. It is clear from ***Airedale NHS Trust* v *Bland*** ([1993] AC 789) that a legal distinction is to be drawn between a doctor carrying out an act to kill the patient which is clearly unlawful, and an omission to treat, where there is no duty so to do, which is lawful. Thus it is argued, the MCA cannot be seen to do any more than respect P's autonomy, enabling P, while capable, to make his own treatment choices.

It may be argued that a broader definition of euthanasia should be applied and that the MCA does then promote this, allowing incapable Ps to die as a result of not being given life-sustaining treatment which could well meet the section 4 best interest test and would, but for the AD, be given. However, since all the MCA does here is to put the common law on a statutory footing in this regard, and indeed, as seen above, make it more difficult in a practical sense to make such a valid applicable refusal, then it is difficult to see how the MCA has moved us closer to legalising euthanasia. Indeed, to follow this argument through to its conclusion would result in the argument that allowing a capable P refusing life-sustaining treatment which is objectively in his best interests would also be euthanasia and this flies in the face of the fundamental principle of autonomy recognised at common law.

Ultimately all the MCA does is to place the protection of P's autonomy, recognised at common law, on a statutory footing, with the necessary safeguards to ensure that it cannot be used as a means of promoting euthanasia through the back door.

✓ Make your answer stand out

- Demonstrate that you understand the common law and post-MCA position.
- Make sure your MCA references are appropriately detailed and precise.
- Demonstrate an-up-to date knowledge of relevant case law.
- Include references to the development of the MCA and concerns that led to the inclusion of section 62.

! Don't be tempted to . . .

- Simply recite chunks of the MCA.
- Be too general with references to advance decisions.
- Get bogged down in terminology and the distinction between passive and active euthanasia and different commentators approaches.
- Simply provide your own views on euthanasia without proper reference to the relevant legal provisions.

www.pearsoned.co.uk/lawexpressqa

Go online to access more revision support including additional essay and problem questions with diagram plans, You be the marker questions, and download all diagrams from the book.

12 Organ donation

How this topic may come up in exams

Deceased organ donation is often assessed using a problem question. You may need to discuss how death can be defined. A problem may centre on the 'appropriate consent' requirements to test your knowledge of the Human Tissue Act 2004 and the Codes of Practice. Bear in mind the impact of conditional consent and be aware different consent rules apply for children and adults. A problem may also consider living donation – watch out for issues regarding donors who lack capacity.

An essay question is also possible. Knowledge of the relevant ethical issues is required. Whether an opt-out system should be introduced is a popular topic but be aware of alternative methods to increase the number of organs available for transplantation. For instance, should we be able to sell organs and are they even 'ours' to sell?

Before you begin

It's a good idea to consider the following key themes of organ donation before tackling a question on this topic.

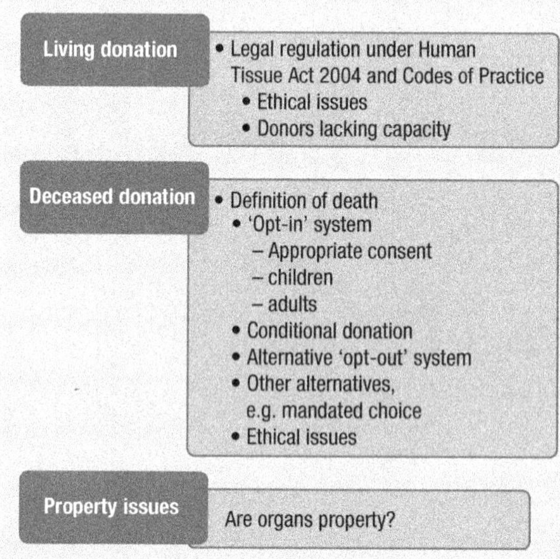

Living donation
• Legal regulation under Human Tissue Act 2004 and Codes of Practice
• Ethical issues
• Donors lacking capacity
Deceased donation
• Definition of death
• 'Opt-in' system
– Appropriate consent
– children
– adults
• Conditional donation
• Alternative 'opt-out' system
• Other alternatives, e.g. mandated choice
• Ethical issues
Property issues
Are organs property?

A printable version of this diagram is available from **www.pearsoned.co.uk/lawexpressqa**

Question 1

Albert and his son Ben (aged 13) are seriously injured in a boating accident and receive emergency treatment in a hospital in the north-east of England. They both undergo extensive clinical diagnostic tests. The clinical team conclude brain stem function has ceased.

Albert is married to Celia. They separated 21 years ago but never divorced. Dina has been living with Albert for 20 years. Albert and Dina have two children, Ben and also a daughter Eve (aged 18). Celia, Dina and Eve attend the hospital. They are informed of the diagnosis and are asked about organ donation.

Dina says she doesn't know what Albert would have wanted. In any event she is adamant she does not want his body to be touched. Celia thinks Albert's organs should be donated. Ben was carrying a donor card. Dina does not want his organs to be removed either, but Eve thinks Ben's wishes should be followed.

Discuss whether it would be lawful to remove Albert and Ben's organs for the purpose of organ transplantation and whether Dina's objection has any impact.

Diagram plan

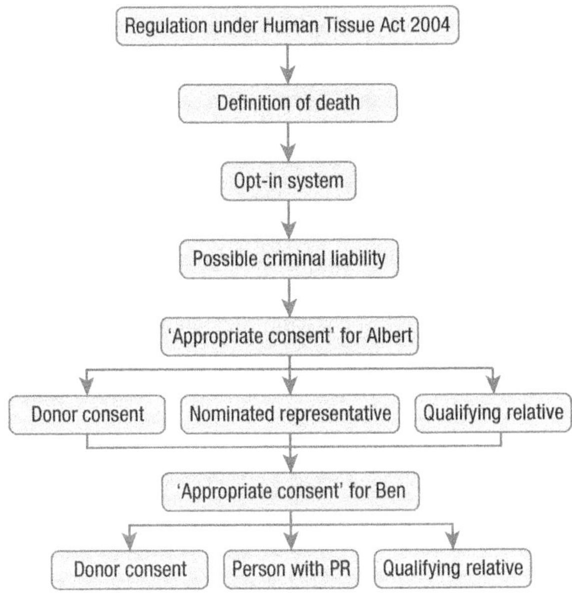

A printable version of this diagram plan is available from **www.pearsoned.co.uk/lawexpressqa**

Answer plan

- Outline the relevance and importance of the Human Tissue Act 2004.
- Confirm the definition of 'death'.
- Introduce the opt-in system for deceased organ donation.
- Mention potential criminal liability.
- Discuss the 'appropriate consent' possibilities for Albert, namely:
  - donor consent;
  - nominated representative;
  - qualifying relative.
- Discuss the 'appropriate consent' possibilities for Ben, namely:
  - donor consent (if *Gillick* competent);
  - person with parental responsibility;
  - qualifying relative.

Answer

The legal regulation of deceased organ donation must be considered.[1] The Human Tissue Act 2004 (the 2004 Act) provides that appropriate consent must be obtained for the removal, storage and use of relevant material from a deceased person to be lawful (section 1 and Schedule 1). Human organs are categorised as 'relevant material' under section 53. Transplantation is a potentially lawful purpose under Part 1, Schedule 1 of the 2004 Act.

Deceased donors fall into two categories. The first category is donors after brain death (DBD) where neurological criteria are used to confirm brain stem death.[2] Albert and Ben fall into this category. The alternative category is donors after circulatory death (DCD) where death is confirmed using cardio-respiratory criteria.

The 2004 Act regulates an 'opt-in' system for organ donation.[3] This means that organs can only be removed with consent. If appropriate consent is not obtained before removing the organs, section 5 provides that a criminal offence[4] would be committed unless the person reasonably believed that there was appropriate consent. The consent requirement is therefore key.

[1] As the question asks you to consider whether it is lawful to remove organs, introduce your intention to focus on issues regarding legal regulation under the Human Tissue Act 2004.

[2] As this is clearly not a living donor situation, it is important to confirm how death is defined as the donor must be deceased.

[3] It is significant the problem question is set in England. It is anticipated Wales will have an opt-out system from December 2015.

[4] Reference to potential criminal liability at an early point helps to establish the importance of the consent problems. Alternatively, it would also be apt to refer to criminal liability at a later point (i.e. to identify potential consequences if consent is not obtained).

1. Albert[5]

[5] Use headings where appropriate to divide your answer. This will help your essay structure and clearly separates coverage of the issues that relate to Albert (as an adult) and Ben (as a child).

The appropriate consent requirements in relation to adults which apply to deceased organ donation are set out in section 3(6). First, we need to see if we can identify whether a decision by Albert to consent or not consent to organ transplantation was in force before he died (section 3(6)(a)). It appears there is no evidence of any consent (or indeed any refusal). Dina is unable to provide any information as to his views. *If* there was evidence he did not wish to consent to organ donation that would be determinative. There is no such evidence, therefore we need to look for alternative sources of appropriate consent.

The next source would be a 'nominated representative' (section 3(6)(b)). Under section 4 an adult can appoint a nominated representative to consent on his behalf after death. The appointment can be in writing or made orally, but there are formal requirements to be met for the appointment to be valid (section 4(4) and section 4(5)). There is no suggestion a nominated representative exists.[6]

[6] As there is no suggestion a nominated representative exists, the issues regarding nominated representatives are dealt with quite briefly (if it were otherwise you would be expected to identify and apply the relevant formal requirements).

Finally, in the absence of Albert's consent (or refusal) or the existence of a nominated representative the hospital will need to seek consent from a person who stood in 'a qualifying relationship' to him before he died (section 3(6)(c)). The relevant qualifying relationships for this scenario are ranked in the following order:[7]

[7] This sets out specific, detailed coverage regarding the ranking in section 27. Given there are various parties in the scenario, it would not be enough to simply say a hierarchy exists. It is vital to carefully consider the respective positions of Celia, Dina and Eve.

- Section 27(4)(a) spouse, civil partner or partner;
- Section 27(4)(b) parent or child.

Dina meets the definition of 'partner' as she and Albert lived as partners in an 'enduring family relationship' (section 54(8)). Celia (Albert's estranged wife) and Dina appear higher in the hierarchical ranking than Eve (his daughter). Eve's consent would have been sought if Celia and Dina did not want to make a decision. That is not the case here, they have both expressed a wish.

Celia provides consent but Dina refuses. Section 27(5) states that relationships in the same paragraph of subsection 4 will have 'equal ranking'. Celia's position as an estranged wife (as they have not divorced) still has the same weighting as Dina's status as Albert's current partner. Section 27(7) provides that where there are at least two people in the same high-ranking category in the hierarchy, it is 'sufficient to obtain the consent of any of them'.[8] The hospital could therefore rely on Celia's consent alone. Dina's objection would not operate as a legal barrier to this even though it appears she had a closer relationship with Albert before his death.

Although Celia's consent would allow the hospital to remove the organs, this does not mean the hospital has an obligation to. The Human Tissue Authority produces Codes of Practice which accompany the 2004 Act. Code of Practice 2 (Donation of solid organs for transplantation)[9] helps indicate how this dispute will be approached. Paragraph 115 states that where there is 'conflict' between those with 'equal ranking' sensitive discussion is needed, although it should be confirmed that the consent of one with equal ranking will suffice. However, paragraph 102 provides that even in cases where the deceased adult consented to donation and relatives do not have the power to overrule this, there may still be cases where donation is viewed as 'inappropriate'. Although this paragraph deals with the situation where the deceased consented (which is not the case here), it does raise the possibility of family objection being considered. Dina's strong objection may cause the doctors to be unwilling to remove Albert's organs.[10]

2. Ben

The 'appropriate consent' requirements which apply to children and deceased organ donation are set out in section 2(7). We are told that Ben has carried a donor card. This may provide the hospital with 'appropriate consent' as section 2(7)(a) requires the hospital to first consider whether a child's decision to consent or refuse was in force before he died. The common law principles to determine a child's competence set out in ***Gillick* v *West Norfolk and Wisbech Area Health Authority*** [1986] AC 112 would apply. ***Gillick*** competence would be established if Ben has 'sufficient understanding and intelligence'[11] to make the decision and the hospital would then be able to rely on his consent. As acknowledged by Jackson (2013), once a child has died, it will be difficult to establish whether they were ***Gillick*** competent to make the relevant decision when they were alive (see Jackson, E. (2013) *Medical Law: Texts, Cases and Materials*. (3rd edn). Oxford: Oxford University Press). A child cannot appoint a nominated representative (unlike an adult).

[8] Dispute between those close to the deceased is a key issue in the scenario. This demonstrates detailed knowledge of section 27 and how it is relevant when dealing with family conflict in relation to consent to donation.

[9] The examiner will be impressed if you refer to relevant parts of the Code of Practice, rather than rely on the 2004 Act alone.

[10] Demonstrate good focus on the instruction in the question which asks whether Dina's objection will have *any* impact. This issue strays beyond legal regulation under the 2004 Act alone. Stress there may be a distinction between what the law permits (referring to legal regulation under the 2004 Act) and what clinicians are prepared to do in the face of family objection (and refer to the Code of Practice in this regard).

[11] The examiner will like you to use your knowledge in other areas, i.e. assessing the competence of children at common law.

[12] Again, it is important to recognise that although it may be lawful to remove organs under the 2004 Act, it does

If ***Gillick*** competence *can* be established the hospital will be able to rely on that consent and remove, store and use organs lawfully, however they are not obliged to do so. Paragraph 118 of Code of Practice 2 states it is 'essential' to discuss the child's consent with the family and 'take their views and wishes into account' when determining how to proceed. It may therefore be that Dina's strong views against donation mean that the doctors are reluctant to act.[12]

If Ben was *not* ***Gillick*** competent,[13] section 2(7)(b) provides that appropriate consent can instead be given by a person who has parental responsibility (PR) for him. Code of Practice 2, paragraph 119 confirms that the consent of only one person with PR is needed. Dina is the only person with PR in any event. Dina refuses to consent and this will be determinative – Ben's organs will not be used. Eve stood in a qualifying relationship with Ben as his sister (section 27(4)(c)). However, the hospital would only be able to rely on the consent of someone who stood in a qualifying relationship where there was no person with PR. This is not the case here – Eve cannot override Dina's refusal.[14]

not mean that this will always happen. The examiner would be pleased you had considered the Code of Practice coverage regarding children and tried to apply it to this scenario.

[13] This shows a consideration of alternatives, which is important as the scenario did not provide you with information to enable you to draw any conclusions regarding *Gillick* competence.

[14] It is appropriate to confirm why Eve's agreement would not be sufficient to allow organ donation to proceed. This means you have dealt with the full range of issues raised by the different family members involved.

Make your answer stand out

- There is little case law in this area, so the examiner will expect to see detailed reference to the Human Tissue Act 2004 and relevant parts of the Codes of Practice instead. Code of Practice 1 (Consent) and Code of Practice 2 (Donation of solid organs for transplantation) are of particular relevance.
- Consent is key in relation to authorising the removal of organs. Be prepared to demonstrate your knowledge of issues relating to consent and capacity (both in relation to adults and children). In this scenario you needed to comment on how a child's competence is assessed at common law; in a different scenario you may have to draw upon your knowledge of the Mental Capacity Act 2005 provisions regarding assessing capacity.
- Focus on the instruction in the question. As well as considering whether it would be *lawful* to remove organs (which required consideration of whether the requirements of the 2004 Act were met) you were also asked whether Dina's objections would have *any impact*. Show your understanding that although appropriate consent under the 2004 Act may allow the removal of organs, this does not mean the hospital are under an obligation to do so.

! Don't be tempted to . . .

- Mistakenly apply other areas of the Human Tissue Act 2004. The 2004 Act deals with a range of issues, including living donation and use of human material for purposes other than transplantation. Make sure you are referring to the correct provisions. This also applies to your use of the Codes of Practice, ensure you are dealing with advice regarding deceased organ donation.
- Make assumptions. You must consider alternatives where the scenario does not give you sufficient information to draw conclusions. For example, you would be unable to say whether or not Ben was *Gillick* competent.

Question 2

Part (i) Frank and his brother George are very close. George suffers from kidney disease and has to undergo kidney dialysis. Frank decides to look into the possibility of being a living donor so he can donate a kidney. However, before he has the chance to do this he is injured in a serious accident and subsequently dies. Frank was carrying a donor card in an envelope accompanied by a note attached explaining his wishes, namely he would like to donate to his brother.

There is disagreement among the clinical team as to whether they have to comply with Frank's request. Dr James thinks George should receive one of Frank's kidneys. Dr Lee thinks the team can rely on the donor card to authorise removal of Frank's organs but believes Frank's kidneys should be given to patients at the top of the transplant waiting list.

Discuss the legal impact of Frank's request.

Part (ii) Consider whether directed donation to a particular individual (or alternatively attaching conditions regarding class of recipient) *should* be permitted.

Answer plan

Part (i)

- → Introduce directed donation and the relevance of the Human Tissue Act 2004.
- → Highlight and apply relevant policy.
- → Consider the position if consent is unconditional.
- → Analyse the legal position if consent is conditional and the condition is complied with.
- → Consider the legal impact if consent is conditional and the condition is ignored.

Part (ii)

- Introduce the distinction between conditional donation (where the condition relates to class of recipient) and directed donation.
- Refer to previous difficult ethical dilemmas.
- Consider the impact of the altruism principle.
- Discuss the relevance of the 'greatest need' principle.
- Analyse the extent to which autonomy is/should be respected.

Diagram plan

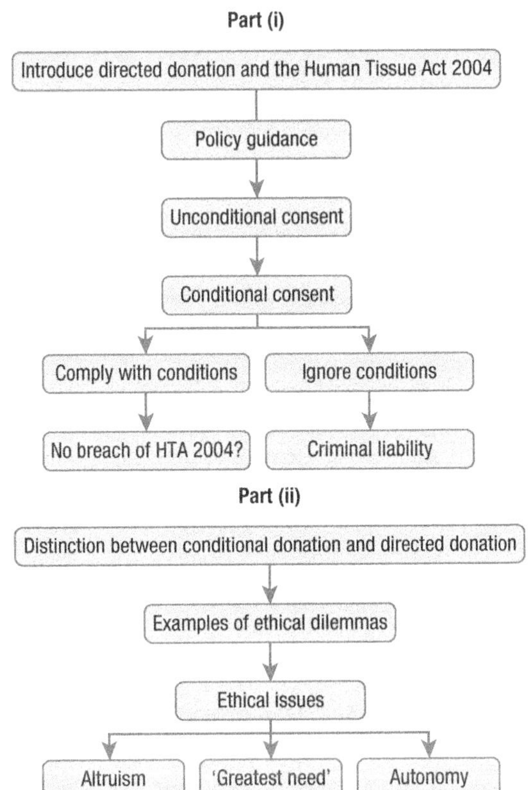

A printable version of this diagram plan is available from **www.pearsoned.co.uk/lawexpressqa**

Answer

Part (i)

[1] This introduces and defines the particular issue raised in the scenario, i.e. directed donation.

[2] This demonstrates you understand the importance of obtaining Frank's consent, before you focus on the particular request he has made.

[3] The examiner would be impressed if you refer to relevant policy documentation.

[4] It is important that you highlight where you feel you need more information, particularly where this may be critical to the outcome.

[5] You will need to consider alternatives, given you cannot draw firm conclusions as to whether the consent was conditional.

Directed donation is where a donor has expressed a wish for his/her organs to be given to a particular individual.[1] Directed donation may involve a 'condition' being attached to the donor's consent or could be a more generally expressed desire that a particular individual is considered. Section 1 of the Human Tissue Act 2004 (the 2004 Act) provides that appropriate consent allows a hospital to remove, store and use organs lawfully. Frank's donor card demonstrates his decision to consent was in force[2] before he died (section 3(6)(a)). The 2004 Act is silent on the issue of whether conditions can be attached.

A policy document on the subject of 'Requested Allocation of a Deceased Donor Organ' was issued in March 2010.[3] This states it is a fundamental principle that deceased organ donation is unconditional. Further investigation of the nature of Frank's request is required.[4] Was it expressed as a desire that his brother be considered as a recipient (and therefore unconditional)? Alternatively, was a condition attached to Frank's consent whereby his consent would be vitiated if a kidney was not offered to George?

MacLean (1999) argues a distinction can be drawn between 'conditions precedent' to the donation which form part of it and cannot be separated and 'conditions subsequent' which are an 'afterthought' to the unconditional offer and can be disregarded (see MacLean, A. (1999) Organ donation, racism and the Race Relations Act. *NLJ*, 149: 1250–52). Cronin and Douglas (2010) suggest this is a 'contrived attempt' to reach a solution (see Cronin, A.J. and Douglas, J.F. (2010) Directed and conditional deceased organ donations: laws and misconceptions. *Medical Law Review* 18(3): 275–301).

If Frank's consent is *unconditional*,[5] the 2010 policy provides that where there is a request that an organ be given to a particular individual this can be considered in 'exceptional circumstances': where there is no other person in urgent clinical need; where the deceased had indicated a wish to donate to a specific named relative or friend; and that person is either on the transplant waiting list (or could be placed on the list).

If Frank's consent is *conditional*, what would be the legal position if the hospital complied with Frank's request, as suggested by Dr James, so that George receives a kidney?[6] This would seem to breach the 2010 guidance which states donation must be unconditional. However, this may not breach the 2004 Act.[7] Cronin and Douglas (2010) argue that the principle of unconditional donation is 'certainly lawful, but only amounts to an operational policy'. Pattinson (2011) suggests the guidance 'lacks legal force' as the donor's consent would be a 'complete answer' to any civil or criminal law issues (see Pattinson, S.D. (2011) Directed donation and ownership of human organs. *Legal Studies*, 31(3): 392–401). He notes that once appropriate consent is present the 2004 Act does not demand approval from the Human Tissue Authority (whereas such approval is needed for living donation).

[6] Make sure you signpost your application of the principles to the scenario clearly.

[7] The examiner would like to see you critically consider the impact of the guidance – bearing in mind the question asks you to consider the *legal impact*.

Turning to Dr Lee's suggestion, if Frank's consent was *conditional* would the hospital act unlawfully if it ignored the condition and removed his organs anyway (considering the 2010 policy opposes conditions being attached to donation)? It appears that potential criminal liability could arise. If the condition was ignored, it seems Daniel's consent would be vitiated and there would be no 'appropriate consent' to render the removal and use of organs lawful under section 1 of the 2004 Act. Cronin and Douglas (2010) argue it is impossible to 'accept the donation while ignoring the restriction' and criminal liability could arise under section 5[8] as an offence is committed where 'appropriate consent' is not established before removing organs.

[8] It is important to address potential criminal liability as this is a significant legal effect of failure to comply with the consent requirements.

Part (ii)

To consider whether conditional and directed organ donation *should* be permitted, ethical issues also become relevant.[9] Can an ethical distinction be drawn between conditional donation where the donor wants his/her organs to be given (or not given) to a particular class of recipient and directed donation where a donor wants a particular individual to benefit?

[9] Acknowledge this part of the question requires you to consider issues beyond legal regulation.

Conditional donation has been criticised. This originates from a case where consent to remove organs was given on the condition that organs would only be given to white recipients. A subsequent investigation found that the white recipients who received organs were at

[10] The examiner will be pleased if you show you have read a wide range of material.

[11] It will impress the examiner if you critically consider the conclusions that have been drawn in a report.

[12] Support your analysis by referring to academic commentary.

[13] In the absence of reported case law refer to reported incidents which have generated some controversy.

the top of the waiting list in any event. The report which followed[10] (Department of Health (2000) *An Investigation into Conditional Organ Donation, the Report of the Panel*, London: DoH) confirmed that conditional donation was not permissible and *all* conditions should be rejected. It is easy to agree with this conclusion when faced with a condition based on race. However, should all conditions be impermissible? Paragraph 6.1 of the report states that attaching conditions is contrary to 'the fundamental principle that organs are donated altruistically and should go to patients in the greatest need'.

Is this reasoning sound?[11] Conditional donation does not automatically conflict with altruism. As Wilkinson (2003)[12] notes, 'wanting organs to go to a child . . . is not a violation of altruism any more than donating to a children's charity is' and argues that altruism does not demand that actions follow a greatest needs principle (see Wilkinson, T.M. (2003) What's not wrong with conditional organ donation? *Journal of Medical Ethics*, 29: 163–4). Also, it is difficult to see how the 'greatest need' principle is met if conditional donation is not permitted. If a condition is attached to donation it cannot be ignored without incurring criminal liability (as stated above). The net result of refusal to comply with a condition is that nobody receives the organ, whereas, as stated by Wilkinson, 'accepting the offer allows someone's needs to be met'.

This line of argument applies in relation to directed donation. Applying the 'altrusim' element of donation it is difficult to see how donating to a sick relative offends altruism. In 2008 Rachel Leake was unable to receive a kidney from her deceased daughter Laura Ashworth despite suffering end stage renal failure, due to the policy that organs should be distributed on the basis of the greatest need.[13] Laura had considered the possibility of living donation before her death. A new policy followed in March 2010 (referred to in Part (i) above) which allowed close relatives/friends to be potential recipients in exceptional circumstances provided the donation was unconditional and there was no other person in urgent need. Does this still pay insufficient respect to the donor's wishes? The needs of an unknown potential recipient can potentially outweigh the wishes of a donor and the needs of their relative/friend.

As lawful authority for removal, storage and use of organs rests on 'appropriate consent', it appears respect for autonomy underpins the 2004 Act. If the deceased objected to donation when alive, this refusal must be respected. This demonstrates the wishes of the donor can outweigh the needs of a potential recipient. Considering the respect given to donor choice it is difficult to justify why decisions about who should benefit are not respected after death. In relation to living donation,[14] it is commonplace for a donor to donate to a relative or friend. It is unclear why this autonomous choice is not respected in relation to deceased donation.

[14] It is helpful to draw comparisons with living donation to help support your point – this also shows the breadth of your knowledge.

Make your answer stand out

- When considering relevant policy in this area try to engage in analysis. Whether you agree or disagree with it, you must show you have critically considered the basis of the policy.
- Demonstrate your understanding that policy documentation may not necessarily reflect the legal position.
- Draw comparisons with the position in relation to living donation. This is very relevant when considering the extent to which we do (or should) respect autonomous choices after death.
- Read Cronin, A.J. and Douglas, J.F. (2010) Directed and conditional deceased organ donations: laws and misconceptions. *Medical Law Review*, 18(3): 275–301; Pattinson, S.D. (2011) Directed donation and ownership of human organs. *Legal Studies*, 31(3): 392–401; and Wilkinson, T.M. (2003) What's not wrong with conditional organ donation? *Journal of Medical Ethics*, 29: 163–4. Make reference to the arguments advanced in these articles.

Don't be tempted to . . .

- Take a narrow approach regarding your reading. As the 2004 Act does not deal specifically with conditions attached to donation, you need to engage in wider research. Relevant source material for you to consider is referred to in the body of this answer.
- Only summarise the policy and the basis of the policy. You need to engage in your own analysis to determine whether a sound approach has been taken.
- Lose sight of the particular instructions in each part of the question. Part (i) asked you to consider the *legal* impact of the request, whereas Part (ii) asked you to consider whether conditions *should* be permitted. The issues in Part (ii) therefore extended beyond legal regulation and require you to look at ethical issues too.

Question 3

An opt-out system for organ transplantation should now be introduced to replace the current opt-in system in England. Discuss.

Answer plan

- Consider the current opt-in system and identify any criticisms.
- Introduce what an opt-out scheme is and distinguish between hard and soft opt-out.
- Evaluate whether an opt-out scheme respects autonomy.
- Critically consider whether the deceased have interests which survive after death.
- Refer to relevant moral and ethical theories such as utilitarianism.
- Discuss the potential practical effect of an opt-out scheme.
- Consider a possible alternative to the opt-in scheme – a mandated choice system.

Diagram plan

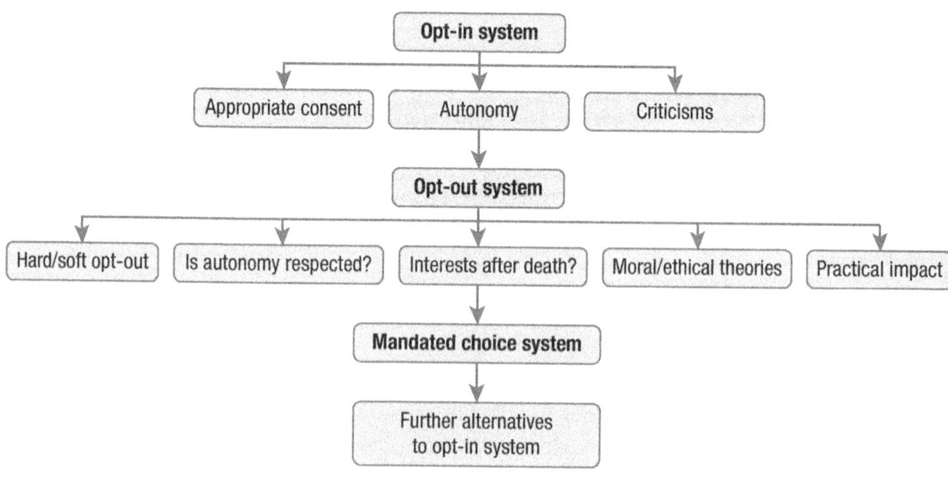

A printable version of this diagram plan is available from **www.pearsoned.co.uk/lawexpressqa**

Answer

There is a well-documented shortage of organ donors. An opt-out system has been identified as a solution. Would this be better than the current opt-in system or would it raise new problems?

It is important to consider the current opt-in system.[1] If it has flaws, it becomes easier to justify change. Under the Human Tissue Act 2004 organs can only be removed with 'appropriate consent'. For adults[2] the first step is to identify whether the deceased had consented or refused before death (section 3(6)(a)). Otherwise, consent can be given by a nominated representative (section 3(6)(b)) or, if there is no representative appointed, a person who stood in a qualifying relationship to the deceased (section 3(6)(c)). The relevant qualifying relationships are 'ranked' and consent is sought from the relative who features highest in the ranking (section 27).

Arguably, the advantage of this system is it respects the wishes of a potential donor as the first step is to ascertain donor consent. However, it is apparent that even in the absence of the deceased's consent, organ donation can go ahead with the consent of a relative (provided the deceased had not refused during their lifetime). There is no guarantee this reflects what the deceased would have wanted. A second issue concerns the potential power of relatives to override the organ donation, even if the deceased had consented to donation. Although the deceased's consent gives doctors the power to remove organs, they may choose not to where the family object. Finally, if the donor did want to donate but never indicated this wish when alive and the family do not provide consent, the organs will not be used. Even an opt-in system cannot guarantee the deceased's wishes will be respected.

An alternative 'opt-out' system is proposed. This would allow the removal of organs provided the deceased had not registered an objection[3] during their lifetime. There are different types of opt-out system.[4] Under a hard opt-out system there is no need to consult the deceased's family, so even if relatives thought the deceased would object, donation would go ahead. An independent report by the Organ Donation Taskforce (DoH, 2008)[5] which considered the potential impact of an opt-out system suggested that a hard opt-out system could be challenged under the European Convention on Human Rights (see Department of Health (2008)) *The Potential Impact of an Opt Out System for Organ Donation in the UK: An Independent Report from the Organ Donation Taskforce*. London: DoH. A soft opt-out system would allow relatives to object even if the deceased had not. Legislation permitting the introduction of a soft

[1] An evaluation of the current system is relevant to the question set. If it can be criticised – perhaps reform should be considered?

[2] There are slightly different appropriate consent requirements for children. However, to illustrate your point regarding respecting autonomy reference to adults will suffice.

[3] It is important for you to explain key terms.

[4] It is good to highlight there are different types of opt-out scheme – each type may generate different criticisms.

[5] The examiner will be impressed if you show you have read widely and identified relevant points from your research.

opt-out system in Wales has been enacted. Transplantation will be lawful on the basis of 'deemed consent' where the deceased has not registered an objection (Human Transplantation (Wales) Act 2013, section 3). The scheme is due to commence in December 2015. Use of the term 'presumed consent' or 'deemed consent' to describe an opt-out system can be criticised. Consent is generally viewed as having some positive element to it.

A key argument raised against an opt-out system centres on the importance of autonomy and consent. The British Medical Association (BMA) have supported the introduction of 'an opt-out system with safeguards', i.e. the soft opt-out approach. In *Building on Progress: Where next for organ donation policy in the UK?* (February 2012) the BMA state the public would have 'the same choice . . . to donate or not to donate – but the way that choice is registered differs'.[6] Individuals are therefore able to exercise autonomous choices in either system. The ODT report suggests that currently many people may wish to donate and due to inertia this desire is not registered, therefore an opt-out scheme could be described as 'consent for the disorganised'. To argue that an opt-out scheme respects autonomy it is important to ensure that individuals are equipped with knowledge about the new scheme, so that if an individual does not register an objection this is because they are happy for organs to be used and not due to ignorance.[7]

[6] It is a good idea to refer to the BMA approach – this gives some indication of the views of the medical profession.

[7] This demonstrates careful consideration of whether failure to object can be said to equal consent.

Competing moral and ethical theories exist regarding the extent to which any interests the potential donor has after death should continue to be protected. The arguments are significant if we cannot be sure that the deceased would have been happy to consent simply because they have failed to register an objection. A real possibility exists that it is only those with a strong objection who make the effort to register an objection. Those who are indifferent may not.

Glannon (2003) suggests some interests can survive death, such as a surviving interest in bodily integrity (see Glannon, W. (2003) Do the sick have a right to cadaveric organs? *Journal of Medical Ethic*, 29: 153–56). However, even though Harris (2003) accepts that 'persisting interests' remain after death[8] it is argued these are 'relatively

[8] The examiner will be impressed if you refer to academic authority on the issue of interests which survive death.

weak' compared to the interests of the potential recipient who could be harmed (see Harris, J. (2003) Organ procurement: dead interests, living needs. *Journal of Medical Ethics*, 29: 130–134). Glannon (2003) suggests the rights of a potential donor not to be interfered with could be categorised as a 'negative right' which carry more 'moral force' than any 'positive right' of the potential recipient to be helped. This is particularly relevant if failure to register an objection is due to ignorance or lethargy (rather than willingness to donate).[9] There may well be negative rights which deserve protection. Competing moral theories exist. Utilitarianism considers whether the costs of any scheme are low compared to the benefits to balance utility over disutility. There is great benefit where lives can be saved, however Glannon (2003) suggests any surviving interest the potential donor has regarding what happens to his body places 'deontological constraints' on what can be done.

[9] This applies the issue to the particular problem posed by an opt-out scheme – the deceased may not have wanted his organs to be donated.

Realistically, an opt-out system will only be of benefit if it results in more organs available for transplantation. The opt-out system in Spain has been viewed as successful as donation rates increased; but as noted by the ODT report, this increase coincided with the later development of new infrastructure (an increase did not arise at the time opt-out legislation was passed.) The ODT report considered that an opt-out system could potentially damage the trust between clinicians and families,[10] concluding that it would not yet recommend the introduction of such a system.

[10] This shows you have tried to anticipate the potential practical consequences of such a system.

Would an alternative 'mandated choice' scheme better protect the deceased's interests?[11] This system would demand that individuals make a choice whether or not to donate. There would be practical difficulties in implementation as 'forcing' people to decide could be problematic. Arguably the right to respect autonomous choices should also extend to respect the choice to *not* make a decision.

[11] It is a good idea to consider whether there is a better alternative.

An opt-out system can only be successful if it increases donation rates, however it must also be morally and ethically defensible. Significantly, there are doubts about whether the opt-in system always protects autonomy in any event. There are legitimate concerns regarding the extent to which an opt-out scheme respects patients' wishes. It seems clear we cannot assume that the deceased no longer have any interests to protect.

✓ Make your answer stand out

- There is scope to develop coverage of the competing ethical and moral issues at stake, e.g. utilitarianism versus rights-based theories.
- Refer to a range of source material, for example articles in non-legal journals such as the *Journal of Medical Ethics.* Read Harris, J. (2003) Organ procurement: dead interests, living needs. *Journal of Medical Ethics*, 29: 130–34.
- Incorporate consideration of alternatives to an opt-out system. Mandated choice is referred to in the answer, but there are other (more extreme?) options too, e.g. payment to donors.
- Discuss whether there are any property rights in a dead body or its parts. This would be a relevant line of argument to develop as this may impact on how we approach the body of the deceased. You should be conscious of time in an exam situation though and not try to cover too many angles at the expense of depth. Plan your time carefully to see what is feasible.

! Don't be tempted to . . .

- Leave out introduction of key terms. You need to explain what is meant by opt-in and opt-out.
- Only consider issues regarding an opt-out scheme. The question asks you to consider whether the opt-in scheme should be replaced. Discussion of the flaws of an opt-in scheme therefore falls within the scope of the question. If there are problems this enhances the need to consider alternative approaches.

www.pearsoned.co.uk/lawexpressqa

Go online to access more revision support including additional essay and problem questions with diagram plans, You be the marker questions, and download all diagrams from the book.

Bibliography

Alghrani, A. and Harris, J. (2006) Reproductive liberty: should the foundation of families be regulated? *Child and Family Law Quarterly*, 18(2): 191.

Asch, A. (2003) Disability Equality and Prenatal Testing: Contradictory or Compatible? *Florida State University Law Review*, 30: 315–42.

Bartlett, P. and Sandland, R. (2013) *Mental Health Law: Policy and Practice* (4th edn). Oxford: Oxford University Press.

Brazier, M. and Miola, J. (2000) Bye Bye *Bolam*: A Medical Litigation Revolution? *Medical Law Review*, 8(1): 84–115.

British Medical Association (2012) *Building on Progress: Where next for organ donation policy in the UK?* London: BMA.

Coggon, J. (2006) Could the right to die with dignity represent a new right to die in English Law? *Medical Law Review*, 14.

Coggon, J. and Miola, J. (2011) Autonomy, liberty and medical decision making. *Cambridge Law Journal*, 70: 523–47.

Cronin, A. J. and Douglas, J. F. (2010) Directed and Conditional Deceased Organ Donations: Laws and Misconceptions. *Medical Law Review*, 18: 275–301.

Department for Education (2013) *Working Together to Safeguard Children*. Statutory guidance, London: DfE.

Department of Health (2000) *An Investigation into Conditional Organ Donation, the Report of the Panel*. London: DoH.

Department of Health (2004) *Best Practice Guidance for Doctors and other Health Professionals on the Provision of Advice and Treatment to Young People under 16 on Contraception, Sexual and Reproductive Health*. London: DoH.

Department of Health (2008) *The Potential Impact of an Opt Out System for Organ Donation in the UK: An Independent Report from the Organ Donation Taskforce*. London: DoH.

Department of Health (2010) *Confidentiality: NHS Code of Practice Supplementary Guidance: Public Interest Disclosures*. London: DoH.

Department of Health (2010) *Requested Allocation of a Deceased Donor Organ*. London: DoH.

Department of Health (2013) *Mental Capacity Act 2005 Code of Practice*. London: DOH.

Department of Health (2014) *Guidance in Relation to Requirements of the Abortion Act 1967*. London: DoH.

Department of Health & Social Security (1984) *Report of the Committee of Inquiry into Human Fertilisation and Embryology*. London: Her Majesty's Stationery Office.

Department of Health (2015) *Mental Health Act 1983: Code of Practice*. London: DOH.

Donnelly, M. (2009) Best interests, patient participation and the Mental Capacity Act 2005. *Medical Law Review*, 17: 1–29.

Dyer, C. (1999) British GP cleared of murder charge. *British Medical Journal*, 318: 1306.

Edis, W. (2005) *Gregg* v *Scott*: loss of a chance, chance of a loss or a lost chance? *Solicitors Journal*, 11(2): 166.

Eekelaar, J. (2006) *Family Law and Personal Life*. Oxford: Oxford University Press.

Ellis Cameron-Perry, J. (1999) Return of the burden of the blessing. *New Law Journal*, 149: 1887.

Fortin, J. (2009) *Children's Rights and the Developing Law* (3rd edn). Cambridge: Cambridge University Press.

Foster, C. (2004) It should be, therefore it is. *New Law Journal*, 5(11): 1644.

Foster, C. (2005) Last chance for lost chances: (*Gregg* v *Scott* in the House of Lords). *New Law Journal*, 18(2): 248.

Foster, S. (2014) Case Comment (*R (on the application of Nicklinson)* v *Ministry of Justice*) [2014] UKSC 38. *Coventry Law Journal*, 19(1): 73–6.

Francis, R. (2006) *Report of the Independent Inquiry into the Care and Treatment of Michael Stone*. South East Coast Strategic Health Authority.

Freeman, M. (1992) Taking children's rights more seriously. *International Journal of Law, Policy and the Family*, 6(1): 52–71.

Freeman, M. (1999) Does surrogacy have a future after Brazier? *Medical Law Review*, 7: 1–20.

General Medical Council (2009) *Confidentiality*. London: GMC.

Gilmore, S. and Herring J. (2012) Children's refusal of treatment: the debate continues. *Family Law*, 42: 973–8.

Glannon, W. (2003) Do the sick have a right to cadaveric organs? *Journal of Medical Ethics*. 29: 153–6.

Greasley, K. (2011) Medical abortion and the 'golden rule' of statutory interpretation, *BPAS* v *the Secretary of State for Health* [2011] EWHC 235. *Medical Law Review*, 19: 314–25.

Gurnham, D. and Miola J. (2012) Reproduction, Rights, and the welfare interests of children: the times they aren't a–changin. *KLJ*, 23: 29–35.

Harris, J. (2003) Consent and end of life decisions. *Journal of Medical Ethics*, 29: 10–15.

Harris, J. (2003) Organ procurement: dead interests, living needs. *Journal of Medical Ethics*, 29: 130–34.

Health and Social Care Information Centre (2013) *A Guide to Confidentiality in Health and Social Care*. London: HSCIC.

Herring, J. (2012) *Medical Law and Ethics* (4th edn). Oxford: Oxford University Press.

Herring, J. and Foster, C. (2012) Welfare means relationality, virtue and altrusim. *Legal Studies*, 32 (3): 480–498.

Hewitt, D. (2008) Too young to decide? *Solicitors Journal*, 30(9).

Hoyano, L.C.H. (2002) Misconceptions about wrongful conception. *Modern Law Review*, 65: 883–906.

Human Fertilisation and Embryology Authority [HFEA] (2003) *Sex Selection: Options for Regulation*. London: HFEA.

Human Fertilisation and Embryology Authority [HFEA] (2012) *Code of Practice* (8th edn). London: HFEA.

Information Commissioner's Office (2014) Human Tissue Authority Code of Practice 2 (Donation of solid organs for transplantation), *Guide to Data Protection*. London.

Jackson, E. (2002) Conception and the irrelevance of the welfare principle. *Modern Law Review*, 65: 176–203.

Jackson, E. (2013) *Medical Law: Texts, Cases and Materials* (3rd edn). Oxford: Oxford University Press.

Jones, C. (2003) Tightropes and tragedies: 25 years of Tarasoff. *Medicine, Science and the Law*, *43*(1): 13–22.

Jones, R. (2013) *Mental Health Act Manual* (16th edn). London: Sweet & Maxwell.

Laing, J.A. and Oderberg, D.S. (2005) Artifical reproduction, the 'welfare principle', and the common good. *Medical Law Review*, *13*(3): 328–56.

Laurie, G.T. (1996) The most personal information of all: an appraisal of genetic privacy in the shadow of the Human Genome Project. *International Journal of Law, Policy and the Family*, *10*(1): 74–101.

MacLean, A. (1999) Organ donation, racism and the Race Relations Act. *NLJ*, 149: 1250–52.

Maclean, A.R. (2008) Advance directives and the rocky waters of anticipatory decision-making. *Medical Law Review*, *16*(1): 1–22.

Maskrey, S. and Edis W. (2005) *Chester* v *Afshar* and *Gregg* v *Scott*: mixed messages for lawyers. *Journal of Personal Injury Law*, 205: 223.

Mason, J.K. and Laurie G.T. (2006) *Mason & McCall Smith's Law and Medical Ethics* (7th edn). Oxford: Oxford University Press, paragraph 10.52.

Mason, J.K. and Laurie G.T. (2013) *Mason & McCall Smith's Law and Medical Ethics* (9th edn), Oxford: Oxford University Press.

McGuiness, S. (2013) Law, Reproduction and disability: fatally 'handicapped'? *Medical Law Review*, 21: 213–42.

Miola, J. (2009) On the materiality of risk – paper tigers and panaceas. *Medical Law Review*, 17: 76–108.

Morgan, D. (1990) Abortion: the unexamined ground. *Criminal Law Review*: 687–94.

Newdick, C. (2005) *Who Should We Treat? Rights, Rationing and Resources in the NHS* (2nd edn). Oxford: Oxford University Press.

Newdick, C. (2007) Judicial review: low priority treatment and exceptional case review. *Medical Law Review*, 15(2): 236.

Ngwena, C. and Chadwick R. (1993) Genetic diagnostic information and the duty of confidentiality: ethics and law. *Medical Law International*, 73.

Pattinson, S.D. (2011) Directed donation and ownership of human organs. *Legal Studies*, (3): 392–401.

Pattinson, S.D. (2014) *Medical Law and Ethics* (4th edn). London: Sweet and Maxwell.

Peay, J. (2003) *Decisions and Dilemmas: Working with Mental Health Law*. Oxford: Hart Publishing.

Priaulx, N.M. (2005) Damages for the unwanted child: time for a rethink? *Medico–Legal Journal*, 73(4).

Royal College of Obstetricians and Gynaecologists (2010) *Termination of Pregnancy for Fetal Abnormality in England, Scotland and Wales*. London: Royal College of Obstetricians and Gynaecologists.

Royal College of Physicians, Royal College of Pathologists and British Society for Human Genetics (2011) *Consent and Confidentiality in Clinical Genetic Practice: Guidance on Genetic Testing and Sharing Genetic Information* (2nd edn). Report of the Joint Committee on Medical Genetics, London: Royal College of Physicians, Royal College of Pathologists.

Sexual Health Policy Team, Public Health Directorate 10250 (2014) *Guidance in Relation to Requirements of the Abortion Act 1967*. London: Department of Health.

Shaw, M. (2004) Sick Pay. *Solicitors Journal*, 29(10): 1228.

Sheldon, S. and Wilkinson, S. (2001) Termination of pregnancy for reason of foetal disability: are there grounds for a special exception in law? *Medical Law Review*, 9: 85–109.

Sheldon, S. and Wilkinson, S. (2004) Hashmi and Whitaker, an unjustifiable and misguided distinction? *Medical Law Review*, 12(2): 137–63.

Sheldon, S. (2012) The Abortion Act's paternalism belongs to the 1960s. *Guardian*, 22 March.

Skene, L. (2001) Genetic secrets and the family: a response to Bell and Bennett. *Medical Law Review* 9(2): 162.

Sommerville, A. and English V. (1999) Genetic privacy: orthodoxy or oxymoron? *Journal of Medical Ethics*, 25: 144–50.

Swift, K. and Robson M. (2012) Why doctors need not fear prosecution for gender-related abortions. *Journal of Criminal Law*, 76(4): 348–57.

Taylor, R. (2007) Reversing the retreat from Gillick? *CFLQ*, 19: 81.

Thornton, S. (1997) The Child B case – reflections of a chief executive. *British Medical Journal*, 314: 1838.

Wicks, E., Wyldes, M. and Kilby, M. (2004) Late termination of pregnancy for fetal abnormality: medical and legal perspectives. *Medical Law Review*, 12(3): 285–305.

Wilkinson, T.M. (2003) What's not wrong with conditional organ donation? *Journal of Medical Ethics*, 29: 163–4.

Index

Tried and tested

What law students across the UK are saying about the **Law Express** and **Law Express Question&Answer** series:

'I personally found the series very helpful in my preparation for exams.'

Abba Elgujja, University of Salford

'Law Express are my go-to guides. They are an excellent supplement to my course material.'

Claire Turner, Open University

'This is the best law Q&A series in my opinion. I think it's helpful and I will continue to use it.'

Nneka H, University of London

'These revision guides strike the right balance between enough detail to help shape a really good answer, but sufficiently brief to be used for last-minute revision. The layout is user friendly and the use of tables and flowcharts is helpful.'

Shannon Reynolds, University of Manchester

'I find them easy to read, yet very helpful.'

Rebecca Kincaid, University of Kent

'The information is straight to the point. This is important particularly for exams.'

Dewan Sadia Kuraishy, University of Manchester

'In the modules in which I used these books to revise with, generally the modules I found the most difficult, I got the highest marks in. The books are really easy to use and are extremely helpful.'

Charlotte Evans, Queen Mary University of London